AF867440

ICONLOGIC™

Version: 021725b
Page Count: 260
9781960604323 (Kindle Perfect-Bound Print Book)
97819606043231 (VitalSource PDF)
9781960604330 (Kindle eBook)

QuarkXPress 2025: The Essentials & Beyond

Kevin Siegel

ICONLOGIC
"Skills and Drills" Learning

Contents

NOTES

NOTES

NOTES

NOTES

ICONLOGIC

"Skills and Drills" Learning

Rank Your Skills

Before starting this book, complete the skills assessment on the next page.

Skills Assessment

How This Assessment Works

Below you will find 10 course objectives for *QuarkXPress 2025: The Essentials & Beyond*. **Before starting the book:** Review each objective and rank your skills using the scale next to each objective. A rank of ① means **No Confidence** in the skill. A rank of ⑤ means **Total Confidence**. After you've completed this assessment, go through the entire book. **After finishing the book:** Review each objective and rank your skills now that you've completed the book. Most people see dramatic improvements in the second assessment after completing the lessons in this book.

Before-Class Skills Assessment

1. I can add images to a layout.	①	②	③	④	⑤
2. I can create an item style.	①	②	③	④	⑤
3. I can create paragraph styles.	①	②	③	④	⑤
4. I can create a PDF output.	①	②	③	④	⑤
5. I can track text.	①	②	③	④	⑤
6. I can create master pages.	①	②	③	④	⑤
7. I can create a Pantone color.	①	②	③	④	⑤
8. I can create a numbered list.	①	②	③	④	⑤
9. I can create wrap text around an image.	①	②	③	④	⑤
10. I can link text across columns and pages.	①	②	③	④	⑤

After-Class Skills Assessment

1. I can add images to a layout.	①	②	③	④	⑤
2. I can create an item style.	①	②	③	④	⑤
3. I can create paragraph styles.	①	②	③	④	⑤
4. I can create a PDF output.	①	②	③	④	⑤
5. I can track text.	①	②	③	④	⑤
6. I can create master pages.	①	②	③	④	⑤
7. I can create a Pantone color.	①	②	③	④	⑤
8. I can create a numbered list.	①	②	③	④	⑤
9. I can create wrap text around an image.	①	②	③	④	⑤
10. I can link text across columns and pages.	①	②	③	④	⑤

IconLogic, Inc.
www.iconlogic.com
ksiegel@iconlogic.com

ICONLOGIC
"Skills and Drills" Learning

About This Book

This Section Contains Information About:

NOTES

The Author

Kevin Siegel is the founder and president of IconLogic, Inc. He has authored hundreds of step-by-step computer training books covering applications such as Adobe Captivate, Articulate Storyline, Adobe RoboHelp, Articulate Rise, QuarkXPress, and TechSmith Camtasia.

Kevin served for five years in the U.S. Coast Guard as an award-winning photojournalist. He has three decades of experience as a print publisher, technical writer, instructional designer, and eLearning developer. He is a certified technical trainer, a veteran classroom instructor, and frequently speaks at trade shows and conventions.

Kevin holds multiple certifications from Adobe and CompTIA and is a Certified Online Training Professional (COTP) with the International Council for Certified Online Training Professionals (ICCOTP). You can reach Kevin at **ksiegel@iconlogic.com**.

IconLogic

Founded in 1992, IconLogic is a global training, development, and publishing company.

As a training provider, IconLogic has trained tens of thousands of professionals both on-site and online across a wide range of applications. Our clients include some of the largest companies in the world, such as Adobe Systems, Urogen, Agilent, Sanofi Pasteur, Kelsey Seybold, FAA, Office Pro, Adventist Health Systems, AGA, AAA, Wells Fargo, VA.gov, American Express, Lockheed Martin, General Mills, Grange Insurance, Electric Boat, Michigan.gov, Freddie Mac, Fannie Mae, ADP, ADT, the Federal Reserve Bank of Richmond, Walmart, Kroger, Duke Energy, US Coast Guard, US Marine Corps, Canadian Blood Services, PSA, the Department of Homeland Security, and the Department of Defense.

In our development capacity, IconLogic has created eLearning modules and technical documentation for clients such as Duke Energy, the World Bank, Heineken, EverFi, Bank of America, Fresenius Kabi, Wells Fargo, Federal Express, Fannie Mae, American Express, Microsoft, the Department of For-Hire Vehicles, DC Child and Family Services, DCORM, Canadian Blood Services, Cancer.org, MLB, Archrock, NEEF, CHUBB, Canadian Natural Resources, and Hagerty Insurance.

As a publishing company, IconLogic has published hundreds of critically acclaimed books and has developed technical documents for both print and digital formats. Some of our most popular titles over the years include books on HTML, Dreamweaver, QuarkXPress, PageMaker, InDesign, Word, Excel, Access, Publisher, RoboHelp, RoboDemo, iSpring Suite, Adobe Presenter, Storyline, Rise, Captivate, and PowerPoint.

To learn more about the diverse services offered by IconLogic, please visit www.iconlogic.com.

Book Conventions

In my experience, people learn best through hands-on activities rather than simply by watching or listening. With this principle in mind, instructors and authors with extensive experience in training adult learners have created IconLogic books. IconLogic books typically contain minimal text and are filled with practical activities, screen captures, and challenge exercises designed to reinforce newly acquired skills.

This book is organized into modules, with each module building on the lessons from the previous one. Therefore, it is recommended that you complete each module in sequence.

The step-by-step instructions in this book look like this:

❒ choose **File > Open**

If you are expected to type anything or if something is important, it is set in bold type like this:

❒ type **9** into the text field

If you are expected to press a key on your keyboard, the instruction looks like this:

❒ press **[shift]**

Confidence Checks

As you progress through this book, you will encounter an image indicating a Confidence Check. Throughout each module, you will be guided through several hands-on activities. To ensure you grasp the book's lessons, these Confidence Checks encourage you to complete a process or steps independently. Since some activities build on previous Confidence Checks, it's important to complete them in the specified order.

Software & Asset Requirements

To run QuarkXPress 2025 efficiently, your computer must meet specific system requirements. You will need a 64-bit operating system; QuarkXPress 2025 is compatible with Windows 10 and later, or macOS Monterey (12.0) and later. It's essential to have at least 8 GB of RAM, though 16 GB is recommended for optimal performance, especially when working on complex layouts.

For storage, the software requires approximately 3 GB of available hard disk space for installation, but it's advisable to have additional space for your project files. A high-resolution monitor with a minimum resolution of 1280x800 pixels is necessary; however, a higher resolution will enhance your workflow.

A reliable Internet connection is also required for software activation and updates. While a dedicated GPU is not mandatory, it can improve performance when working with high-resolution graphics. Lastly, ensure that your machine has a multi-core CPU (Intel or equivalent) to effectively handle the robust capabilities of QuarkXPress 2025.

Asset files that support the activities in this book are available for download. Please see the "Download the Free Book Assets" on page xii for download instructions.

Asset Files

You're likely feeling excited—and maybe a bit anxious—about diving into QuarkXPress to start creating layouts, and I completely understand that enthusiasm. But hold on a moment! Do you have all the necessary assets to get started? For example, beyond the QuarkXPress software, do you have some QuarkXPress projects to experiment with? What about images? Have you gathered text files to import and edit? If you answered "no" to most of these questions, I have you covered with several support assets. Just follow the steps below to download them.

Download the Free Book Assets

1. Download the student assets necessary to use this book.

   ❒ use a web browser and go to **https://www.iconlogic.com/**

   ❒ click the **Data Files** link

   ❒ select your platform (PC or Mac)

   ❒ expand the **QuarkXPress Data Files** menu

   ❒ click **QuarkXPress 2025: The Essentials & Beyond**

   A dialog box may open, asking if you want to Save or Open (or Run) the file. On some computers and some browsers, the file simply downloads to your Downloads folder without question.

2. If necessary, download/save the file to your computer. After the file downloads, close the web browser.

3. Locate the **QuarkXPress 2025 Book Assets.zip** file you just downloaded and extract the contents. Note that downloaded files *typically* go to your Downloads folder. On the Mac, zipped files tend to extract automatically.

4. Move the unzipped **QuarkXPress 2025 Book Assets** folder to your **desktop** and you're done.

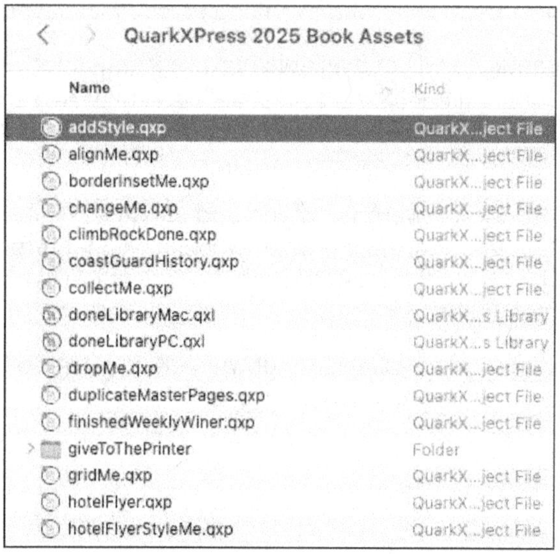

Before starting the lessons in this book, review "How Software Updates Affect This Book" on page xiii.

How Software Updates Affect This Book

This book has been created to teach you how to use QuarkXPress 2025.

With each major release of QuarkXPress, my goal is to write a companion book that supports that version, making it available within 30 to 60 days of the software's launch by Quark. Occasionally, Quark may issue service releases or patches for QuarkXPress that address bugs or introduce new features.

Typically, these software updates consist of minor bug fixes and have little to no impact on the lessons presented in this book. However, Quark may implement significant changes to how QuarkXPress looks or functions, even with patches.

Since it is not feasible for me to update printed books, some instructions provided in this book may not match the version you have after updates or patches. If something on your screen differs from what is shown in this book, please feel free to email me at the address below for clarification.

Contacting IconLogic

IconLogic, Inc.
Phone: 410.956.4949
Web: **www.iconlogic.com**
Email: **ksiegel@iconlogic.com**

NOTES

Notes

ICONLOGIC

"Skills and Drills" Learning

Module 1: An Introduction to QuarkXPress

In This Module You Will Learn About:

And You Will Learn To:

NOTES

The Interface

Working with QuarkXPress, the sky—or your imagination—is the limit. You can create newsletters, magazines, posters, business cards, letterhead, certificates, brochures—just about any print media.

During this first module, you'll learn your way around the QuarkXPress interface, open an existing project, work with palettes, and even create your first new project (including adding text and inserting an image).

> **Note:** QuarkXPress does not come with this book. You can either subscribe to the software or download a free trial. If you still need to do so, visit the Quark website and download the QuarkXPress software. The trial version, while limited, will work for most of this book's activities.

Guided Activity 1: Explore a Project and Layout Views

1. Start QuarkXPress.

   The **Welcome Screen** is typically the first thing you will see after starting QuarkXPress. The Welcome Screen lets you create or open a project and provides access to valuable resources. If the Welcome screen is not open, choose **Window > Welcome Screen**.

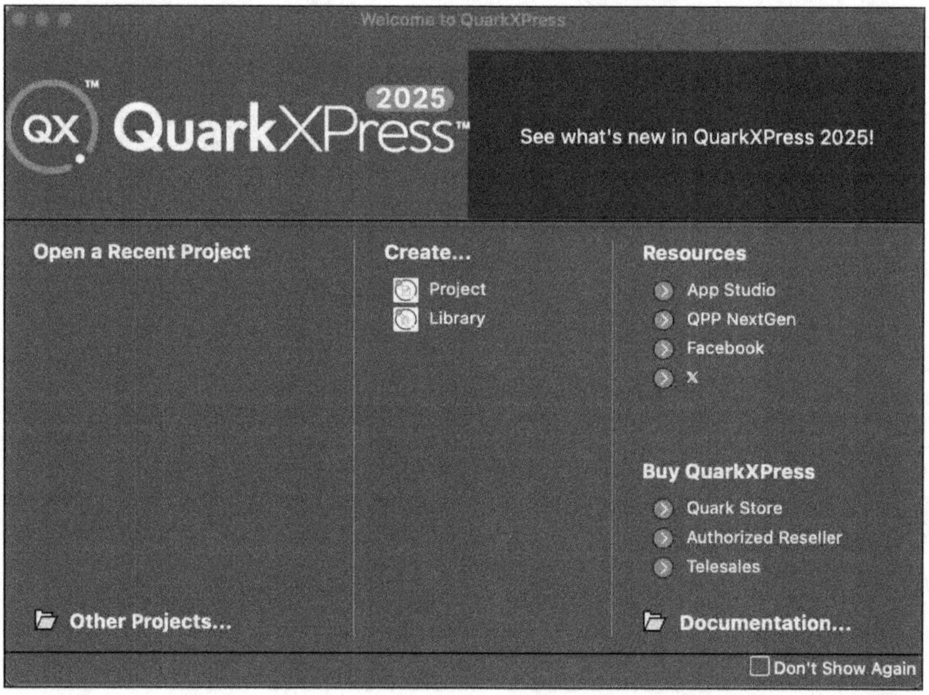

   Note: You are about to open a project from the **QuarkXPress 2025 Book Assets** that come with this book. Ensure the assets have been downloaded to your computer and extracted by following the steps in the **About This Book** section, **page xii**.

2. Open a QuarkXPress project from the QuarkXPress 2025 Book Assets folder.

   ❒ on the **Welcome Screen**, click **Other Projects**

   ❒ from the **QuarkXPress 2025 Book Assets** folder, open **finishedWeeklyWiner.qxp**

The QuarkXPress interface remembers how it looked when you last worked in the program. The QuarkXPress main window may be relatively clean, with just a few open windows (palettes). On the other hand, several open windows may make the entire interface visually overwhelming. You can close open palettes, reposition them, and customize what you see onscreen. Let's start by closing any open windows.

3. Close all open palettes.

   ❒ click the **Window** menu and remove any checkmarks from the palette names

   ❒ resize the QuarkXPress window as large as you can make it

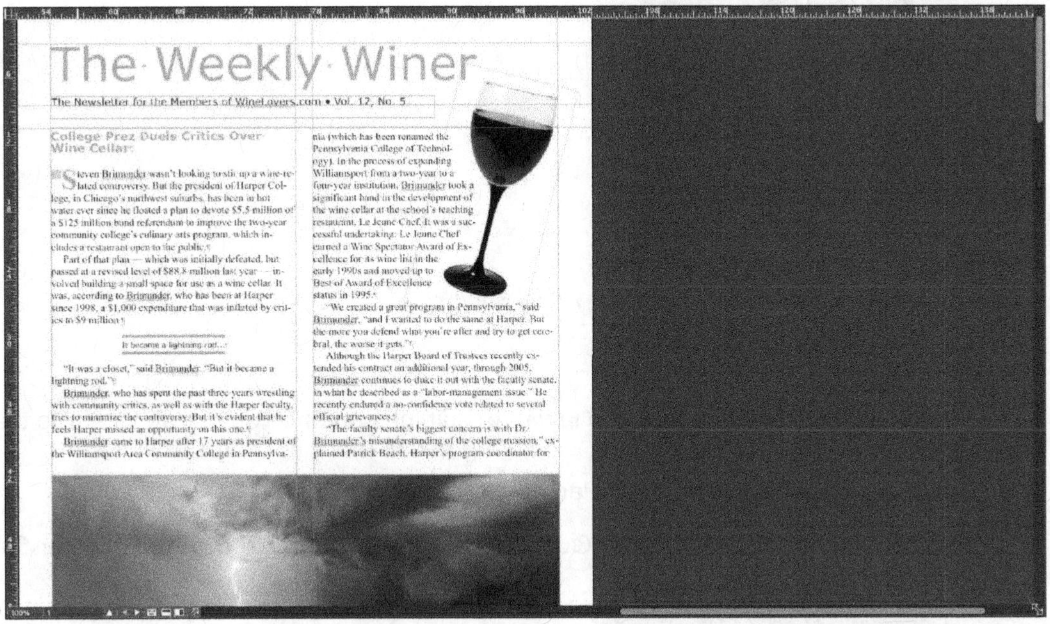

In this book, you will acquire the necessary skills to complete this project. The project includes multiple document pages, images, text, styles, master pages, specific colors, a numbered and bulleted lists, and more.

Currently, you are viewing the layout at a reduced zoom level. Generally, the closer you zoom in on a QuarkXPress layout, the more accurately the screen representation will match the final design. Conversely, if you zoom out, you can scroll faster and view more of the layout, but the accuracy of the final output will decrease.

There are several ways to adjust the zoom level, including using menu commands, keyboard shortcuts, and input fields where you can specify a particular zoom percentage.

4. Change the layout view to Fit in Window.

   ❒ choose **View > Fit in Window**

   The view changes and the first layout page centers within the application window.

NOTES

NOTES

5. Use Thumbnail view.

   ❒ choose **View > Thumbnails**

You can now see miniatures of your page layout.

❒ choose **View > 50%**

While still too far away from the layout to edit the content, you're now closer to the layout.

6. Change the view via the View Percent Field.

   ❒ from the **bottom left** of the QuarkXPress window, double-click the number **50%**

❒ type **227** and press **[return]**

Now you're "up close and personal" to the page.

Note: You are about to use keyboard shortcuts to change the view of the document. This book is written for both Mac and PCs. While QuarkXPress is nearly the same on both platforms, there are minor differences, such as the keys available on the keyboard. The term **[command]** is used in this book as a neutral term for **[ctrl]** (PC) and **[cmd]** (Mac). The term **[alt]** is used as a neutral term for **[alt]** (PC) and **[option]** (Mac). The term **[return]** is used as a neutral term for **[enter]** (PC) and **[return]** (Mac).

7. Use keyboard shortcuts to switch the layout view between Fit in Window and Actual size.

   ❒ press **[command] [zero]** on your keyboard to change the view to Fit in Window

You can now see your entire page.

❒ press **[command] [1]** to change the view to Actual size (100%)

8. Scroll through the layout by dragging the page.

   ❒ **PC** users, press **[alt]**; **Mac** users, press the **[option]**

❒ with the **[alt]** key pressed, drag the page

As long as you keep the **[alt]** key pressed, you can scroll through the layout. This is a great way to move around your layout, especially when you are zoomed close to a page.

❒ release **[alt]**

❒ press **[command] [zero]** on your keyboard to change the view back to Fit in Window

9. Scroll using the scrollbars.

❒ use the scrollbars at the bottom of the window to scroll from left to right

❒ use the scrollbars at the right of the window to scroll from vertically through the layout

❒ scroll back up to page 1 of the layout

10. Switch to preview mode.

❒ choose **View > View Sets > Output Preview**

All of the page guides and boxes that surround page items are hidden. Except for the red underlined text, indicating a potentially misspelled word), Output Preview is how your document will look when printed or output as a PDF.

The Weekly Winer

The Newsletter for the Members of WineLovers.com • Vol. 12, No. 5

College Prez Duels Critics Over Wine Cellar

Steven Brimunder wasn't looking to stir up a wine-related controversy. But the president of Harper College, in Chicago's northwest suburbs, has been in hot water ever since he floated a plan to devote $5.5 million of a $125 million bond referendum to improve the two-year community college's culinary arts program, which includes a restaurant open to the public.

Part of that plan — which was initially defeated, but passed at a revised level of $88.8 million last year — involved building a small space for use as a wine cellar. It was, according to Brimunder, who has been at Harper since 1998, a $1,000 expenditure that was inflated by critics to $9 million.

It became a lightning rod...

"It was a closet," said Brimunder. "But it became a lightning rod."

Brimunder, who has spent the past three years wrestling with community critics, as well as with the Harper faculty, tries to minimize the controversy. But it's evident that he feels Harper missed an opportunity on this one.

Brimunder came to Harper after 17 years as president of the Williamsport Area Community College in Pennsylvania (which has been renamed the Pennsylvania College of Technology). In the process of expanding Williamsport from a two-year to a four-year institution, Brimunder took a significant hand in the development of the wine cellar at the school's teaching restaurant, Le Jeune Chef. It was a successful undertaking: Le Jeune Chef earned a Wine Spectator Award of Excellence for its wine list in the early 1990s and moved up to Best of Award of Excellence status in 1995.

"We created a great program in Pennsylvania," said Brimunder, "and I wanted to do the same at Harper. But the more you defend what you're after and try to get cerebral, the worse it gets."

Although the Harper Board of Trustees recently extended his contract an additional year, through 2005, Brimunder continues to duke it out with the faculty senate, in what he described as a "labor-management issue." He recently endured a no-confidence vote related to several official grievances.

"The faculty senate's biggest concern is with Dr. Brimunder's misunderstanding of the college mission," explained Patrick Beach, Harper's program coordinator for

❒ choose **View > View Sets > Authoring View**

NOTES

Guided Activity 2: Explore Palettes

1. Open several palettes.

   ❒ choose **Window > Tools**

   The Tools menu item is close to the bottom of the menu.

   ❒ choose **Window > Measurements**

   ❒ choose **Window > Style Sheets**

   ❒ choose **Window > Page Layout**

   ❒ choose **Window > Colors**

   ❒ choose **Window > Lists**

   ❒ choose **Window > Guides**

   ❒ choose **Window > Stock Images**

   Your screen should now have several palettes open, which also means your screen is fairly cluttered. Next you will organize the appearance of the palettes by creating a Palette Set.

Palette Sets

As you have seen, there are several palettes are available in QuarkXPress. The palettes can be opened, closed, resized, and repositioned as needed (even moved across multiple displays). You can save the size and screen position of palettes as a custom palette set. After you save the palette set, you can access it at any time through Window > Palette sets.

Guided Activity 3: Create and Use a Palette Set

1. Show just the Tools and Style Sheets palettes.

   ❒ close all of the palettes on your screen except for **Tools** and **Style Sheets**

   ❒ drag the two palettes to any location on your screen that you like

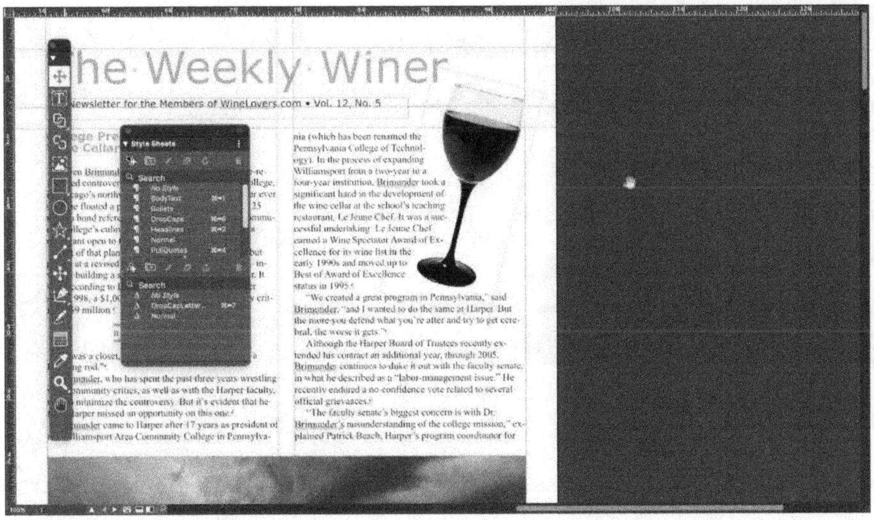

2. Save a Palette Set.

   ❒ choose **Window > Palette Sets > Save Palette Set As**

   The **Save Palette Set As** dialog box opens.

   ❒ name the Palette Set **Tools and Styles**

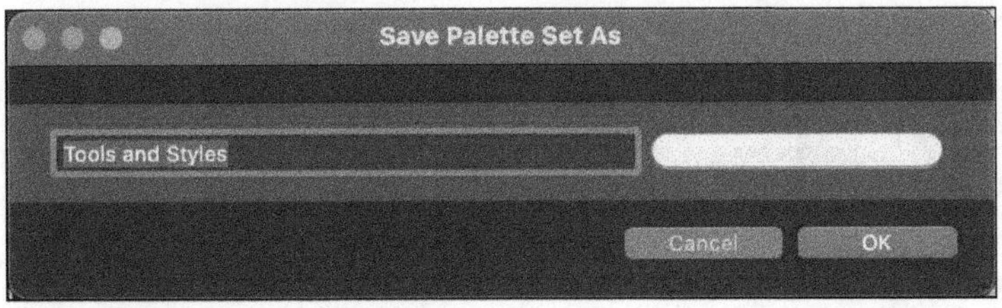

   ❒ click **OK**

3. Close both the **Tools** and **Style Sheets** palette, along with any other open palettes.

4. Recall a Palette Set.

   ❒ choose **Window > Palette Sets > Tools and Styles**

   The Tools and Style Sheets reappear, exactly where you left them.

NOTES

Greeking

Depending on your monitor's screen resolution, and your view percentage, you may or may not be able to make out actual letters on the page. If you cannot make out the letters, there isn't anything wrong with your vision. Quark assumes that at a reduced view, you are not interested in reading the text in your layout. This assumption is called *greeking.* Good assumption or not, I do not recommended reading or editing text at reduced views such as Fit in Window. In my world, there are two types of print publishers: those who have glasses, and those who will. Working with text while in a reduced view will hasten your journey into the "have glasses" club.

Guided Activity 4: Enable Greek Text Below

1. Enable greeking.

   ❐ Windows users, choose **Edit > Preferences**;
   Mac users, choose **QuarkXPress > Settings**

   The Preferences dialog box opens. There are several categories.

   ❐ select **General > Print Layout**

   ❐ from the **Display** area, select **Greek Text Below**

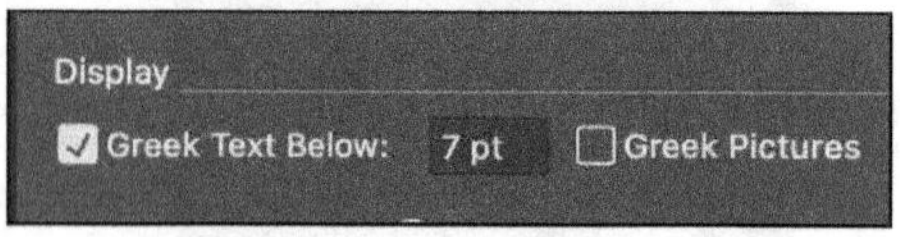

   ❐ click **OK**

   If you are viewing any of your pages at actual size, you can read the text onscreen.

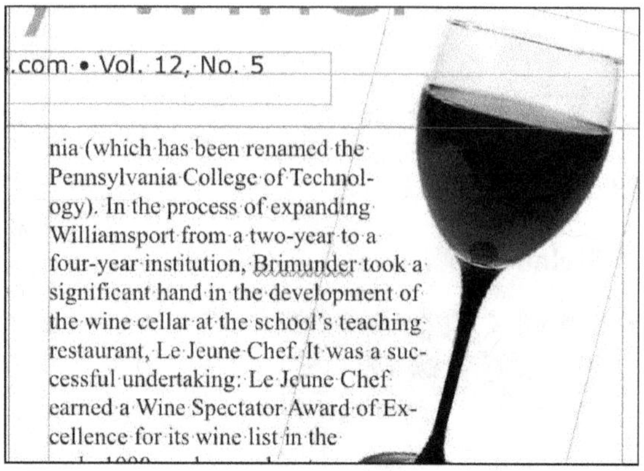

2. View the "greeked" text.

   ❐ choose **View > 50%**

   At this reduced view, the letter shapes disappear and instead you see gray bars—greeking. If you can still see letter shapes instead of gray bars, try zooming out a bit more by changing your View Percentage lower. Moving forward, if you prefer to see letter shapes (greeking off) or gray bars (greeking on), disable or enable the Greek Text Below feature as appropriate.

Managing Windows

You can have several QuarkXPress projects open at one time. While you can switch between open projects easily, you can only edit in one project at a time. In addition to easily switching between open projects, you can split the QuarkXPress application window into panels so you can view multiple open projects at one time.

Guided Activity 5: View Multiple Project Windows

1. Open a second project using a keyboard shortcut.

   ❒ choose **File > Open**

   ❒ from **QuarkXPress 2025 Book Assets**, open **Vonnie**

   Two projects are currently open: **Vonnie** and **finishedWeeklyWiner**.

2. Tile your projects.

   ❒ PC users: choose **Window > Tile Vertically**;
   Mac users: choose **Window > Tile**

   Observe your screen. Both project windows occupy equal space on your screen.

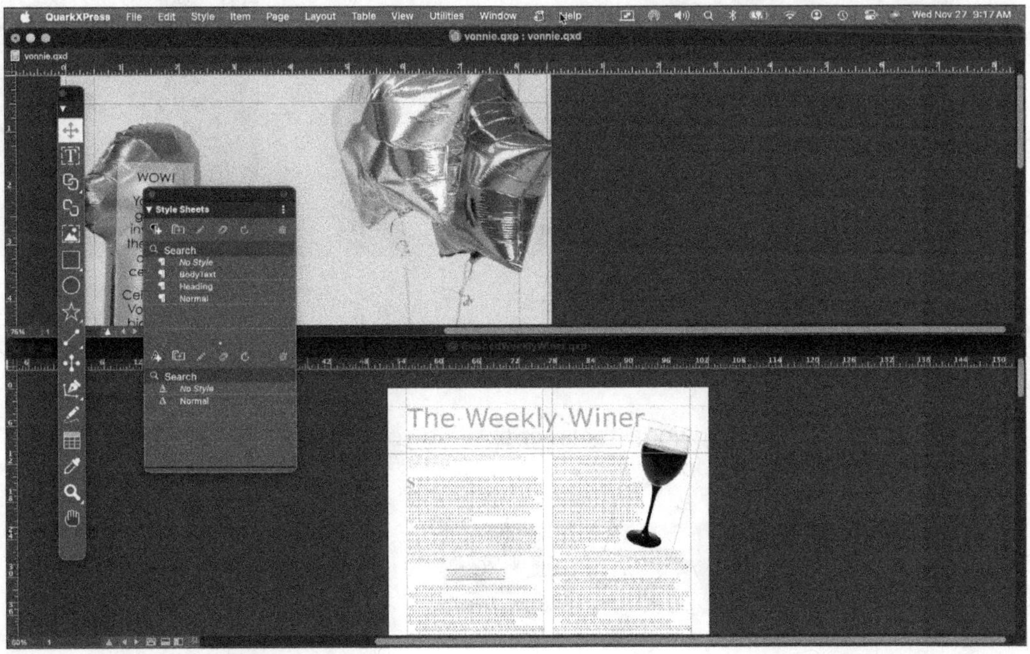

3. Switch between projects.

   ❒ click on each project's window to make it active

4. Select and then close a project.

   ❒ choose **Window > Vonnie**

   ❒ choose **File > Close Window** (if prompted, do not save the Vonnie project)

   The **finishedWeeklyWiner** project should still be open.

NOTES

5. Maximize the **finishedWeeklyWiner** layout.

   ❒ choose **Window > Tile**

6. Split the layout window horizontally.

   ❒ choose **Window > Split Window > Horizontal**

   The layout window is split into two. You can use this nifty feature to work in one part of the layout while reading another. Notice that you have two sets of scroll bars that allow you to scroll both windows independently.

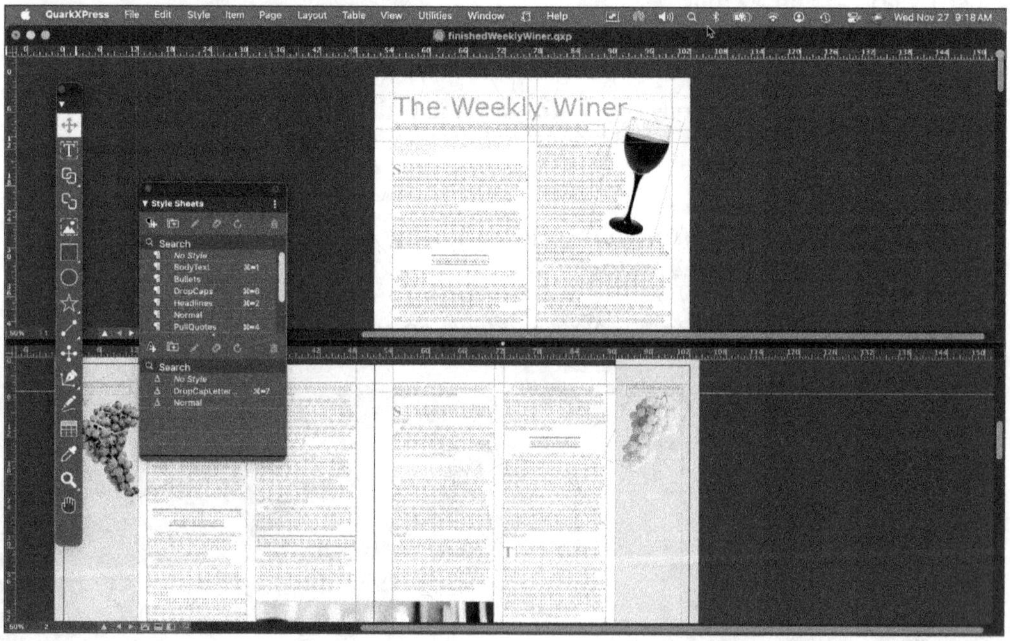

7. Remove the window split.

   ❒ choose **Window > Split Window > Remove All**

   Note: You will find additional tools for splitting your window views at the bottom of the QuarkXPress window.

8. Close the **finishedWeeklyWiner** project without saving it.

New Projects

When creating new QuarkXPress projects, you need to make a host of decisions regarding the look of your layout. Prior to making those decisions in the New Project dialog box, it's a good idea to meet with your designer so that you understand such things about the project as its size, margins, number of columns needed, and more. While you can modify the look and feel of your layout at any time, it is easier if you know the project's specifications and requirements before creating the new project.

Guided Activity 6: Set the Application Measurements

1. Ensure that the horizontal and vertical measurement systems is set to inches.

   ❒ Windows users, choose **Edit > Preferences**;
   Mac users, choose **QuarkXPress > Settings**

   ❒ from the **Default Print Layout** category, click **Measurements**

   ❒ if necessary, select **Inches** from the Horizontal drop-down menu

   ❒ if necessary, select **Inches** from the Vertical drop-down menu

   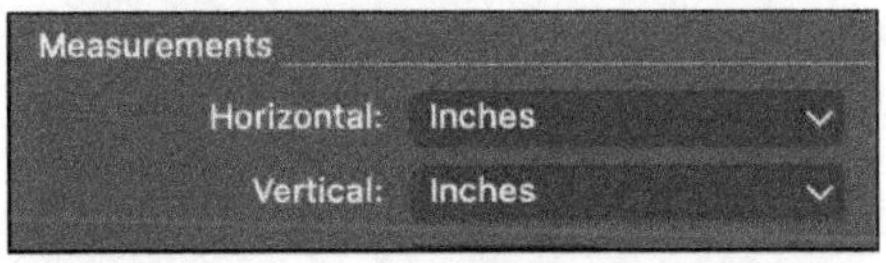

   ❒ click **OK**

   You just confirmed a preference with no projects open, but it doesn't appear you have done anything. However, you ensured that all new projects use inches as the measurement system. Existing projects using a different measurement system will not be changed.

   Because most new US-based QuarkXPress users are comfortable working with inches, the projects you learn to create during the first several modules in this book rely on the inch measurement system. However, points or picas are the preferred units of measurement for publishers.

   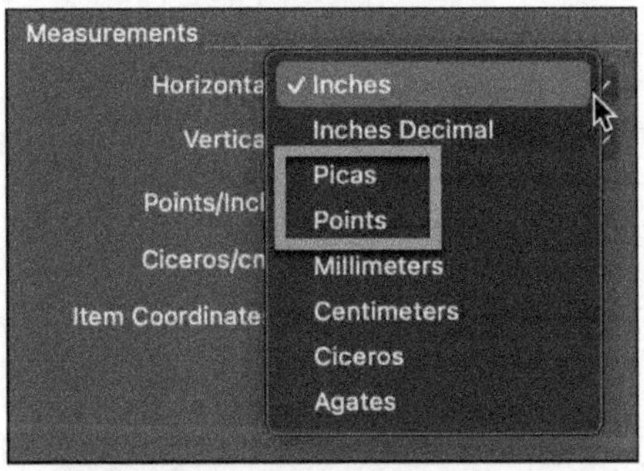

   Inches are typically used to define larger dimensions, such as page sizes, margins, and column widths. For example, a letter-size page is 8.5 inches wide by 11 inches tall. Points are a smaller unit of measurement used mainly for font sizes and line spacing. Picas are a unit of measurement that fall between inches and points and are often used to measure the width of columns or elements in page layout. Picas provide a more precise measurement than inches but might be easier to manage than points for larger layouts. You will learn more about picas and points beginning on page 136.

NOTES

NOTES

Guided Activity 7: Create a New Project

1. Explore the New Project dialog box.

    ❒ choose **File > New > Project**

    The New Project dialog box opens. There are two choices in the **Layout Type** drop-down menu: Print and Digital.

    ❒ if necessary, change the **Layout Type** to **Print**

    Print layouts are perfect when creating documents such as brochures, flyers, magazines, and books. These kinds of documents use measurement units like inches, millimeters, or points. Print documents also support CMYK and spot colors. These documents are static and lack interactive elements such as hyperlinks or videos.

    Digital layouts are meant to be accessed and viewed onscreen and are typically used for creating websites, presentations, eBooks, and interactive documents. Digital projects typically measure in pixels and are designed for viewing on computers and mobile devices. Regarding color, digital layouts use RGB colors and support hyperlinks, buttons, audio, video, and animations.

    ❒ select **Single Layout Mode**

    Single Layout Mode is ideal when creating projects that do not require multiple layouts, such as a single brochure, flyer, magazine, or web page. For projects requiring various layouts (for instance, creating both print and digital layouts of one project), use **Project Mode**, which allows for managing and synchronizing multiple layouts within the same file.

    The lessons in this book focus on Print layouts and Single Layout Mode.

    ❒ from the **Page Size** drop-down menu, select **Legal**

    Notice that the values in the Width and Height fields change to **8.5** and **14**. The Page Size is also known as the **trim**. As it stands now, the trim size of this layout would be 8.5 x 14 inches.

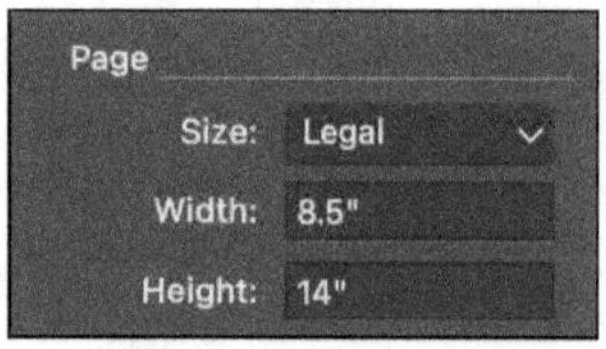

    Next you will specify the page Margin Guides. Margin Guides will appear as non-printing blue lines on your layout. They will serve as the buffer between the trim—the extreme edges of the layout—and the working area remaining within the page area.

2. Change the page margins.

    ❒ change the **Top** Margin Guide to **1** (1 inch)

    ❒ change the **Bottom** margin **1**

- ❐ change the **Left** margin to **1**
- ❐ change the **Right** margin to **1**

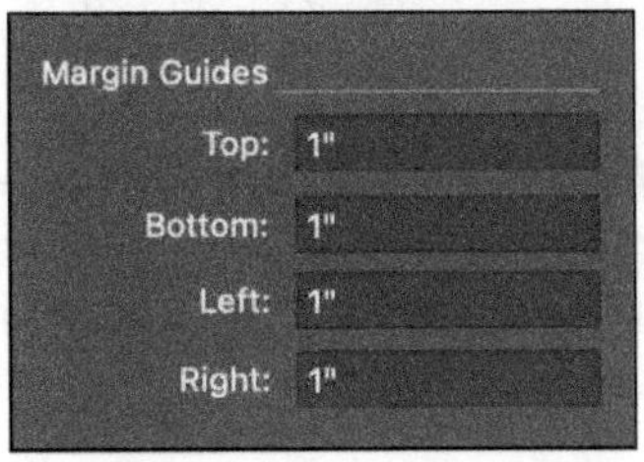

3. Set page specifications.

- ❐ click the **Facing Pages** check box (You will learn about Facing Pages on page 148.)
- ❐ click the **Automatic Text Box** check box (You will learn about Automatic Text Boxes on page 90.)

You will either put in or remove a check in the boxes. A check means the option is active or "turned on." It's like saying: "Yes, I want this."

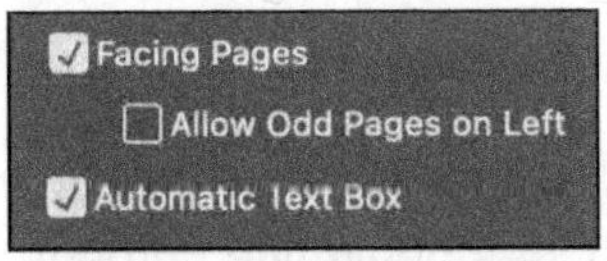

- ❐ select **Letter** from the **Page > Size** drop-down menu
- ❐ confirm that the Orientation is set to **Portrait**
- ❐ confirm that Columns is set to **1**

The Gutter Width is not important now, but it cannot be blank or zero.

- ❐ if necessary, **remove** the check marks from both **Facing Pages** and **Automatic Text Box**
- ❐ change all four of the **Margin Guides** to **.5** (one-half inch)
- ❐ click **OK**

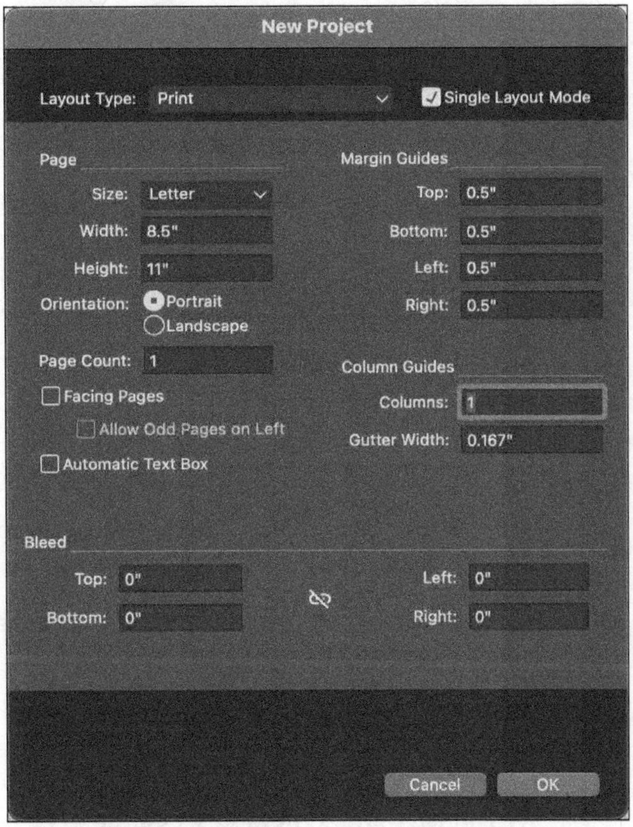

NOTES

NOTES

Guided Activity 8: Change Page Orientation and Margins

1. Change the layout's orientation.

   ❒ choose **Layout > Layout Properties**

   The Layout Properties dialog box opens. You can change the page Size, Width, Height and Orientation, and select Facing Pages. But also notice that options for changing your page margins are NOT available. You'll have to go someplace else to change those.

   ❒ change the **Orientation** to **Landscape**

   ❒ click **OK**

2. Change the layout's view to **Fit in Window**.

   Note that your layout is now flipped on its side.

3. Change the layout's Margin Guides.

   ❒ choose **Page > Display > A-Master A**

   The master page appears. You will learn about master pages beginning on page 148. For now, it's enough to know to change the margins for a page, you must be on a master page.

   ❒ choose **Page > Master Guides & Grid**

   The **Master Guides & Grid** dialog box opens.

   ❒ change the Top Margin Guide to **2** and press [**tab**] on your keyboard to move to the next field

   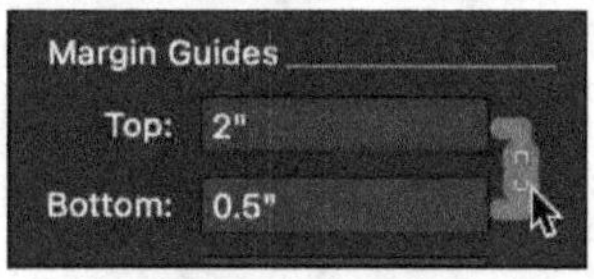

   ❒ click the **Link** icon between the Top and Bottom fields

   The Bottom margin should automatically switch to **2** to match what you typed in the Top Margin Guide field.

   ❒ change the **Left** margin Guide to **2** and then click the Link icon between the Left and Right fields

   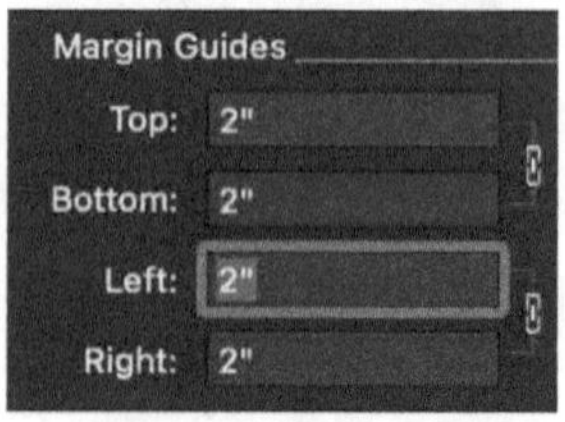

   The Right Margin should automatically switch to **2**.

   ❒ click **OK**

   ❒ choose **Page > Display > Layout**

   The layout should now have very large, 2-inch margins.

Confidence Check

1. Change the Orientation of your layout to **Portrait**.
   If you need help, refer to page 14.
2. Change all of the margins to **one-half** inch.
   If you need help, refer to page 14.

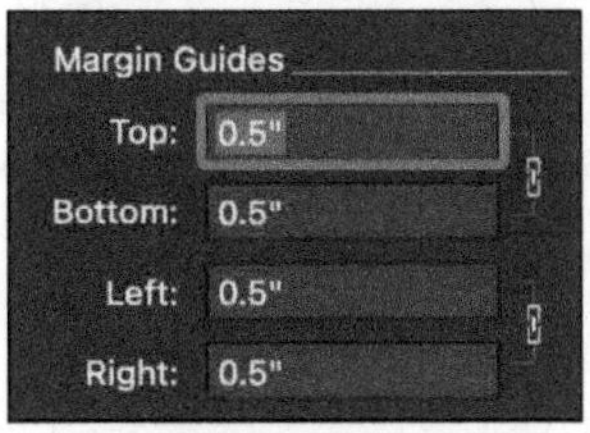

3. Ensure you are displaying the **Layout**, not **A-Master A**.

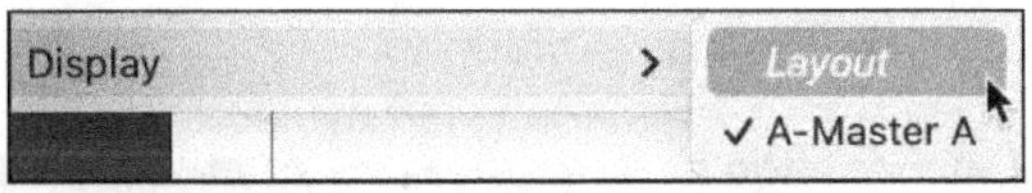

4. If necessary, change your view to **Fit in Window**.
5. Show the **Tools window**. (**Window > Show Tools** or press **[F8]** on your keyboard.)

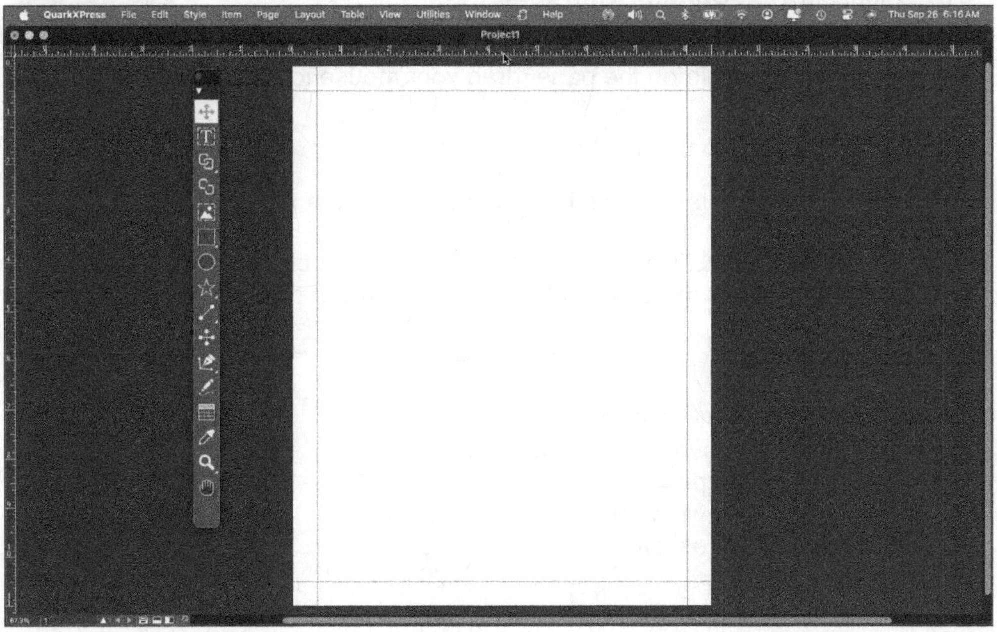

NOTES

Text and Picture Content

Text goes into text boxes; pictures go into picture boxes. You draw text boxes on your layout using the Text Content Tool on the Tools window. When you have finished drawing the text box, it will contain a blinking insertion point—indicating that you can either type text into the box or import the text from a word processor. Similarly, you draw picture boxes using the Picture Content Tool on the Tools window. While picture boxes cannot contain text, you can import several picture formats into a picture box.

Guided Activity 9: Create and Modify a Text Box

1. Change your view to **Actual Size**.

2. Ensure the Tools window is showing. (Window menu)

3. Use Tool Tips to learn about each tool.

   ❒ move your mouse pointer over any tool on the Tools window

   When you point to (hover above) a tool, a message appears next to the tool telling you the name of the tool.

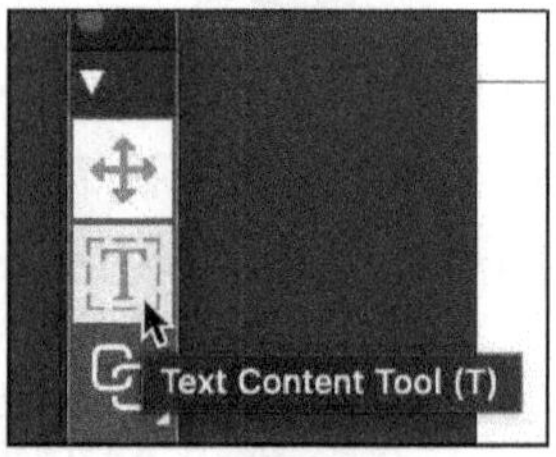

4. Draw a text box.

   ❒ select the **Text Content Tool**

   ❒ position your pointer anywhere on the layout and draw a square or rectangle on the page (drag your mouse to draw)

5. Type text content into the text box.

   ❒ with the Text Content Tool still selected, click inside the text box you drew

   You should be see a blinking insertion point in the text box you drew (you can't type text into a text box unless the Content tool and text box are selected).

   ❒ type **your name**

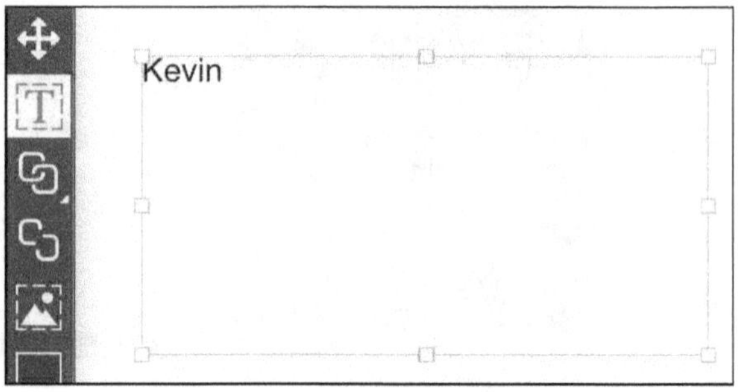

   As you type your name, the blinking insertion point will move to the right, just like you would expect to see in any word processor. You will work more with text and text boxes later.

6. Delete the text box with a keyboard shortcut.

   ❒ press [**command**] [**k**]

   Pressing [command] [k] is a fast, efficient way to delete any selected item. An easy way to remember this keyboard shortcut is to associate the letter "**k**" with "kill." When you press [command] [k], you "kill" the selected object.

Guided Activity 10: Draw and Use a Picture Box

1. Change your view to Fit in window.

2. Draw a picture box.

   ❒ from the Tools window, select the **Picture Content Tool** 

   ❒ using the Picture Content Tool, draw a shape that's approximately **3** inches wide and **5** inches tall

   Unlike Text Content Boxes, notice that a Picture Content Box contains an "X."

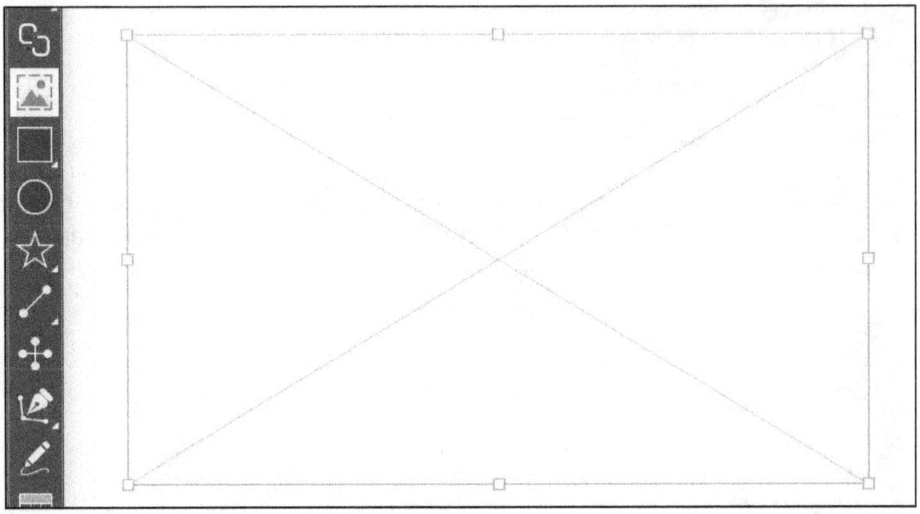

3. Import a picture into the Picture Content box.

   ❒ with the Picture Content box you just drew selected, choose **File > Import**

   The Import dialog box opens.

   ❒ navigate to **QuarkXPress 2025 Book Assets > images**

   ❒ open **kidsOnBeach.jpg**

   The image is imported into the picture box.

   Unless you made your Picture Content box very large, you will notice that part of the image appears clear and the rest is faded out. The faded part of the image does not fit in the box and will not print.

NOTES

NOTES

4. Modify the picture content viability.

   ❒ with the **Picture Content Tool** still selected, move your mouse pointer over the image

   Notice that the shape of your pointer changes to a hand pointer.

   ❒ drag the image any direction to change what appears within the picture box (in the picture below, the image has been cropped so all three of the children appear within the box)

5. Preview the cropped image.

   ❒ click just above, or below, the picture box containing the image of the kids to deselect the item

   With the item deselected, you can now see the part of the image that will print.

6. Save the project.

   ❒ choose **File > Save**

   ❒ name the project **My First QuarkXPress Project**

   ❒ save the project to the **QuarkXPress 2025 Book Assets** folder

Guided Activity 11: Resize and Move Layout Items

1. Resize the picture box.

   ❒ on the **Tools window**, select the **Item Tool**

   ❒ using the Item tool, click on the picture box containing the image of the kids

   Notice the squares that appear around the box. The squares are known as resizing handles.

   ❒ drag the right, center resizing handle right to make the box a bit wider and display more of the image

2. Move an item.

   ❒ ensure the **Item Tool** is still selected

   ❒ using the Item Tool, drag the picture box to a different location within the layout

Confidence Check

1. Draw a few lines on the page using the **Line Tool**.
2. Draw a few rectangles using the **Rectangle Box Tool**.
3. Select and then click and hold the Rectangle Box Tool to display a few more tools.
4. On the Tools window, click and hold the **Star Tool**.

   Additional shape tools appear.

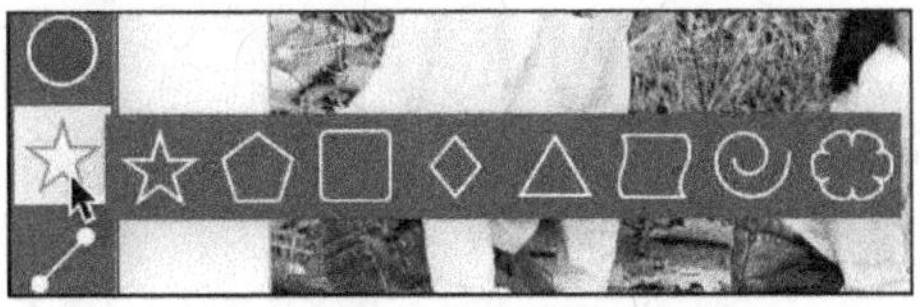

5. Use some of the shape tools to add shapes to the layout.

NOTES

NOTES

Customizing Tools

The easiest way to customize a tool on the toolbar is by double-clicking the tool. If you double-click an editable tool, such as the Zoom Tool, you'll be taken to the Preferences dialog box. Once there, you can customize the tool's behavior to suit your needs.

Guided Activity 12: Customize the Zoom Tool

1. Change the view.

   ❒ choose **View > 75%**

2. Use the Zoom Tool.

   ❒ from near the bottom of the Tools window, select the **Zoom Tool** 

   ❒ click on the layout page a few times

   Each click should move you closer to the page by 25%.

3. Customize the view scale increment.

   ❒ double-click the **Zoom Tool**

   The Preferences dialog box opens. The Zoom Tool is selected from the Tools category.

   ❒ from the **View Scale** area, change the number in the **Increment** area to **50**

   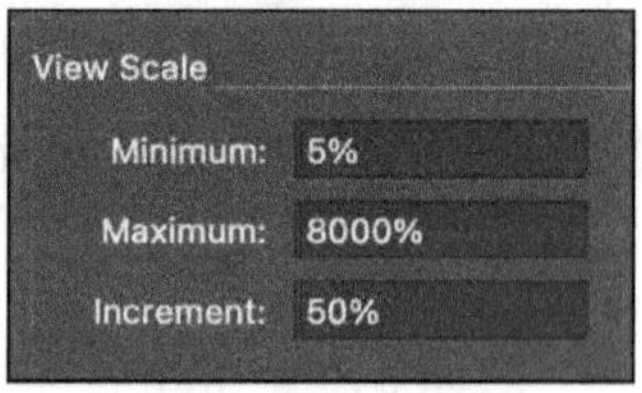

   ❒ click **OK**

4. Use the customized Zoom Tool.

   ❒ if necessary, select the **Zoom Tool**

   ❒ click on the layout page a few times

   Each click takes you closer to the page by 50%.

5. Zoom out with the Zoom Tool.

   ❒ press [**alt**] and click on the layout

   Notice that with the [alt] key pressed, the + (plus) on the Zoom Tool changes to a - (minus) and you zoom out by 50% with each click.

6. Reset tool defaults.

   ❒ double-click the **Zoom Tool**

   The Preferences dialog box reopens.

   ❒ click the **Restore To Default** button 

   ❒ click **OK**

   Any changes made to any of the tools on the Tool palette have been restored to their original settings.

The Zero Point

You can create truly massive layouts using QuarkXPress. But how do you expect to print a huge layout? If you are like most people, your printer is not capable of printing pages larger than legal or tabloid size.

To print a larger page, you can take advantage of two things: the ability to **tile** your pages when you print, and the **zero point area** of the page rulers that lies at the intersection of the horizontal and vertical rulers.

If you choose **File > Print** and select the **Pages** category in the list, you'll see the tiling options near the center of the dialog box. When you choose **Automatic** tiling, QuarkXPress prints your large project as tiles with an **overlap** and prints as many tiles (pages) as necessary until the entire project has printed. When you choose **Manual** tiling, QuarkXPress prints only one page. The part of the project that prints depends on the **zero point**.

You can control the zero point by dragging the **zero point area** to the part of the page you want to print. When you print with Manual tiling, the single sheet of paper that prints contains anything **below and to the right** of the zero point.

Guided Activity 13: Change the Zero Point

1. Change the zero point.

   ❒ change the page view to **Fit in Window**

   ❒ position your pointer on the zero point (the zero point is located where the horizontal and vertical rulers intersect—the vertical ruler is at the left; the horizontal ruler is above the page)

   ❒ drag the zero point to the center of the page

   Observe the two rulers.The zero point, where the two zeros intersect, is now in the middle of the page.

2. Spend a minute or two moving the zero point to different page locations.

   Notice how the rulers change to match the position of the zero point you placed on your page.

3. Restore the zero point to its original location.

   ❒ click one time in the zero point area

   The zero point for both rulers is located in its default position—the upper left of the trim.

4. Move the zero point again, this time dragging it to the middle of your page.

NOTES

5. Explore the tiling options.

❒ choose **File > Print**

The Print Layout dialog box opens.

❒ select the **Pages** category from the list

❒ from the Page Tiling drop-down menu, select **Automatic**

With this option selected, QuarkXPress would print your layout using as many sheets of paper as necessary, regardless of the zero point. The larger the Overlap value, the more paper it will take to print the layout.

❒ from the Page Tiling drop-down menu, select **Manual**

With the Manual option selected, QuarkXPress will print just one sheet of paper based entirely on the position of the zero point, from the zero point down. The preview at the right is an excellent indication of which part of the page would print.

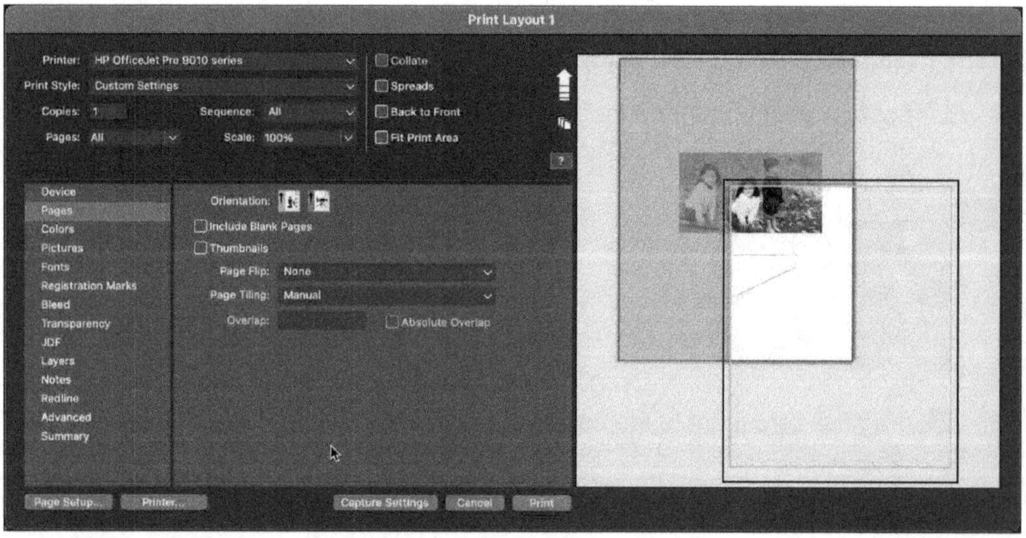

❒ click **Cancel**

6. Save and close the project.

Color Schemes

By default, QuarkXPress uses a dark mode color scheme, which is quite popular today. While the book's screenshots are in dark mode, you can switch modes easily and, on a Mac, customize many interface colors.

Guided Activity 14: Change the Application Color Scheme

1. Change the application color interlace.

   ❒ Windows users, choose **Edit > Preferences**;
   Mac users, choose **QuarkXPress > Settings**

   ❒ Windows users, click the **Display** category;
   Mac users, from the **Application** category, choose **Color Theme**

   ❒ All users, from the **Color Theme** drop-down menu, choose **Light Gray**

   Mac users, the entire QuarkXPress interface immediately updates to the new color scheme. PC users, you will need to restart QuarkXPress to see the changes.

   ❒ All users, click the **OK** button

   ❒ PC users, **restart QuarkXPress** to see the application color theme change

2. Change the application color theme again.

   ❒ Windows users, choose **Edit > Preferences**;
   Mac users, choose **QuarkXPress > Settings**

   ❒ Windows users, click the **Display** category;
   Mac users, from the **Application** category, choose **Color Theme**

   ❒ All users, from the **Color Theme** drop-down menu, choose **Dark**

   ❒ All users, click the **OK** button

   ❒ PC users, restart QuarkXPress to see the application color changes

   As mentioned above, the color theme shown in the screenshots throughout this book uses Dark mode. However, you can use any color theme you like

Confidence Check

1. Open the **coastGuardHistory** project.
2. Scroll through the project.

   This project consists of multiple pages, similar to the Weekly Winer project. It includes master page layouts, complex image wraps, paragraph styles, and item styles. While most of the lessons in this book focus on building the Weekly Winer project, you will work with Coast Guard images and see the elements of this and other projects from time to time.

3. Close the project without saving.

NOTES

Notes

ICONLOGIC
"Skills and Drills" Learning

Module 2: Text Basics

In This Module You Will Learn About:

- Single Layout Mode, page 26
- Adding Text to a Layout, page 28
- Importing Text, page 30
- The Measurements Window, page 31
- Invisibles, page 32
- Selecting Text, page 33
- Character Attributes, page 34
- Glyphs, page 35
- Flowing Text, page 37
- Paragraph Alignment, page 39
- Paragraph Spacing, page 40
- Leading, page 44
- Rules, page 45

And You Will Learn To:

- Enable Single Layout Mode By Default, page 26
- Add Text and Work With Text Box Overflow, page 28
- Import Text, page 30
- Modify Item Attributes, page 31
- Display Invisibles, page 32
- Use Different Text Selection Techniques, page 33
- Change Character Attributes, page 34
- Use the Glyphs Window to Add a Symbol, page 35
- Automatically Flow Text, page 37
- Align Paragraphs, page 39
- Work with Multiple Columns, page 40
- Set a First Line Indent, page 42
- Add Space Between Paragraphs, page 43
- Set Leading, page 44
- Set Paragraph Rules, page 45

NOTES

Single Layout Mode

When creating new projects, you can select Single Layout Mode. This mode benefits users who don't require the complexity of handling multiple layouts and want to streamline the development process. Single Layout Mode reduces distractions and clutter from other layouts and makes it easier to concentrate on the design and formatting of a specific page or layout. However, unless you remember to select Single Layout Mode, you'll be potentially working on multiple layouts. Let's edit the QuarkXPress preferences and enable Single Layout Mode by default. Later, when you're more comfortable with QuarkXPress, edit the Preferences and disable Single Layout Mode as appropriate.

Guided Activity 15: Enable Single Layout Mode By Default

1. Ensure QuarkXPress is still running. No projects should be open.

2. Change the QuarkXPress application preferences so that new projects all use Single Layout Mode.

   ❒ Windows users, choose **Edit > Preferences**;
   Mac users, choose **QuarkXPress > Settings**

   The Preferences dialog box opens.

   ❒ from the **Project** category, select **General**

   ❒ select **Single Layout Mode**

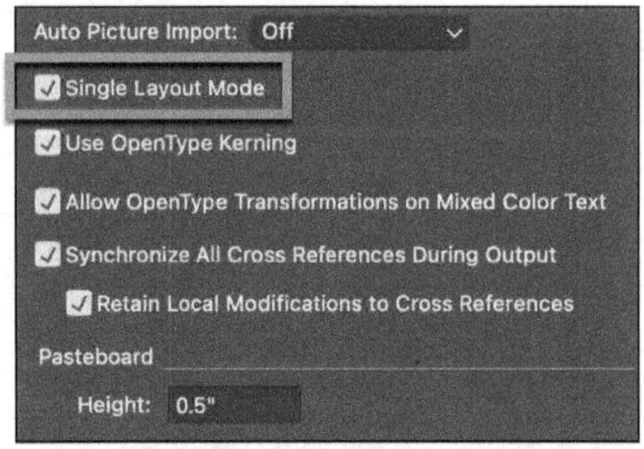

   ❒ click **OK**

3. Create a new project.

   ❒ choose **File > New > Project** (or press [**command**] [**n**])

   Thanks to the preference change you made during the last step, notice that **Single Layout Mode** is already selected. 

   ❒ ensure the **Layout Type** is **Print**

   ❒ ensure the **Page Size** is **Letter**

   ❒ if necessary, change the margins to **0.5"** (one-half inch)

   ❒ ensure the **Orientation** is **Portrait**

   ❒ ensure that both **Facing Pages** and **Automatic Text Box** are **not selected** (if necessary, remove the check mark from both)

❒ ensure the **Column Guides** are set to **1** column

❒ ensure the **Gutter Width** is **.167"**

Because you are only using one column, the gutter width (the space between columns) is not important. However, the field cannot be left blank.

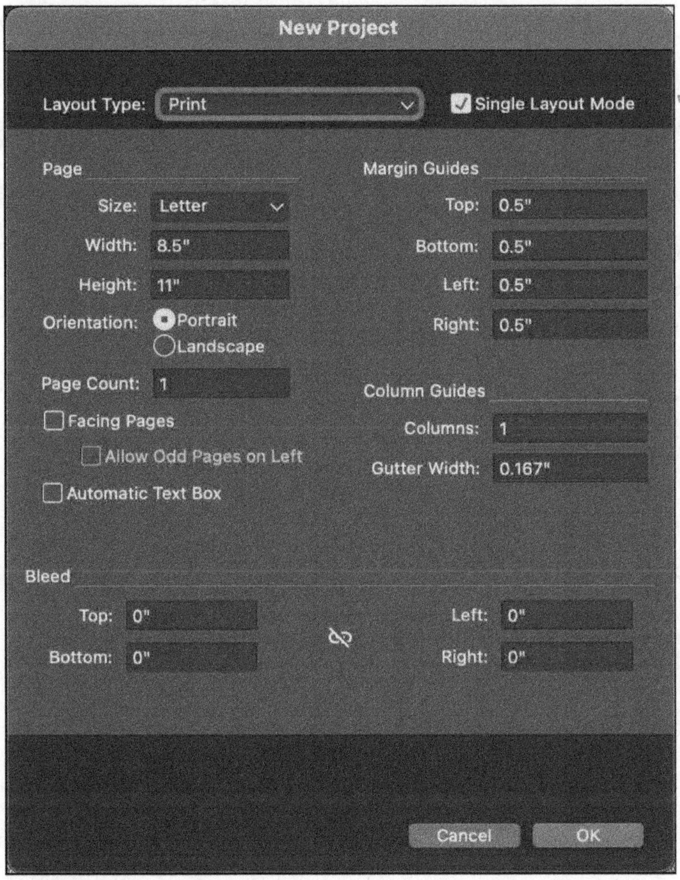

❒ click **OK**

NOTES

NOTES

Adding Text to a Layout

Typing text in a text content box works the same as typing in typical word processors. If you've got a blinking insertion point, you can type text. As you type, the insertion point moves to the right. As you near the right edge of a text box, the insertion point automatically wraps to the next line.

There is no limit to the amount of text you can add to a text box. However, if the text box is small and you add more text than will fit, the extra text will disappear and an overflow box will appear on the bottom right of the text box.

Guided Activity 16: Add Text and Work With Text Box Overflow

1. Add text to the layout.

   ❒ Select the **Text Content Tool** on the Tools window and draw a large text box anywhere on the page

   ❒ type the following text into the text box:

   The United States Coast Guard is the nation's oldest and premier maritime agency. The history of the Service is very complicated because it is the amalgamation of five Federal agencies.

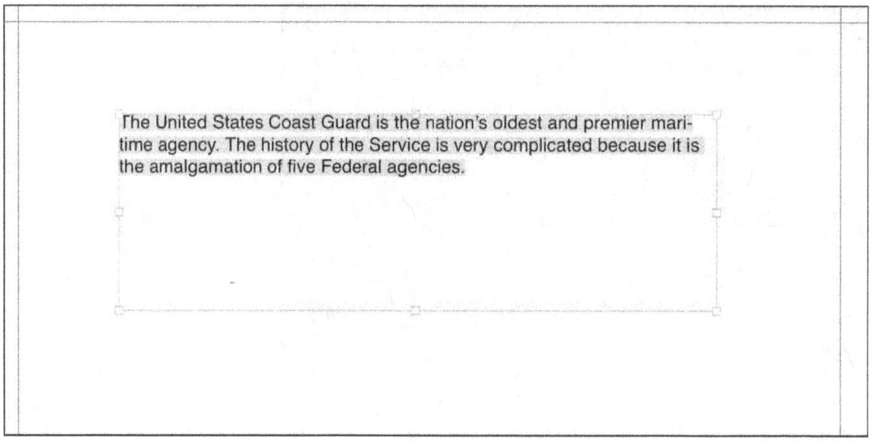

2. Save the project to the **QuarkXPress 2025 Book Assets** folder as **My Text Basics**.

3. Resize the text box vertically.

   ❒ point your mouse on the bottom, center resizing square of the text box

   A double-headed arrow appears indicating that you can make the text box taller or shorter.

   ❒ drag the square **up** until the height of your text box is no taller than **one inch**

   Notice the overflow text alert—the red X—that appears in the lower right of the text box.

4. Use the Line Check Utility to alert you of overflow text.

   ❒ choose **Utilities > Line Check > Search Criteria**

   The Search Criteria dialog box opens.

   ❒ deselect all of the options except **Text Box Overflow**

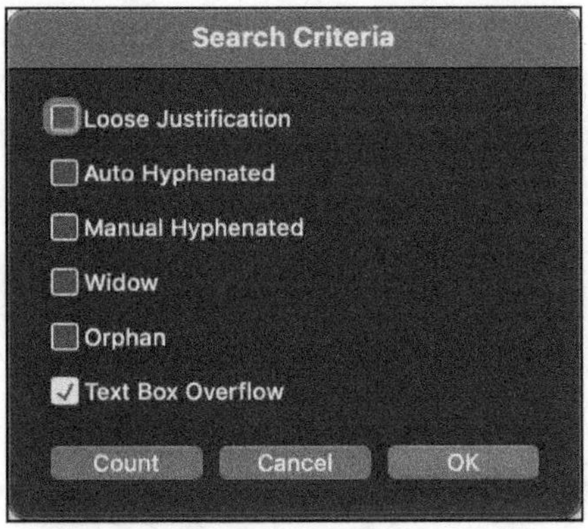

   ❒ click **Count**

   The number 1 appears to the right of Text Box Overflow, an indication that one text box in your layout has text overflowing the box. It's a good idea to run this utility prior to printing your project. Any number greater than 0 should be investigated.

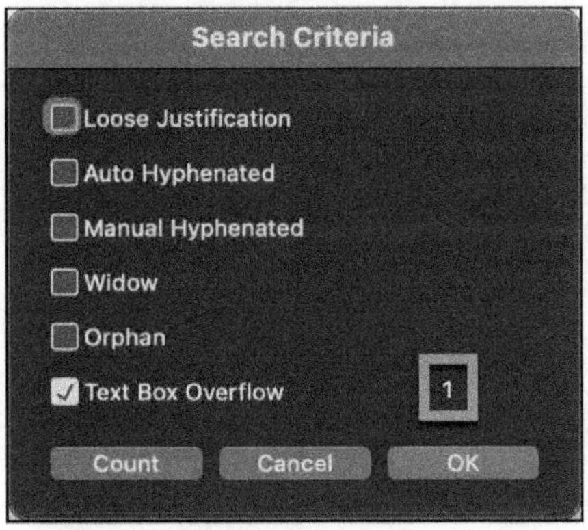

   ❒ click **OK**

5. Using the **Item Tool**, drag the bottom, center square of the text box **down**, making the text box tall enough to remove the overflow text alert.

6. Use the Line Check Utility again to confirm there are no text overflows.

   ❒ choose **Utilities > Line Check > Search Criteria**

   ❒ ensure all of the options are deselected except **Text Box Overflow**

   ❒ click **Count**

   The number **0** appears to the right of Text Box Overflow.

   ❒ click **OK**

NOTES

NOTES

Importing Text

You have now learned that you can easily type as much text as you need into a text content box. However, instead of typing all of the content yourself, it is more likely that you will be provided the existing text for use in the project. You can import text files from just about any word processor. Alternatively, you can also copy and paste text into a text content box.

Guided Activity 17: Import Text

1. Ensure that the **My Text Basics** project is open.

2. Import text into the text content box.

   ❒ using the **Text Content Tool**, click anywhere within the layout's text box

   ❒ choose **Edit > Select All** to select the text that you typed

   ❒ choose **File > Import**

   ❒ from the **QuarkXPress 2025 Book Assets > text** folder, open **textContent.txt**

   The selected text within the text box has been replaced with new content.

3. Resize the text box as necessary to remove the text overflow alert.

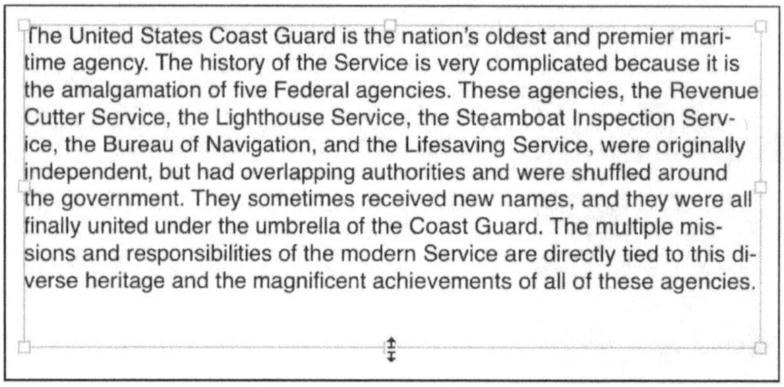

4. Save the project.

The Measurements Window

You can use the **Item Tool** to move and resize a selected layout item. If you need to move an item, change its color, and its size all at the same time, the Item tool isn't very efficient because you can only perform one task at a time. An excellent alternative to the Item tool is the Measurements window where you can change quickly control several object properties from page position, box size, color, and more.

Guided Activity 18: Modify Item Attributes

1. Ensure that the text box you have been working with is still selected.

2. Change the page location of the text box.

   ❒ choose **Window > Measurements**

   The Measurements window typically appears at the bottom of the QuarkXPress window. There several tabs including Character, Paragraph, Rules, and Text Box.

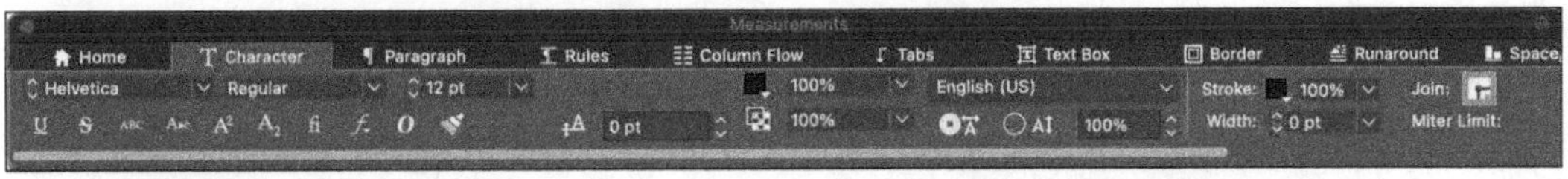

   ❒ select the **Text Box** tab

   ❒ change the **X** value to **1**

   ❒ change the **Y** value to **1** and then press [**return**]

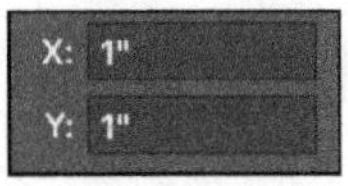

   The **X** and **Y** values control where the selected item appears on the page. The larger the value, the farther away from zero the item will be. Currently the **zero point** of the page is the upper left of the page trim. (You learned about the zero point on page 21.) The upper left of the text box is now positioned one inch from the left of the page trim and one inch down from the top of the page trim. Why did I specifically say the upper left of the text box? On the Measurements window, there is a **proxy area** that lets you select which part of an item is being "measured." By default, the proxy (shown in the box) is the upper left of the selected item.

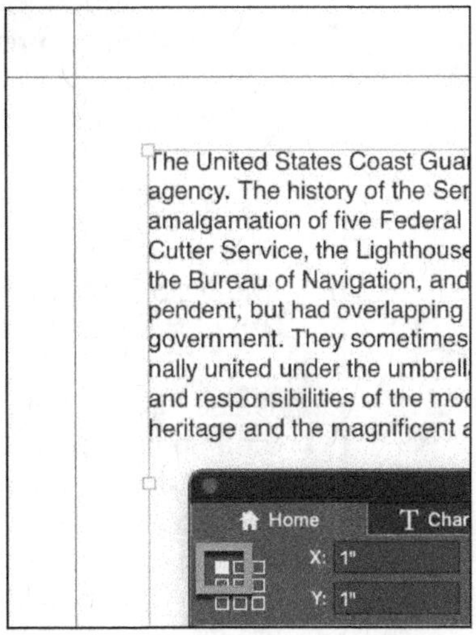

The proxy area is shown highlighted above.

3. Change the size of the text box.

   ❒ ensure the text box is still selected

   ❒ on the **Measurements** window, change the **W (Width)** to **5.5**

   ❒ change the **H** (Height) to **4.5** and then press [**return**]

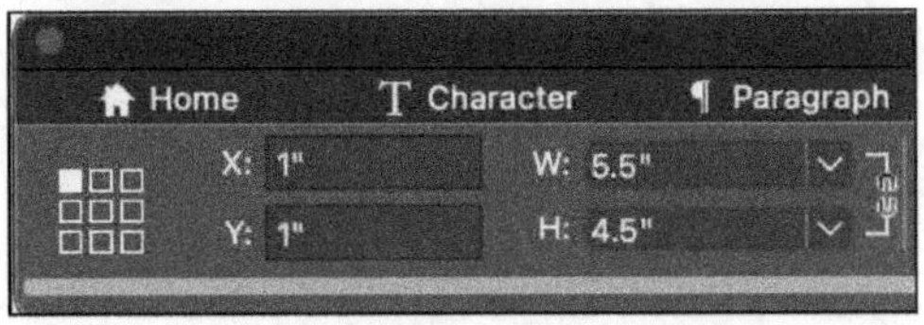

Invisibles

Just as with any word processor, you can edit text directly within QuarkXPress. If you have a blinking insertion point in a content box, you can type, import, edit, cut, copy, and format text. When working with text, it's helpful to see the non-printing characters that separate words and paragraphs. These characters are known as invisibles.

Guided Activity 19: Display Invisibles

1. The **My Text Basics** project should still be open and you should have saved your work after the Confidence Check from the previous page.

2. Change your view to **Actual Size**.

3. Remove a word.

   ❒ using the **Text Content Tool**, double-click the word **automatically** to select it

   ❒ press [**backspace**] (PC) or [**delete**] (Mac) to remove the word

4. Break the one paragraph into two.

   ❒ position your mouse to the left of the phrase **These agencies** and click **once**

   Your insertion point should now appear just in front of the word "These."

   ❒ PC users, press [**enter**] twice; Mac users, press [**return**] twice

5. Show invisibles.

   ❒ choose **View > Invisibles**

   Notice that non-printing symbols, such as hard returns and spaces, appear.

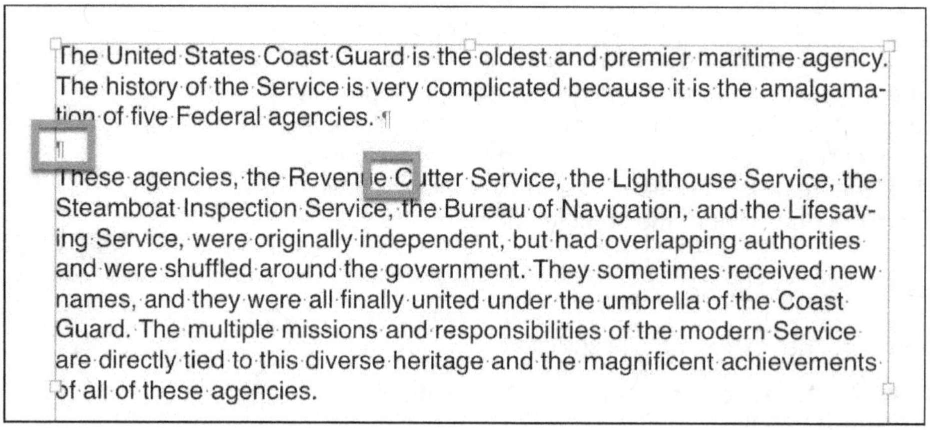
The·United·States·Coast·Guard·is·the·oldest·and·premier·maritime·agency. The·history·of·the·Service·is·very·complicated·because·it·is·the·amalgamation·of·five·Federal·agencies.·¶
¶
These·agencies,·the·Revenue·Cutter·Service,·the·Lighthouse·Service,·the·Steamboat·Inspection·Service,·the·Bureau·of·Navigation,·and·the·Lifesaving·Service,·were·originally·independent,·but·had·overlapping·authorities·and·were·shuffled·around·the·government.·They·sometimes·received·new·names,·and·they·were·all·finally·united·under·the·umbrella·of·the·Coast·Guard.·The·multiple·missions·and·responsibilities·of·the·modern·Service·are·directly·tied·to·this·diverse·heritage·and·the·magnificent·achievements·of·all·of·these·agencies.

6. Hide invisibles with a keyboard shortcut.

   ❒ press [**command**] [**i**] on your keyboard

   If you press the [**command**] [**i**] again, you will show the invisibles.

Selecting Text

There are several ways to select text in QuarkXPress. Using the Text Content Tool, you can **drag** over text, **shift-click** to select a range of text, **double-click** to select a word, **triple-click** to select a line, **four-click** to select a paragraph, or **five-click** to select an entire story.

Guided Activity 20: Use Different Text Selection Techniques

1. The **My Text Basics** project should still be open.

2. Select text by dragging.

   ❒ select the **Text Content Tool** and **drag** over some of the text to highlight it

   ❒ click anywhere in the text to deselect the selected text and move the insertion point to a new location

3. Select text by clicking.

   ❒ using the Text Content Tool, **double-click** any word in your text to highlight one word

   ❒ **triple-click** any word to highlight one line

   ❒ **four-click** any word to highlight one paragraph

   ❒ **five-click** any word to highlight the entire story

4. Select text by shift-clicking.

   ❒ using the Text Content Tool, click anywhere in the text

   ❒ point anywhere else in the story (but don't click just yet)

   ❒ press [**shift**] on your keyboard, click one time, and then release [**shift**]

   The text between your starting and ending clicks is highlighted.

5. Select text by using the keyboard.

   ❒ using the Text Content Tool, click anywhere in the story

   ❒ press [**command**] [**a**]

   The entire story highlights. You can get the same result by choosing **Edit > Select All**.

6. Select text by using the keyboard.

   ❒ using the Text Content Tool, click in the middle of your story

   ❒ hold [**shift**] and press the right arrow key [➔] on your keyboard a few times

   Text is selected one character at a time.

   ❒ hold [**command**] [**shift**] and press the right arrow key [➔]

   Text is selected, one word at a time.

   ❒ hold [**command**] [**shift**] and press the down arrow key [🡇]

   Text is selected, one paragraph at a time.

NOTES

NOTES

Character Attributes

Before you can change the font for any text in your story, you need to select it. After the text is selected, changing fonts is as simple as choosing the font you want from the Style, menu or Measurements window.

While there are thousands of fonts, there are only two categories of font: serif (fonts with feet) and sans-serif (without feet). The two most popular fonts are Times New Roman (serif) and Arial (sans-serif). Here is an example of both:

This is an example of Times New Roman, a serif font.

This is an example of Arial, a sans-serif font.

You learned about points and picas on page 11. Typefaces are measured in points and while both lines of text above are 18 points, Arial looks larger because Arial has a larger x-height (the height of lowercase letters). In addition, the letters themselves tend to be more spread out. In printed materials, sans-serif fonts like Arial are typically used for headlines and subheads (because they look good bigger). Serif faces guide the eye across the page and typically make ideal body text.

Guided Activity 21: Change Character Attributes

1. The **My Text Basics** project should still be open.

2. Change the font and font size of selected text.

   ❒ using the **Text Content Tool**, click one time in the **first paragraph**

   ❒ click **four times** in the paragraph to select it

   ❒ if necessary, open the **Measurements** window

   ❒ select the **Character** tab

   ❒ use the **Font** drop-down menu to change the font to **Times New Roman**

   ❒ from the **Size** area, change the size to **14 pt**

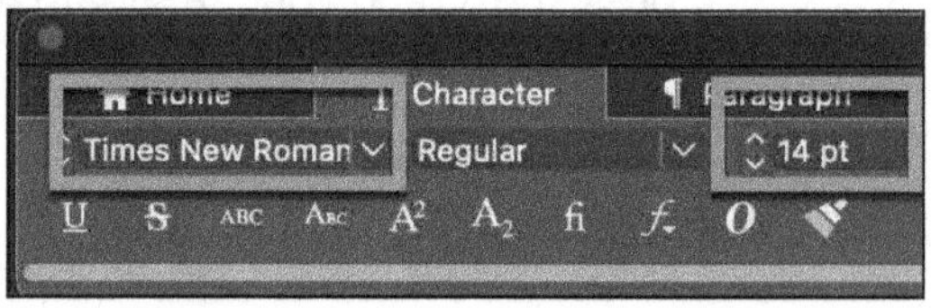

3. Change the character style of selected text.

   ❒ using the **Text Content Tool**, double-click any word to select it

   ❒ on the **Measurements** window, **Character** tab, click the drop-down menu between the Font and Size menus and choose **Bold**

   ❒ click the **Styles** icon drop-down menu and choose **Shadow**

   ❒ click the **Styles** icon drop-down menu and choose **ALL CAPS**

Glyphs

A glyph is the visual representation of a character in a typeface, including letters, numbers, symbols, or decorative elements. It can vary by typeface and style, such as bold, italic, or ornate designs. Glyphs also include special characters like copyright symbols and trademark symbols. During the activity that follows, you will use the Glyphs window to add a registered symbol.

Guided Activity 22: Use the Glyphs Window to Add a Symbol

1. The **My Text Basics** project should still be open.

2. Use the Glyphs window to add a registered mark.

   ❒ replace any word in the text box with **your company name**

   ❒ click just to the right of the text you just typed

   ❒ choose **Windows > Glyphs**

   The Glyphs window opens.

   ❒ ensure **Entire Font** is selected in the drop-down menu beneath the **Font** name

   ❒ click the **Zoom in** icon a few times to zoom closer to the Glyph characters

   ❒ scroll down and find the ® symbol

   ❒ double-click the ®

   The ® symbol is added next to your company name.

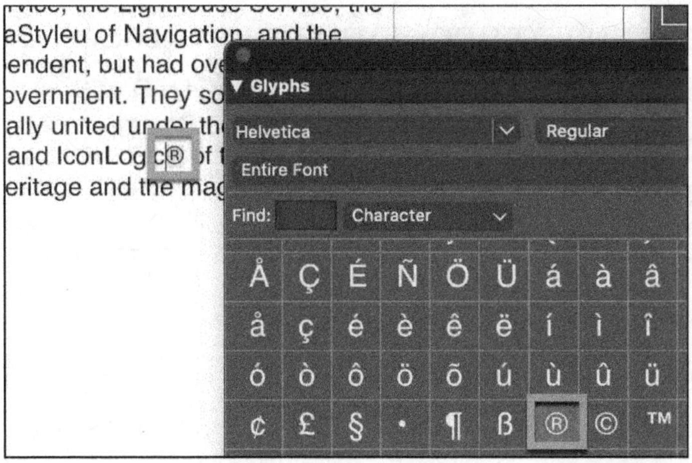

   ❒ close the **Glyphs** window

3. Raise the symbol above the baseline and make it smaller.

   ❒ on the **Measurements** window, **Character** tab, click the **Styles** icon and choose **Superior**

   The registered mark is smaller and is superscript.

NOTES

NOTES

Confidence Check

1. Zoom closer to the text.

   Notice that the size of the registered mark is smaller than the font size of the rest of the text. The size of the text is controlled by the Superior VScale and HScale. You'll modify those settings next.

2. PC users, choose **Edit > Preferences**;
   Mac users choose **QuarkXPress > Settings**

3. From the **Print Layout** category, select **Character**.

4. Change the Superior VScale and HScale to **75%** and then click **OK**.

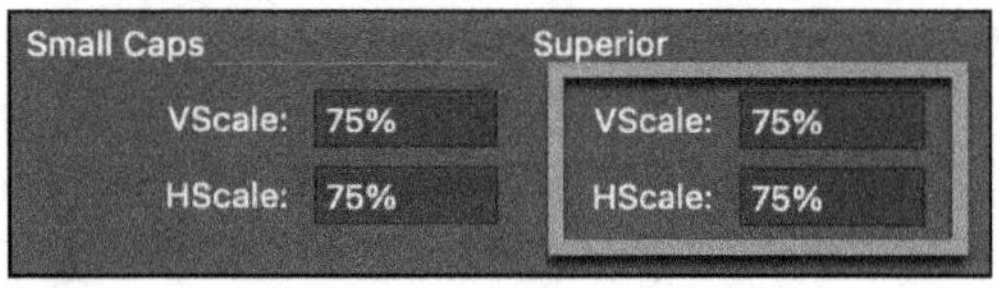

   The size of the registered mark should now be larger.

5. Here's a cool feature: click at the end of the text, press [**spacebar**] and then type **1/2**.

   The text you just typed is the numeral 1, a slash, and a 2.

   But what if you need a true fraction?

6. Ensure your insertion point is just after the fraction you typed.

7. Choose **Style > Type Style > Make Fraction** to convert the text you typed into a fraction.

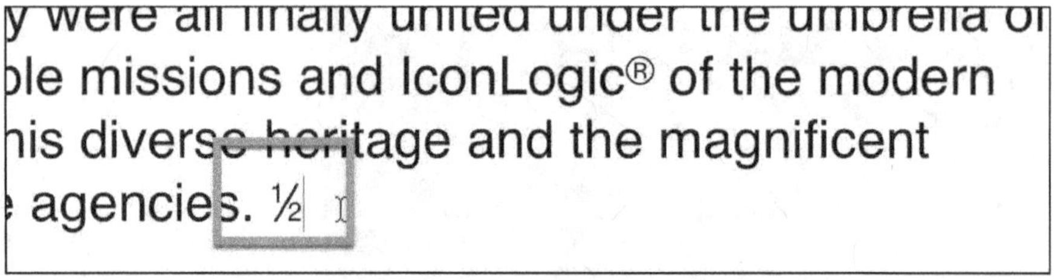

8. Save and close the project.

Flowing Text

You have already learned that QuarkXPress allows you to import text into a content box (page 30). When text reaches the end of a text box, you learned that the overflow disappears and an overflow text alert appears at the bottom right of the text box (page 28). During the next few activities, you will learn how to account for overflow text by allowing to text to flow from one text box to another both automatically and manually.

Guided Activity 23: Automatically Flow Text

1. Create a new project with an automatic text box.

   ❒ choose **File > New > Project** (or press [**command**] [**n**])

   ❒ ensure the **Layout Type** is **Print**

   ❒ ensure **Single Layout Mode** is selected

   ❒ ensure the **Page Size** is **Letter**

   ❒ if necessary, change the **Margin Guides** to **0.5**" (one-half inch)

   ❒ ensure the **Orientation** is **Portrait**

   ❒ ensure that **Facing Pages** is **not selected**

   ❒ select **Automatic Text Box** (put a check mark in the box)

   The Automatic Text Box option will add a text content box to the page. As text is added to the box, pages will automatically be added to account for any overflow text.

   ❒ ensure the **Column Guides** are set to **1** column and the Gutter Width is **.167"**

   ❒ click **OK**

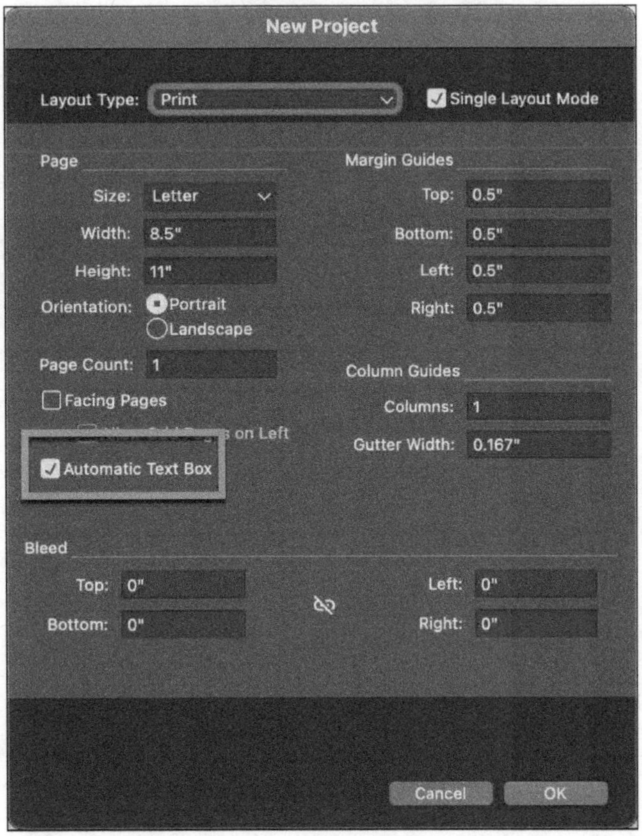

2. Change your view to Fit in Window.

   On the page, notice that a large text content box has automatically been added to the page.

NOTES

3. Import text.
   - ❒ select the **Text Content Tool** and click anywhere on the page
   - ❒ choose **File > Import** (or press **[command] [e]**)

   The Import Text dialog box opens.

   - ❒ from the **QuarkXPress 2025 Book Assets** > **textFiles**, open **getMe.doc**

   The text is imported into the automatic text box.

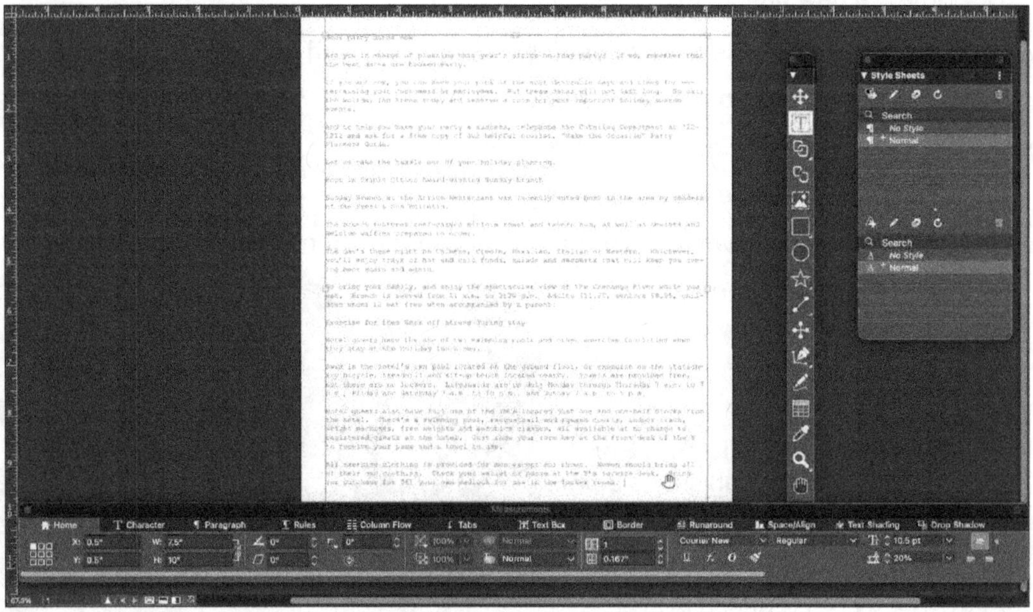

4. Save the Project to the **QuarkXPress 2025 Book Assets** folder as **myParagraphFormatting**.

Paragraph Alignment

To align a single paragraph, it is not necessary to select it—you need only select the Text Content Tool and click anywhere in the paragraph. If, however, your intent is to format more than one paragraph at a time, you'll need to use the selection techniques you learned on page 33 to highlight at least part of the paragraphs you intend to align.

Guided Activity 24: Align Paragraphs

1. The **myParagraphFormatting** project should still be open (you were working on this document during the last activity).

2. Align paragraphs using the **Measurements** window.

   ❒ using the **Text Content Tool**, click anywhere in the first paragraph ("Book party dates now")

   ❒ on the **Measurements** window, select the **Paragraph** tab

   ❒ click the **Centered** alignment icon

   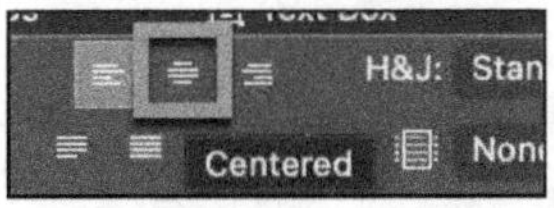

   The paragraph is centered horizontally within the text box.

   ❒ click anywhere in the second paragraph and, on the **Measurements** window, **Paragraph** tab, click the **Right** alignment icon

   The paragraph is aligned to the right of the text box.

   ❒ click anywhere in the next paragraph and, on the **Measurements** window, **Paragraph** tab, click the **Justified** alignment icon

   Justified text looks more formal than the other alignment options. Many newspapers and magazines go with this kind of alignment.

   ❒ click anywhere in the next paragraph and, on the **Measurements** window, **Paragraph** tab, click the **Forced** alignment icon

   Forced alignment forces the last sentence in selected paragraphs to stretch apart and rarely looks good.

3. Select and align paragraphs using keyboard shortcuts.

   ❒ select the Text Content Tool and click anywhere in the story

   ❒ press **[command]** [a] to select all of the text

   ❒ press **[command]** **[shift]** [c] to Center the text

   ❒ press **[command]** **[shift]** [r] to Right align the text

   ❒ press **[command]** **[shift]** [j] to Justify the text

   ❒ press **[command]** **[shift]** [l] to Left align the text

NOTES

Paragraph Spacing

For most people who type their text in word processors, adding the white space necessary to indicate where one paragraph ends and the next begins is accomplished in one of two ways: extra hard returns added between paragraphs (the more white space required, the more hard returns that are typed), or tab characters keyed in front of every new paragraph to indent the first lines of every paragraph. And of course, I've seen people do both—extra paragraph marks and tabs. If I've just described how you type text, you've been adding space the hard way. You only need one hard return between each paragraph, and you don't need to use a tab character for first line indents. As you are about to see, QuarkXPress puts excellent features for both vertical paragraph spacing and first line indentation available at your fingertips.

Guided Activity 25: Work with Multiple Columns

1. The **myParagraphFormatting** project should still be open (you were working on this document during the last activity).

2. View the invisible text symbols.

   ❒ choose **View > Invisibles**

   Notice that extra paragraph marks are between each of the paragraphs (two instead of one). The person who typed this text most likely learned to type on a typewriter where there was no perfect way to control paragraph spacing. Later in this book, you will learn how to remove the extra paragraph breaks using the Find/Change feature. For this activity, you will replace this text with another text file.

3. Replace the existing text with new text.

   ❒ select the **Text Content Tool** and click anywhere in the text on the page

   ❒ press [**command**] [**a**] to selected all of the text

   ❒ press [**command**] [**e**] to **Import**

   ❒ from the **QuarkXPress 2025 Book Assets** > **textFiles**, open **spaceMe**

   The original text is replaced with this new version. Notice that there is only one paragraph symbol between each of the paragraphs in the story. This text was typed correctly in the word processor.

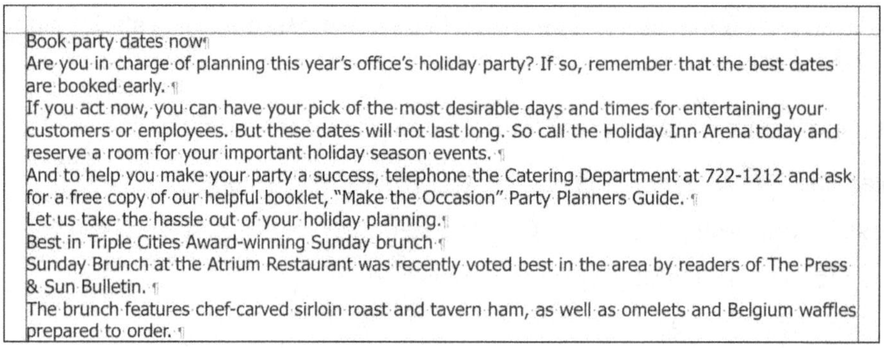
Book party dates now¶
Are you in charge of planning this year's office's holiday party? If so, remember that the best dates are booked early. ¶
If you act now, you can have your pick of the most desirable days and times for entertaining your customers or employees. But these dates will not last long. So call the Holiday Inn Arena today and reserve a room for your important holiday season events. ¶
And to help you make your party a success, telephone the Catering Department at 722-1212 and ask for a free copy of our helpful booklet, "Make the Occasion" Party Planners Guide. ¶
Let us take the hassle out of your holiday planning.¶
Best in Triple Cities Award-winning Sunday brunch ¶
Sunday Brunch at the Atrium Restaurant was recently voted best in the area by readers of The Press & Sun Bulletin. ¶
The brunch features chef-carved sirloin roast and tavern ham, as well as omelets and Belgium waffles prepared to order. ¶

   The problem now is that it will be difficult for anyone reading the text to know where one paragraph ends and the next begins. Let's spend a few moments making the text easier to read by splitting the text box into two columns and adding vertical white space between the paragraphs.

4. Modify the text box so it contains two equal columns.
   - ❒ ensure that the text box on the page is selected
   - ❒ on the **Measurements** window, select the **Text Box** tab
   - ❒ change the number of **Columns** to **2**
   - ❒ change the **Gutter Width** to **.25** (one-quarter inch)

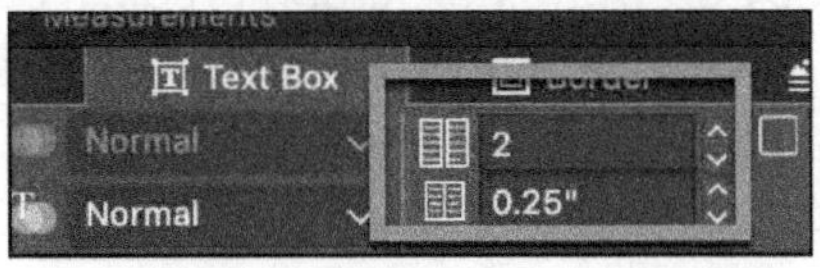

The single column text box is now two equal columns.

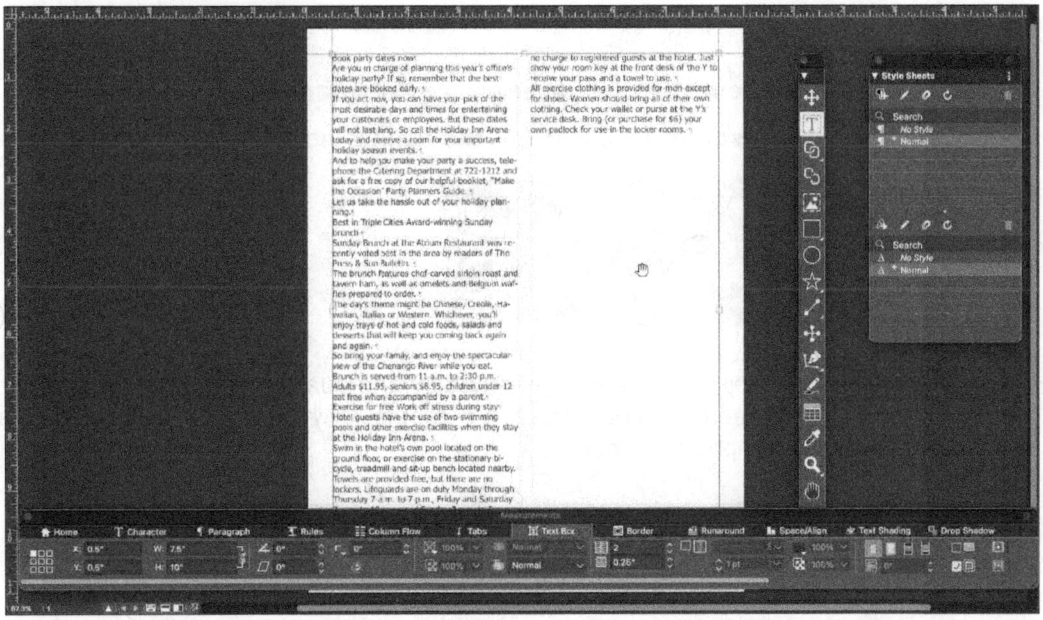

NOTES

NOTES

Guided Activity 26: Set a First Line Indent

1. The **myParagraphFormatting** project should still be open. (You were working on this document during the last activity.)

2. If necessary, show invisibles (press [**command**] [**i**] on your keyboard).

   Again, notice that each paragraph is separated by only one paragraph break. You are about to use spacing commands to control the amount of space between the paragraphs.

3. Select all of the text.

   ❒ select the **Text Content Tool** and click on the page

   ❒ press [**command**] [**a**] to select all of the text

4. Create a First Line indent.

   ❒ on the **Measurements** window, select the **Paragraph** tab

   ❒ change the **First Line** indent to **.25** (one-quarter inch) and press [**enter**]

The first line of every paragraph is indented by one-quarter inch. The visual white space you now see between each paragraph is a popular way to provide visual cues to a reader that a new paragraph has begun.

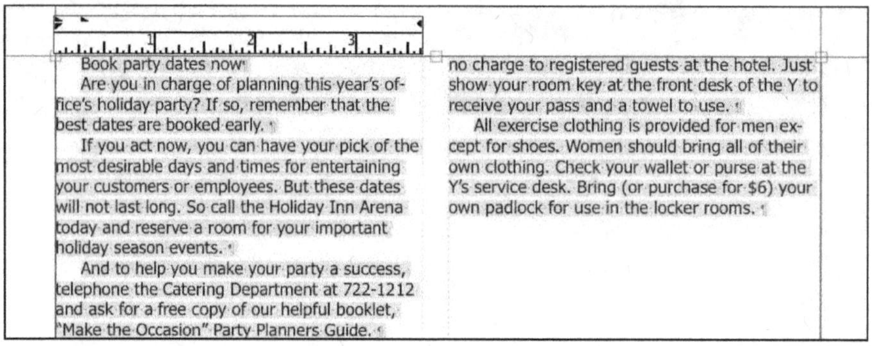

The other way to accomplish this goal is via vertical paragraph spacing. You will learn how to do that next.

Guided Activity 27: Add Space Between Paragraphs

1. The **myParagraphFormatting** project should still be open.

2. Using the Text Content Tool, select all of the text on the page (if necessary).

   ❒ if necessary, press [**command**] [**a**] to select all of the text

3. Remove the First Line indent.

   ❒ on the **Measurements** window, select the **Paragraph** tab

   ❒ change the **First Line** indent to **0** and press [**enter**]

4. Add space below each of the paragraphs.

   ❒ using the Space After area on the **Measurements** window, change the Space After to **.15** and press [**enter**]

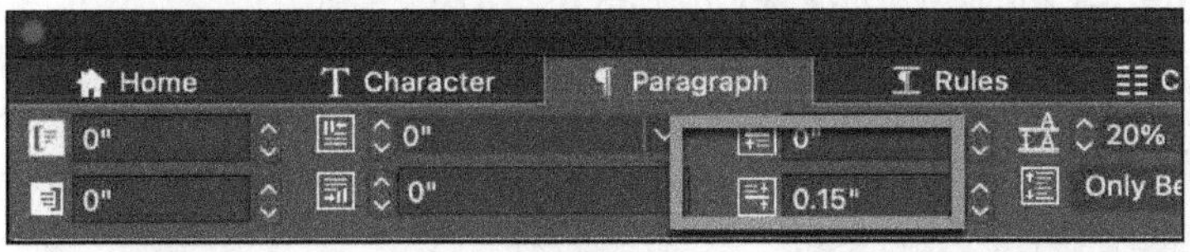

There is now .15 inch of space after all of the selected paragraphs.

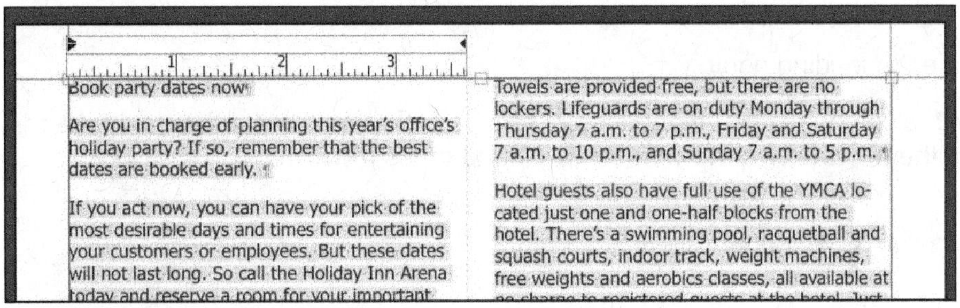

5. Save the project.

NOTES

NOTES

Leading

Leading refers to the space between lines in your text. A simple way to make sure you've got ample leading is to use the "plus two" rule: take your font's point size and add two. The result is a typical amount of leading in body copy layout. For example, if your body text is set at 12 points, 12 + 2 = 14. Typical leading would be 14 points. Many designers will show font size and leading as a fraction. For example, if you see 12/14 written as instructions for you to use in creating a layout, the first number you see is font size (12) and the second number is leading (14).

Guided Activity 28: Set Leading

1. The **myParagraphFormatting** project should still be open (you were working on this document during the last activity).

2. Change the leading.

   ❒ with all of the text in the layout still selected, change the number in the Leading area on the **Measurements** window to **17** and press [**return**]

   There are now 17 points of lead between every selected line of text on the page.

3. Change the leading again.

   ❒ with all of the text in the layout still selected, change the number in the Leading area on the **Measurements** window to **12** and press [**return**]

Confidence Check

1. Change the leading to 14 points.
2. Format all of the paragraphs so that they have .15 inch Space **Before** and **After**.

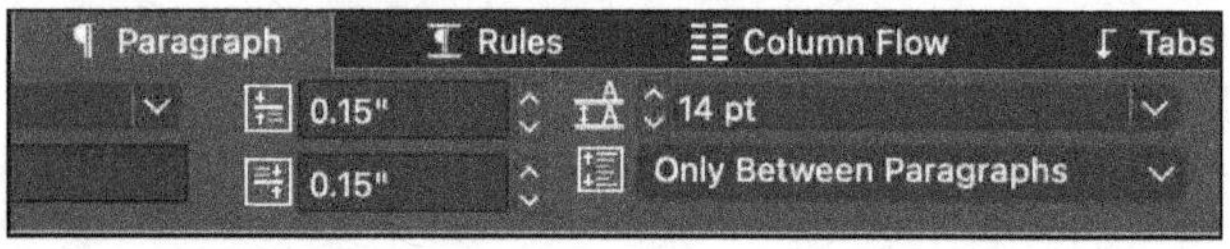

3. Save the project.

Rules

Sometimes you will need to place a line above and/or below your paragraphs. Although you could easily use your line tools to do the job, the minute you add text or move the paragraph, you'll find yourself having to also move the lines. The Rules command simplifies this task. The rules that result look like lines you create with the Line tool, but they will move and resize with the paragraph they are attached to.

Guided Activity 29: Set Paragraph Rules

1. The **myParagraphFormatting** project should still be open.

2. Set the properties for a rule above a paragraph.

   ❒ using the **Text Content Tool**, select the paragraph in the first column "**Are you in**..."

   ❒ on the **Measurements** window, select the **Rule** tab

   ❒ select **Rule Above** (put a check in the box) 

   ❒ from the **Rule Style** drop-down menu, select **All Dots**

   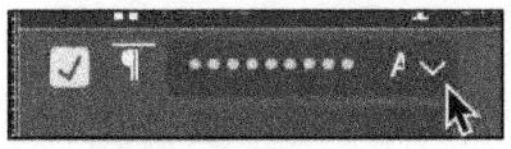

   ❒ change the **Rule Width** to **4 pt**

   ❒ select any color as the **Rule Color**

   ❒ change the **Rule Opacity** to **100%**

   The lower the Opacity, the more see-through and lighter your rule will be. An opacity of 100% shows the rule completely; with a 0%, you wouldn't be able to see the rule at all.

   ❒ change the **Rule Offset** to **50%**

   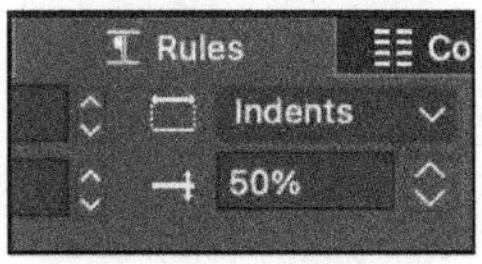

   The Offset option controls how close the rule will be to the text. By changing the Offset to 50%, QuarkXPress positions the rule 50% between the top line in the current paragraph and the last line in the paragraph above. By using a percentage, you can guarantee that there will always be space between the text and the rule, no matter how big the text in the paragraph may get.

   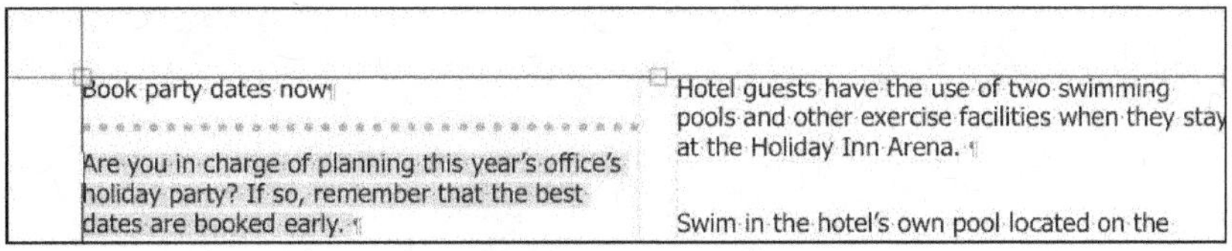

NOTES

Confidence Check

1. Add a rule below the same paragraph using the same Measurement properties.
   - ❒ select **Rule Below**
   - ❒ choose the **All Dots** Style
   - ❒ change the **Width** to **4 pt**
   - ❒ change the **Color** to **Magenta**
   - ❒ change the **Opacity** to **100%**
   - ❒ change the **Offset** to **50%**

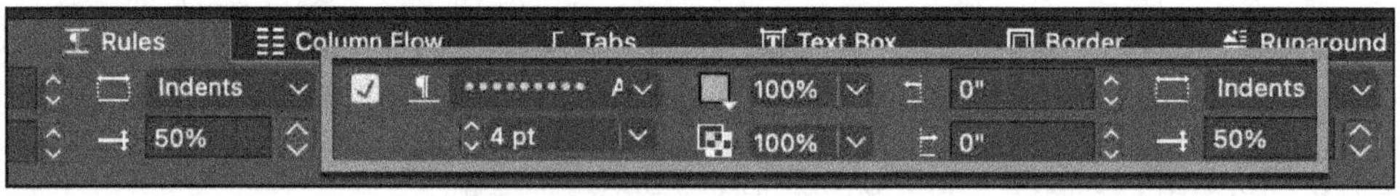

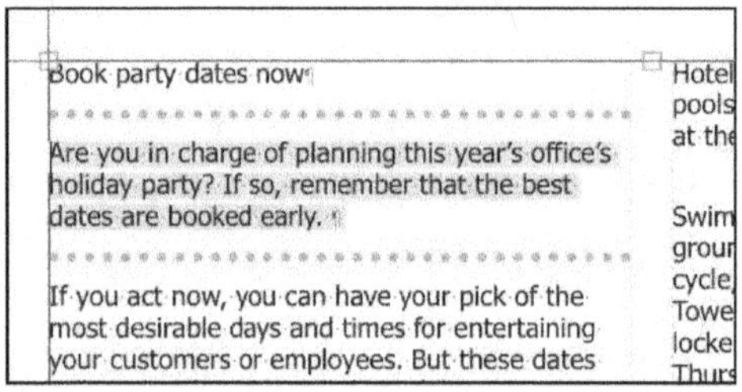

2. Save and close the project.

ICONLOGIC

"Skills and Drills" Learning

Module 3: Image Basics

In This Module You Will Learn About:

And You Will Learn To:

NOTES

Importing, Resizing and Cropping Pictures

You can import a picture into any QuarkXPress picture box, using the Picture Content or Item tools. Once you've imported a picture into a picture content box, you can crop the picture, resize it, reposition it and, depending on its format, even change its color and contrast.

While imported images can be seen onscreen, the image file itself is not embedded in the layout. When you import a picture, QuarkXPress keeps track of the image's file name and location. Should you change the location of the file, modify it, or remove it from your computer, QuarkXPress prompts you to locate the file before the layout can be printed or converted to a PDF. It's a good idea to always keep the original image file in the same folder as the QuarkXPress project.

Guided Activity 30: Import, Resize, and Crop an Image

1. Create a new project without an automatic text box.

   ❒ choose **File > New > Project** (or press [**command**] [**n**])

   ❒ ensure the Layout Type is **Print**

   ❒ ensure **Single Layout Mode** is selected

   ❒ ensure the Page Size is **Letter**

   ❒ if necessary, change the margins to **0.5**" (one-half inch)

   ❒ ensure the **Orientation** is **Portrait**

   ❒ ensure that **Facing Pages** is **not selected**

   ❒ deselect **Automatic Text Box** (remove the check mark from the box)

   ❒ ensure the **Column Guides** are set to **1** column

   ❒ click **OK**

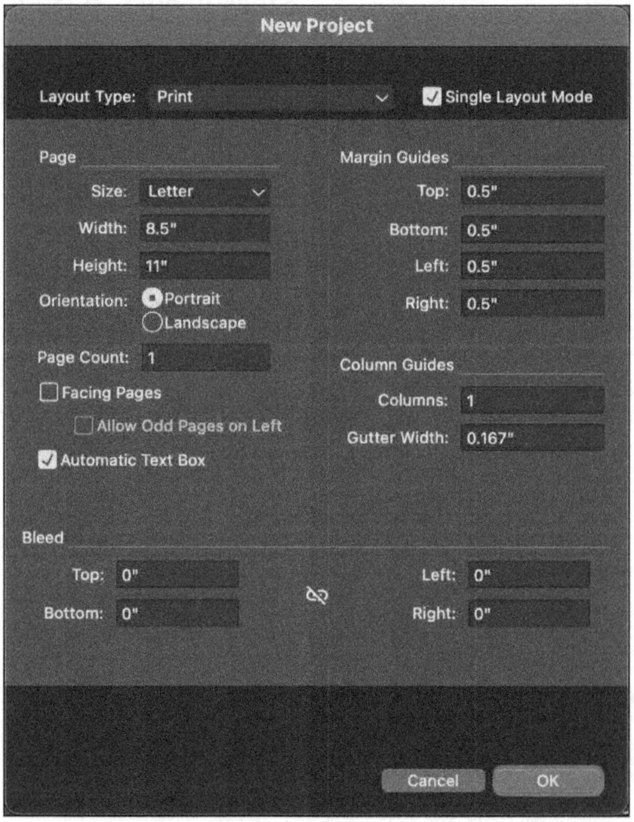

2. Save the project to the **QuarkXPress 2025 Book Assets** folder as **My Images**.

3. Change the layout View to **Fit in Window**. (You learned how to change views on page 3.)

4. Draw a large picture box on the page.

   ❒ on the **Tools window**, select the **Picture Content Tool** and draw a rectangular picture box on your page that is approximately **5** inches wide and **3** inches tall

   Picture boxes contain a large X in the middle until you import an image.

5. Import an image into the picture box.

    ❒ ensure the picture box you just drew is selected, choose **File > Import**

    ❒ from the **QuarkXPress 2025 Book Assets > Images** folder, open **Gallatin2**

    The picture is an image of the Coast Guard Cutter Gallatin. The image is larger than the picture box. Only the part of the image you see within the picture box will print.

6. Change the location of the picture box.

    ❒ select the **Item tool**  and drag the picture box to the upper left of the layout.

    While you have changed the location of the image, notice that this has had no impact on how the image inside the box is cropped or the size of the image.

7. Change the size of the picture box.

    ❒ with the picture box on the page selected, use the **Measurements** window to change the box Width to **6** and the box Height to **3**

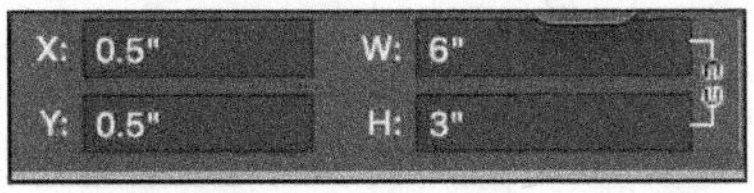

Notice that even though the box has changed size, the change had no impact on the cropping or image size.

NOTES

NOTES

8. Change the size of the image within the picture box.

   ❒ with the picture on the page selected, use the **Measurements** window to change both the X% and Y% to **80%**

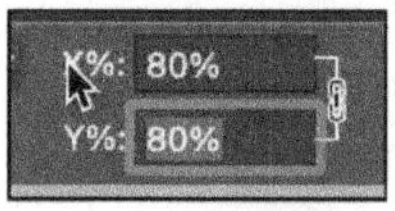

9. Change how a picture is cropped.

   ❒ select the **Picture Content Tool** and drag the center of the image **left** to crop out approximately one-half inch of the water

10. Save the project.

Guided Activity 31: Resize, Center, and Fit a Picture

1. The **My Images** project should still be open.

2. Resize the picture using keyboard shortcuts.

   ❒ with the picture box selected, press **[alt] [command] [shift] [>]** a few times

   The picture gets larger every time you press the keys.

   ❒ press **[alt] [command] [shift] [<]** a few times

   The picture gets smaller every time you press the keys.

3. Center the picture in the box.

   ❒ choose **Style > Center Picture**

   The image should appear perfectly centered in the picture box.

4. Change the scale of the picture so that it fills the picture box.

   ❒ choose **Style > Scale Picture to Fill Box**

NOTES

NOTES

Guided Activity 32: Rotate and Skew a Picture

1. The **My Images** project from the last activity should still be open.

2. Rotate the picture.

   ❒ with the picture box still selected, on the **Measurements** window, change the value in the **Picture Angle** field to **22**

   The picture is rotated but the picture box is not.

3. Skew the picture.

   ❒ on the **Measurements** window, change the **Picture Angle** back to **0** and then change the **Picture Skew** to **25**

   The picture is no longer rotated, but now it's skewed.

4. Remove the picture skew.

   ❒ on the **Measurements** window, change the **Picture Skew** back to **0**

Guided Activity 33: Resize an Item and Content Together

1. The **My Images** project from the last activity should still be open.

2. Resize the picture box and its content at the same time.

   ❒ ensure the picture box on the page is selected

   ❒ point to the resizing handle (the white square) at the right, center of the picture box

   Your mouse pointer should look like a double-headed arrow pointing left and right. 

   ❒ press [**command**] on your keyboard

   ❒ while pressing [**command**], resize the box so that it is smaller (drag the resizing handle **left**)

   ❒ release the mouse and release the [**command**] key

   Both the picture and the box should have resized together.

3. Undo the last step.

   ❒ choose **Edit > Undo Picture Box Change**

4. Proportionally resize the picture box and picture at the same time.

   ❒ ensure the picture box on the page is selected

   ❒ point to the resizing handle (the white square) at the right, center of the picture box

   ❒ press [**command**] [**alt**] [**shift**] on your keyboard

   ❒ while still pressing [**command**] [**alt**] [**shift**], resize the picture so that it is smaller (drag the resizing handle both left and then right)

   ❒ release the mouse and release [**command**] [**alt**] [**shift**]

   Both the picture box and the picture inside the box have resized proportionally.

5. Replace the contents of a picture box with a new picture.

   ❒ with the picture box selected, press [**command**] [**e**] to Import a new picture

   ❒ from the **QuarkXPress 2025 Book Assets > Images** folder, open **beachBunny.jpg**

   ❒ click **Open**

NOTES

NOTES

Confidence Check

1. With the picture box still selected, choose **Style > Scale Picture to Fit Box**.

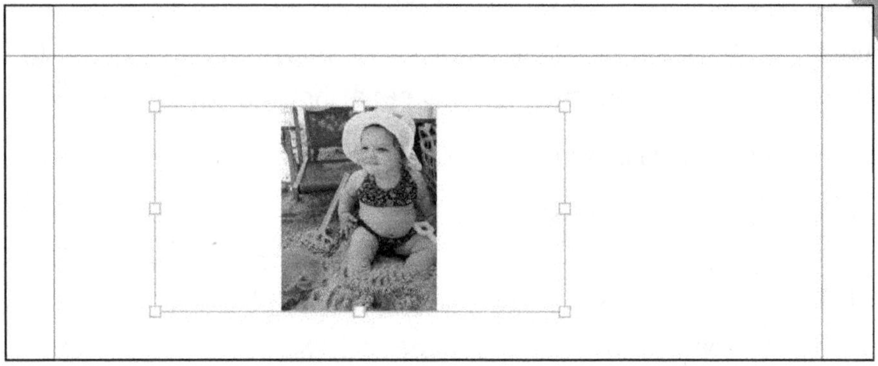

2. Choose **Style > Flip Picture Vertical** to flip the picture upside down.
3. Choose **Style > Flip Picture Horizontal** to force the picture to face the other way.
4. Reverse the flips by choosing **Style > Flip Picture Vertical** and then **Style > Flip Picture Horizontal**.
5. Save and close the project.

Guided Activity 34: Add a Picture to a Layout

1. Open **pictureMe** from the **QuarkXPress 2025 Book Assets** folder and save the file as **myAddedPicture**.

   You have learned most of the skills necessary to create this layout from scratch. To save time, I have added and formatted the text for you. All the layout needs is a picture.

2. Draw a picture box.

   ❒ using the **Picture Content Tool**, draw a picture box in the upper right of the layout as shown below

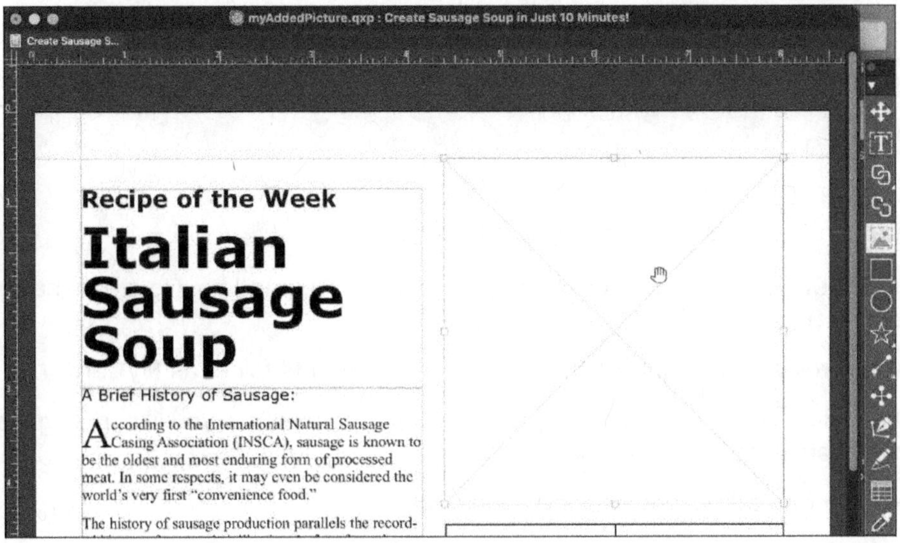

3. Import a picture.

   ❒ with the picture box you drew selected, choose **File > Import Picture** (or press **[command] [e]**)

   ❒ from the **QuarkXPress 2025 Book Assets > Images** folder, open **sausage_soup1.jpg**

4. Save and close the project.

NOTES

Confidence Check

Using the **cello.tiff** graphic from the Images folder, create the business card shown below.

Here are some general steps to make the job a little easier.

1. Create a New, Letter-sized, Portrait project. (You first learned how to create new projects on page 11.)
2. Save the project to the **QuarkXPress 2025 Book Assets** folder as **MyCard**.
3. Draw a picture box. You can make the box as big (or small) as you like, but typical business cards are 3-1/2 x 2 inches.
4. Import the **cello.tiff** picture from the images folder.
5. Go to the **Style** menu and change the cello's shade to **30%**.
6. Resize and crop the graphic to suit your taste.
7. Draw three text boxes and resize them per the sample above.
8. Type the text into each box per the picture above. Use any fonts and font sizes you like.
9. Ensure the Box (background) color of each text box is **None**.
10. When finished, save and close the project.

Stock Images

Finding quality images to use in your project can be a challenge. Sure, it's simple to find images by searching the Internet. However, most of the images you'll find are protected by copyright law and copyright infringement penalties can be severe.

As an alternative to "googling," images, QuarkXPress provides easy access to royalty-free stock images from Pexels and Unsplash.

Before adding images to a project from any resource, review the license agreement. For instance, the license agreement from Pexels (https://www.pexels.com/license/) says that all photos and videos are free to use. Attribution is not required and that giving credit to the photographer or Pexels is not necessary but always appreciated. Also, you can modify the photos and videos. Identifiable people may not appear in a bad light or in a way that is offensive. You are not permitted to sell unaltered copies of a photo or video. You cannot imply endorsement of your product by people or brands in the media. You cannot redistribute or sell the photos and videos on other stock photo or wallpaper platforms. And you cannot use the photos or videos as part of your trade-mark, design-mark, trade-name, business name or service mark.

Guided Activity 35: Download a Stock Image

1. Open **pictureMe** from the **QuarkXPress 2025 Book Assets** folder and save the file as **myStockPicture**.

   Earlier in this module, you imported a supplied image into the sausage soup layout. Let's try that again, but this time you'll download a stock image.

2. Draw a picture box.

   ❒ using the **Picture Content Tool**, draw a picture box in the upper right of the layout as shown below

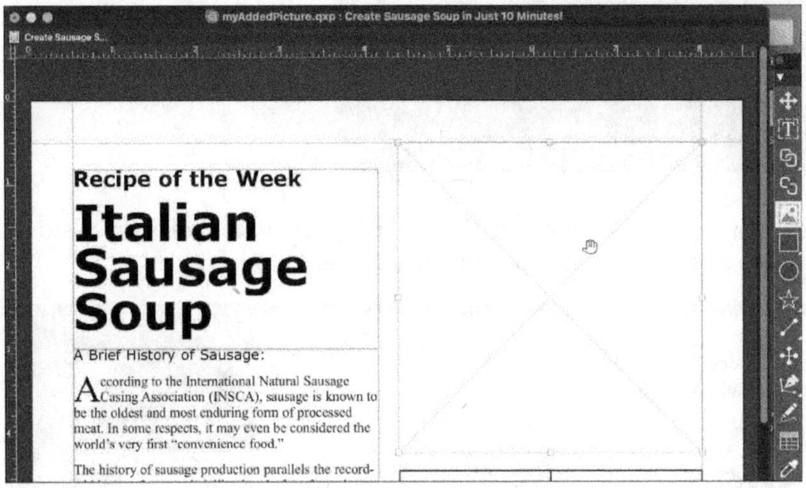

3. Download a stock image.

   ❒ choose **Window > Stock Images**

   ❒ from the menu in the upper left, choose **Pexels**

NOTES

NOTES

❒ click in the **Search** box, type **Sausage Soup**, and then press [**enter**]

❒ with the **Picture Content box** selected, **double-click** any stock image you like

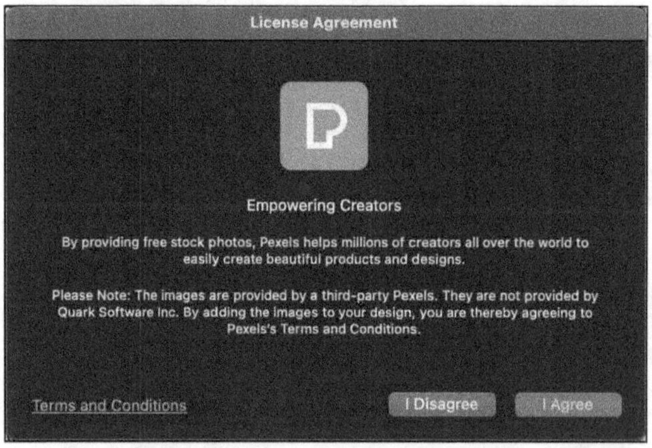

❒ if prompted, agree to the license agreement as appropriate (you may need to double-click the image again to add it to the Picture Content box)

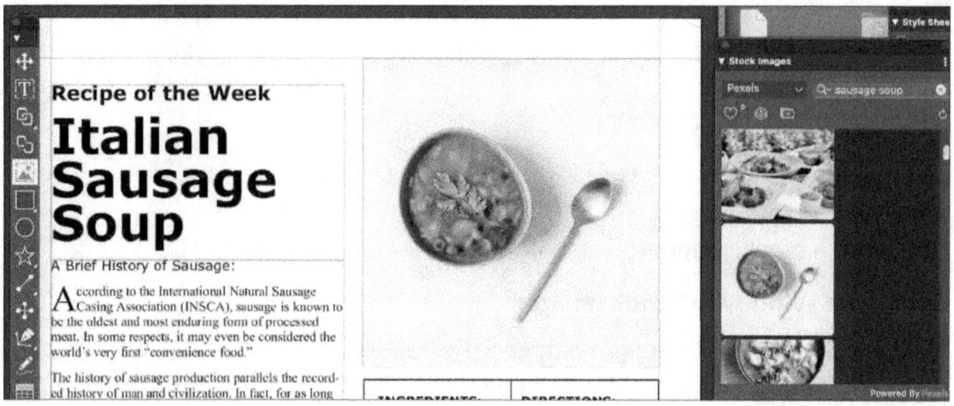

4. Save and close the project.

Opacity

Opacity refers to the transparency level of an object, such as a picture box, text box, or graphic element. In QuarkXPress, adjusting the opacity of an item changes how transparent it is, allowing you to create visual effects where the background or underlying elements are visible through another item.

Guided Activity 36: Change the Opacity of an Item

1. Open **opacityMe** from the **QuarkXPress 2025 Book Assets** folder and save the file as **myOpacity**.

   The text box containing the ingredients and directions overlaps the image of the sausage soup, which is fine. However, it would look even cooler if the text box was just a bit seethrough. Let's take care of that by changing the opacity of the text box.

2. Change the opacity of an item.

   ❒ using the **Item Tool**, select the text box containing the ingredients and the directions

   ❒ on the **Measurements** window, Text Box tab, change the **Box Opacity** to **80%**

   Notice that you can see the sausage soup image through the text box. When applying opacity to an item with an image in the background, it's essential to ensure that the text remains readable. Low opacity can reduce contrast, making text harder to read, especially on busy or high-contrast images.

3. Save and close the project.

NOTES

Notes

ICONLOGIC
"Skills and Drills" Learning

Module 4: Working With Items

In This Module You Will Learn About:

And You Will Learn To:

NOTES

Duplicating

Everything you work with in QuarkXPress, be it a text content box, picture content box, or line, is an item. Learning to control items is an integral part of mastering QuarkXPress.

You can add as many items to a page as you need. Items can get in the way of other items. You may need to duplicate them. You may need to align them.

Copying and deleting are two typical choices for creating replicas of a page item. The difference? If you copy an item (Edit > Copy), the copy does not necessarily appear on the page. Instead, the copy stays in your computer's memory (the clipboard) until you use the Paste command (Edit > Paste). If you get distracted, forget to paste, and copy something else, the item initially on the clipboard is replaced with the newest item you copied. If you duplicate the item (Item > Duplicate), the copy of the item is immediately added to the page without the need for pasting. The main drawback to copying or duplicating is that you have little control over where the duplicated item will appear.

Guided Activity 37: Duplicate an Item

1. Open **stepRepeatMe** from the **QuarkXPress 2025 Book Assets** folder and save the project as **myStepRepeatMe**.

   This project contains a simple circle located in the upper left of the layout where the margins intersect.

2. Duplicate the circle.

   ❒ select the circle with the **Item Tool**

   ❒ choose **Item > Duplicate**

   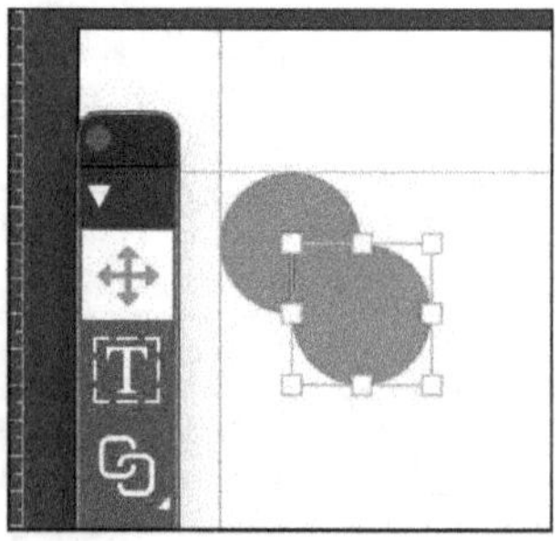

   You should now have two circles on the page. By default, the duplicate is positioned one-half inch from the original circle, overlapping the original.

3. Revert to saved.

   ❒ choose **File > Revert to Saved**

   A dialog box opens asking you to confirm your action.

   ❒ click **OK**

   The duplicated item has been discarded.

   The Revert to Saved option wasn't the only way to eliminate the duplicated item. I could have instructed you to use the **Undo Duplication** command (Edit menu), or you could have used your keyboard to delete the duplicate item. Consider the Revert to Saved option if you have made several edits to a layout and need to remove all of them since your last save.

Super Step and Repeat

If you need multiple items and know where you want them positioned on the page, consider using the Super Step and Repeat option instead of copy/pasting or duplicating. Super Step and Repeat allows you to create multiple duplicate copies of an item *and* control where the duplicates appear on the page along with each repeated item's size, shade, and angle.

Guided Activity 38: Super Step and Repeat Items

1. The **myStepRepeatMe** project should still be open.

2. Use the Step and Repeat command to duplicate the circle.

   ❒ select the circle with the **Item Tool**

   ❒ choose **Item > Super Step and Repeat**

   The Super Step and Repeat dialog box opens.

   ❒ change the **Repeat Count** to **28**

   ❒ ensure that **Horizontal Offset** is set to **.25** inch

   ❒ ensure that **Vertical Offset** is set to **.25** inch

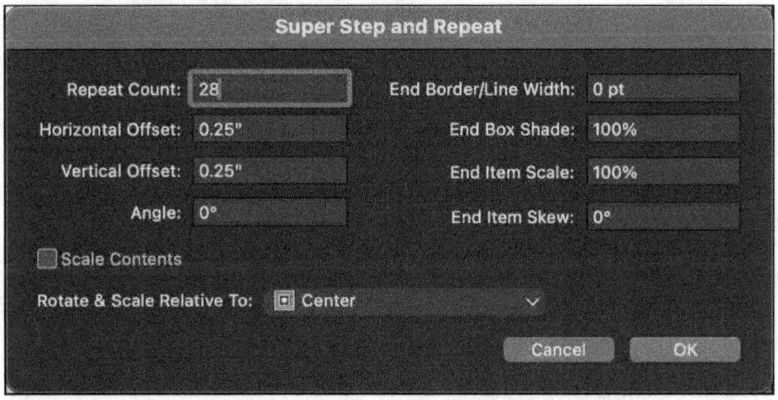

   ❒ click **OK**

   There are 29 circles moving diagonally down the page.

3. Use Super Step and Repeat again.

   ❒ select the last circle

   ❒ choose **Item > Super Step and Repeat**

   ❒ type **9** in the Repeat Count field

   ❒ type **-.25** in the Horizontal Offset field

   ❒ ensure that the Vertical Offset field set to **.25**

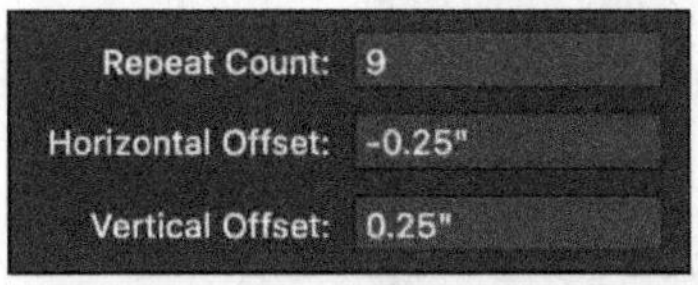

NOTES

NOTES

❒ click **OK**

Now you've got circles on your layout moving down and to the left.

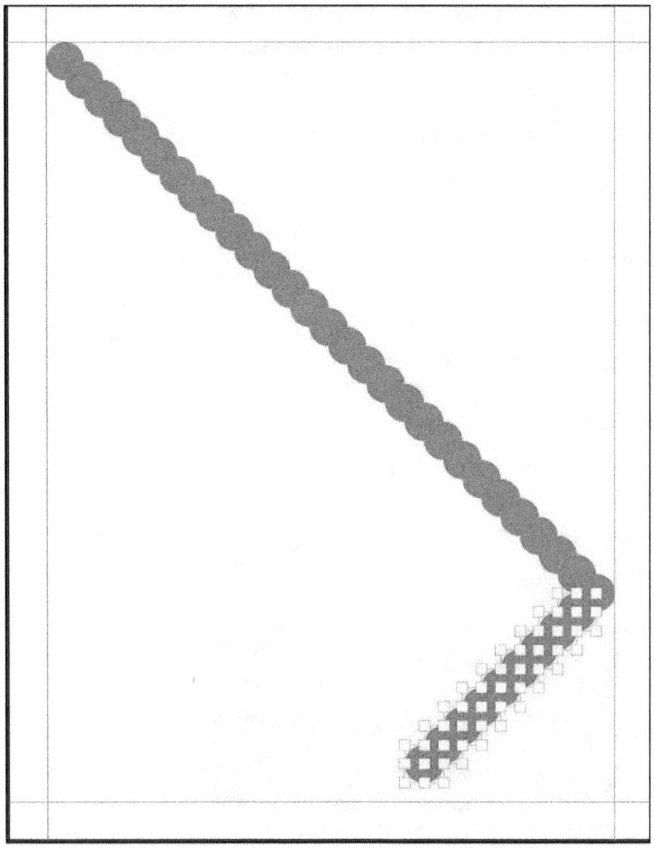

4. Use Super Step and Repeat to change the size and shade of the repeating items.

   ❒ select the last circle

   ❒ choose **Item > Super Step and Repeat**

   ❒ type **18** in the Repeat Count field

   ❒ change **both** the Horizontal Offset and the Vertical Offset to **-.25**

   ❒ change the **End Box Shade** to **20**

   ❒ change the **End Item Scale** to **200**

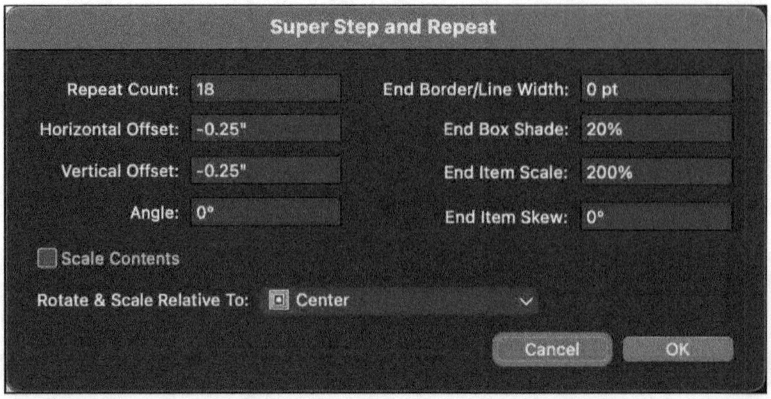

❒ click **OK**

You now have circles moving up and to the left. Each new circle is larger *and* lighter.

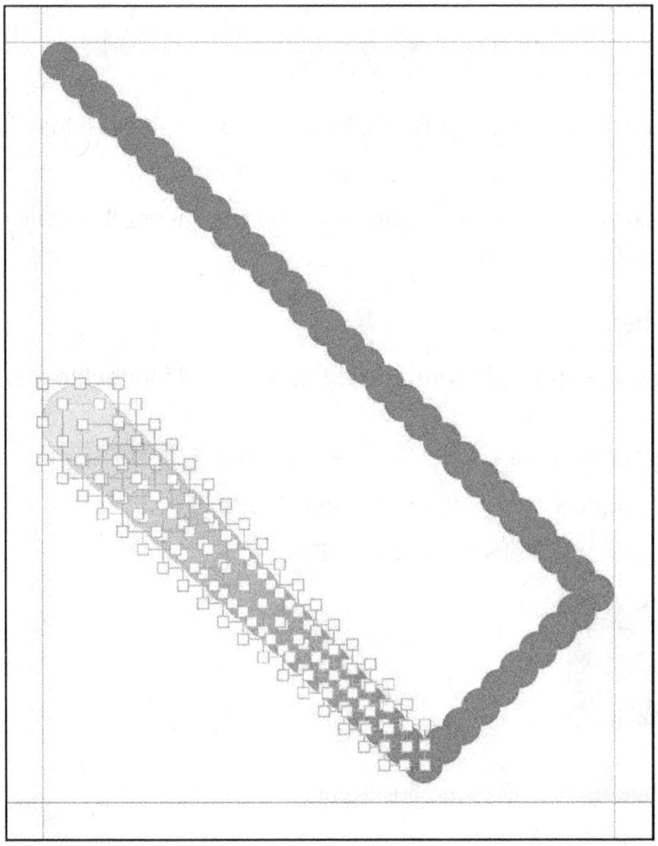

5. Hide guides.

   ❒ choose **View > Guides**

   ❒ click outside of the page layout to deselect all of the page items

   With the page guides hidden from view, you get a better feel for how the page will look if printed.

6. Save and close the project.

NOTES

NOTES

Space/Align

Using the Space/Align option, you can control the amount of horizontal and/or vertical space between multiple selected item.

Guided Activity 39: Space and Align Items

1. Open **alignMe** from the **QuarkXPress 2025 Book Assets** folder and save the file as **myAlign**.

   This project contains four text content boxes. Neither the horizontal nor the vertical space between the items is currently consistent.

2. Align the top edges of the items.

   ❒ select the **Item Tool** and then press [**command**] [**a**] to select all four of the text content boxes on the page

   ❒ on the **Measurements** window, select the **Space/Align** tab Space/Align

   ❒ on the **Measurements** window, select **Item Relative Mode**

   ❒ on the **Measurements** window, select **Align Top Edges**

3. Add an even amount of white space between the items.

   ❒ ensure all of the layout items are still selected

   ❒ on the **Measurements** window, replace the word **Evenly** in the Space field with **.25**

   ❒ on the **Measurements** window, select **Space Horizontally**

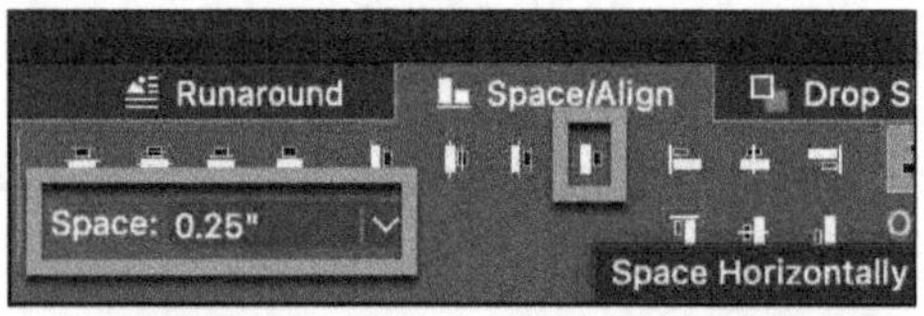

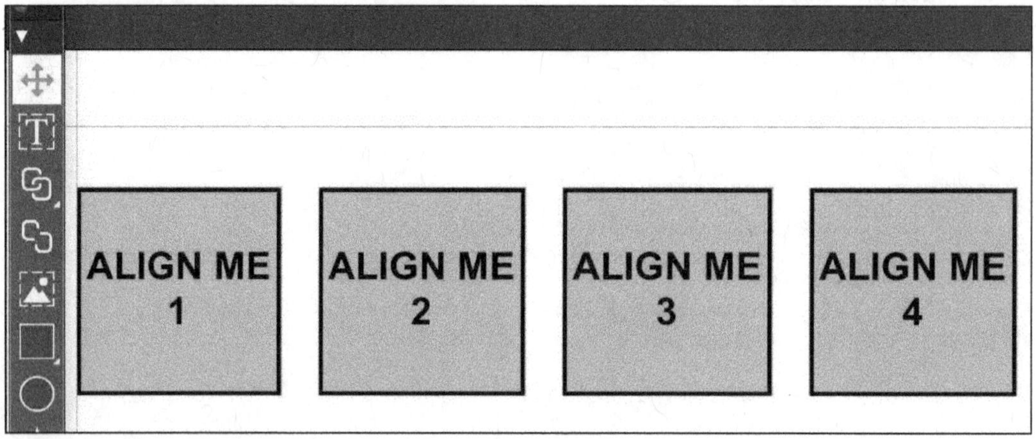

Grouping

You can Group two or more items so that QuarkXPress treats the items as one page object. You can cut, copy, duplicate and even lock a group. And, if you have the Content tool selected, you can resize single elements in the group. Once you have grouped items together, you can easily ungroup them at any time.

Guided Activity 40: Work With Groups

1. The myAlign project should still be open.

   Thanks to the Space/Align activity on page 66, the four items on the page should be nicely spaced and aligned. Even so, the spacing and alignment are okay, they are independent items. Selecting just one of the items and moving it would not move the others, resulting in items that are no longer spaced or aligned properly.

2. Group the items.

   ❒ if necessary, select all of the page items

   ❒ choose **Item > Group**

   The four items become one group.

3. Center the group on the page.

   ❒ choose **Item > Space/Align > Page Relative > Center Align (Vertical)**

   ❒ choose **Item > Space/Align > Page Relative > Center Align (Horizontal)**

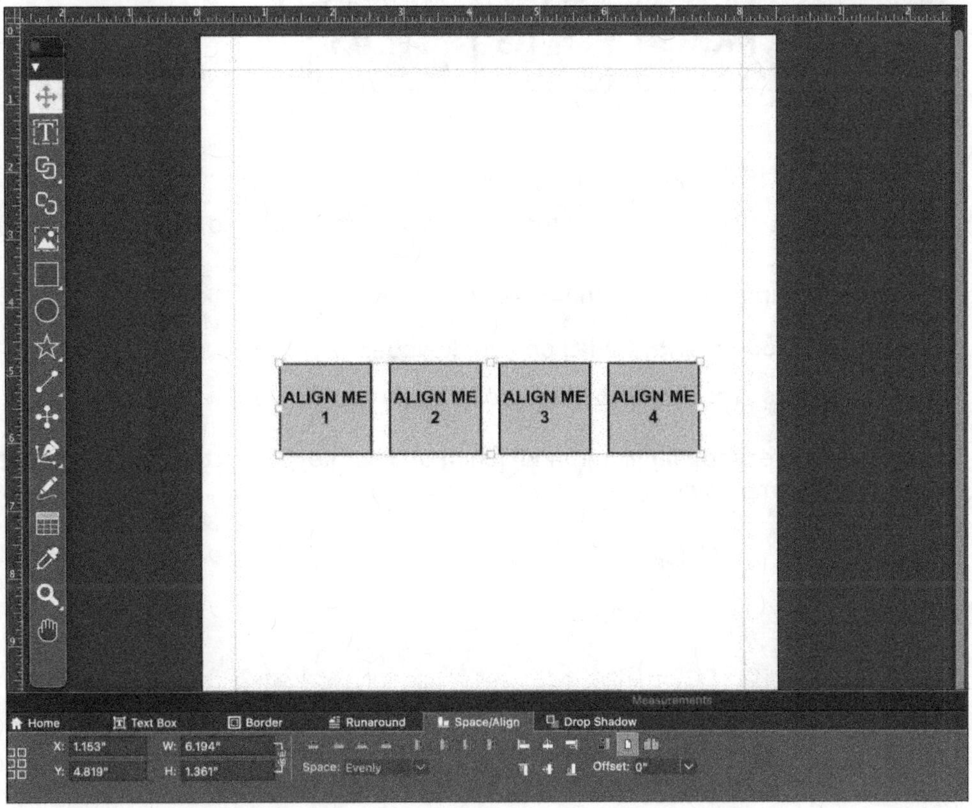

NOTES

4. Lock the group.

   ❒ with the group selected, choose **Item > Lock > Position**

5. Try to move the group.

   Try as you might, you will not be able to move the group with your mouse as long as the group is locked.

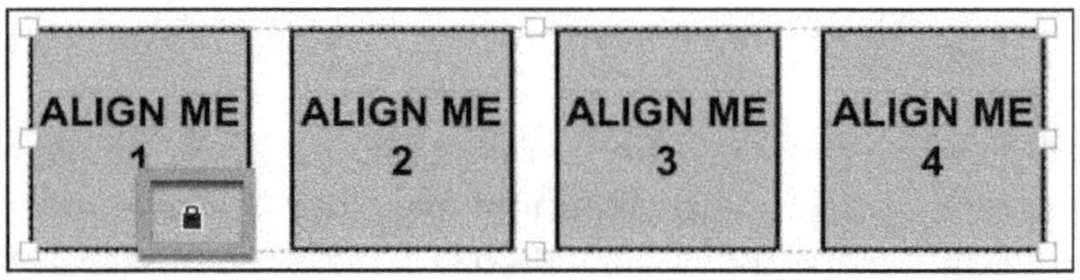

6. Unlock the group.

   ❒ with the group selected, choose **Item > Lock > Position**

7. Resize the group.

   ❒ with the group selected, drag any one of the resize handles to resize the entire group **much smaller**

   Notice that the items in the group have all resized. However, the text in the text content boxes did not get smaller. As a result, the text in each of the boxes is overflowing (hence the red X in each box).

8. Undo the group resize.

   ❒ choose **Edit > Undo** to return the items in the group back to their previous sizes

9. Resize the group and group contents at the same time.

   ❒ press **[alt] [command] [shift]** on your keyboard

   ❒ with the keys pressed, resize the group again

   Because you pressed [alt] [command] [shift] on your keyboard, the text and boxes will all resize at the same time.

10. Save and close the project.

Merging

You can take any selected items and merge them to achieve some pretty amazing results. Among other things, you can merge items where they intersect or combine them.

Guided Activity 41: Merge Items to Create New Shapes

1. Open **mergeMe** and save the file as **MyMerge**.

2. Merge the two items into one.

   ❒ select the **Item Tool**

   ❒ press **[command]** **[a]** to select both of the items on the page

   ❒ choose **Item > Merge or Split Paths > Intersection**

   The two elements become one. All that is left is where the two items intersected.

   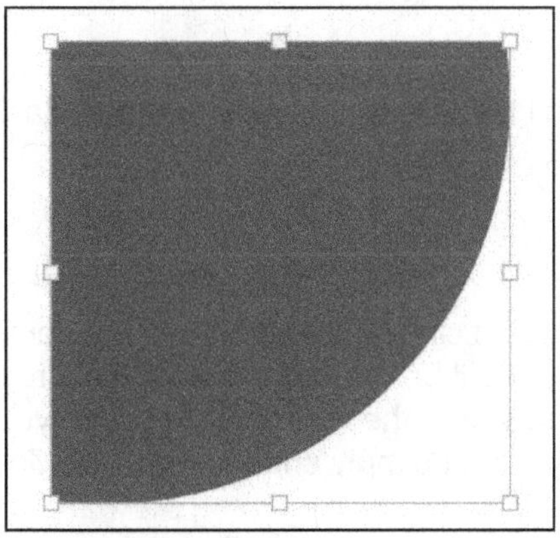

3. Undo your last command.

   ❒ choose **Edit > Undo Merge**

Confidence Check

1. Spend the next few moments playing with the remaining merge commands. (Do not forget to Undo after each change.)

   Pay particular attention to what each merge does to the selected items. Also notice that the item in the background controls the color of the merged item.

2. When finished, save and close the project.

NOTES

NOTES

Stacks

Stacking is the process of placing one item on top of another. There is no limit to the number of items you can stack. However, if you stack several items directly on top of each other, you may find them difficult to manage.

Guided Activity 42: Pass Through a Stack

1. Open **stackMe** and save the project as **myStack**.

   Notice that the page consists of four items stacked on top of one another. The gray circle is on top of the stack.

2. Change the stacking order.

   ❐ using the **Item Tool**, select the gray circle on the top of the stack and then choose **Item > Send & Bring > Send to Back**

3. **Save** your work and **close** the project.

   Now that you have closed the project, you won't be able to undo the Send to Back procedure that you performed in step 2.

4. Reopen the **myStack** project.

   The circle seems to have disappeared. Actually, the circle is behind the other items. Since the circle is no longer selected, or even visible, you'll be unable to select the circle and bring it to the front because all of the other items are in the way. And because you closed the project after completing step 2 above, you cannot simply choose Edit > Undo. It's a real dilemma.

   One solution would be to select the other items in the stack and send them to the back and/or to the front until the circle is once again at the top of the stack. While that solution works, it's not very efficient. What if there were 50 items in front of the item you wanted to work with? Check out this nifty "pass through" trick...

5. Pass through the stack.

   ❐ select the **Item Tool**

   ❐ while pressing **[alt] [shift] [command]** on your keyboard, click the **center** of the **red item**

   ❐ while pressing **[alt] [shift] [command]** on your keyboard, click the **center** of the **red item** again

   Each click of your mouse passes through an item in the stack.

   ❐ continue **[alt] [shift] [command]** clicking the center of the items until the circle you sent to the back is selected

   ❐ once the circle is selected, stop clicking, release the keyboard keys and then choose **Item > Send & Bring > Bring to Front** to bring the circle to the front of the stack

Shape Shifting

QuarkXPress provides an easy way for you to change the shape of any selected item. You can take a circle and instantly transform it into a square, soft-cornered rectangle or a polygon (multi-sided) item. In addition, you can add points to a shape, edit the points and draw just about anything you can imagine.

Guided Activity 43: Change and Edit a Shape

1. The **myStack** project should still be open.

2. Change the shape of an item.

   ❒ if necessary, select the **gray** circle with the **Item Tool**

   ❒ choose **Item > Shape** and then select the **fourth shape** in the list (the concave-corner shape)

   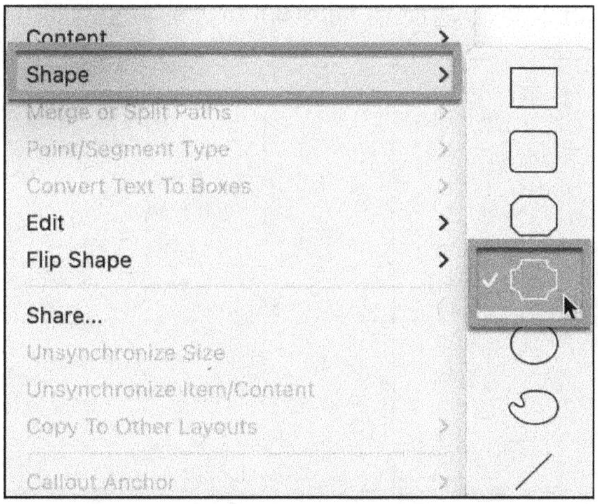

   The circle changes into a concave corner shape. Its background color is not affected.

3. Change another item's shape.

   ❒ select the **red** item in the stack with the **Item Tool**

   ❒ choose **Item > Shape** and then select the **fifth shape** in the list

   The shape changes to a circle.

   ❒ with the red circle still selected, choose **Item > Shape** and then select the **sixth shape** in the list

   Nothing seems to have happened. But you have changed the circle into a free-form shape—you are about to edit it.

NOTES

NOTES

4. Stretch a point.

   ❒ ensure the red circle is still selected

   ❒ on the **Tools** window, select the **Select Point Tool** 

   Note: The Select Point Tool is grouped with other tools on the Tools window. You will find this tool by clicking the **Bézier Pen Tool**.

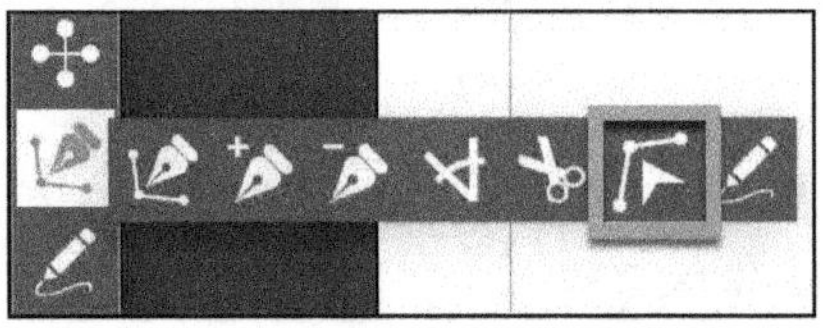

   Multiple points appear around the circle. You can drag the points to create complex shapes.

   ❒ using the **Select Point Tool**, drag a few points to different areas on your page

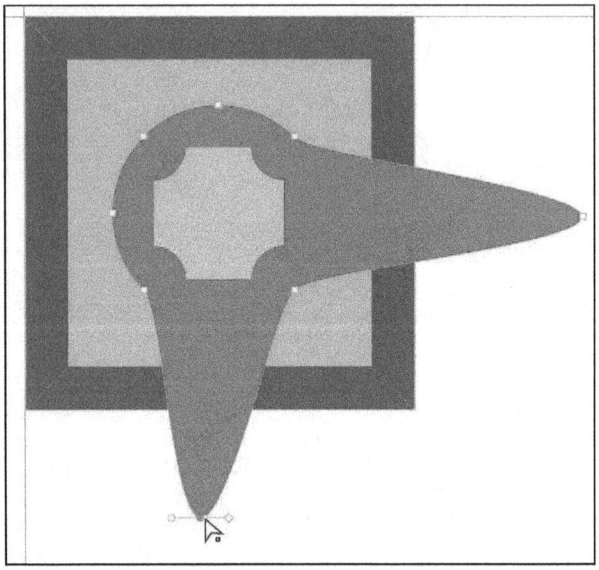

5. Add and remove points.

   ❒ select the **Remove Point Tool**  and then click on a few points to remove them

   Notice that there is a minus sign on the pointer , indicating you will be removing points with every click.

   ❒ select the **Add Point Tool**  and click the path between two points to add a point

   Notice that there is a plus sign on the pointer , indicating you will be adding points along the path with every click)

6. Reshape a curve.

   ❒ select the **Select Point Tool**  and **drag** the point to make the path longer

   Notice that the point has wings on either side of the point that can be dragged to dramatically change the shape.

   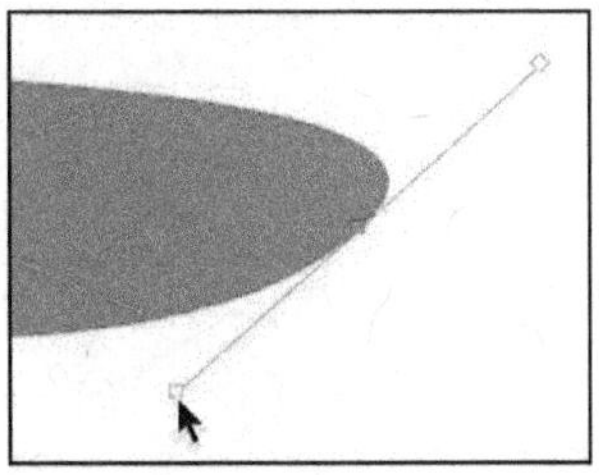

   ❒ drag one of the wings to reshape the curve

   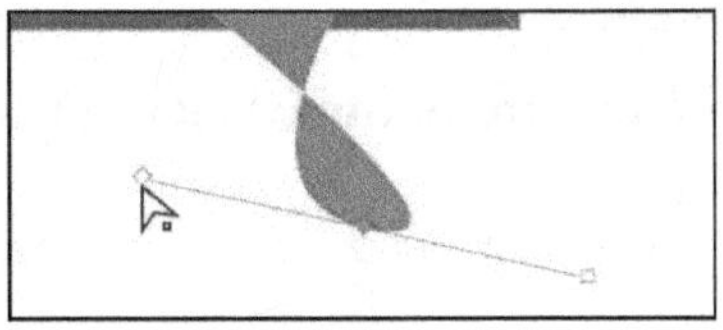

NOTES

Guided Activity 44: Draw a Freehand Line

1. The **myStack** project should still be open.

2. Use the Freehand tool to draw a line.

   ❒ on the Tools window, select the **Freehand Drawing Tool** 

   ❒ draw a squiggly line on the page

3. Change the line's width, style and add an arrowhead.

   ❒ ensure the line you drew is selected and, on the **Measurements** window, change the line's Width to **8**

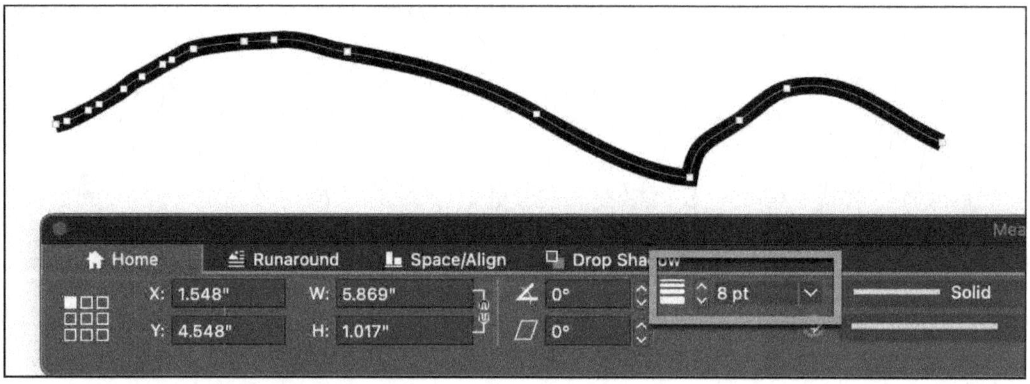

   ❒ on the **Measurements** window, change the line's Style to **All Dots**

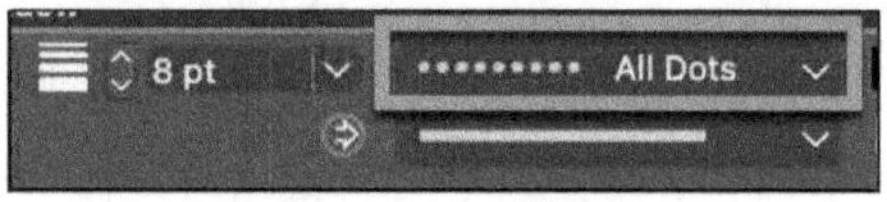

   ❒ on the **Measurements** window, select **any Arrowhead** you like from the Arrowhead drop-down menu

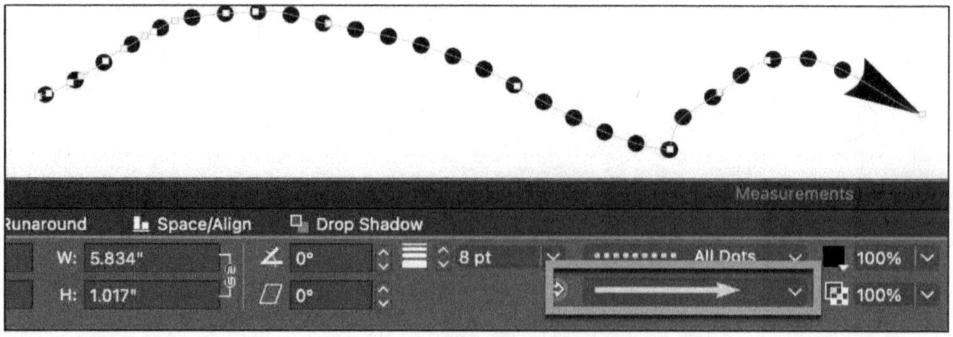

Guided Activity 45: Change Box Content

1. Change the content of a picture box to text.

   ❒ on the Tools window, select the **Picture Content** tool and draw a picture box on the page

   ❒ select the **Text Content Tool**, click in the box and try to type your name

   Since the item is a picture box, you won't be able to type any text at all. Picture boxes can accept only pictures, not text.

2. Change the picture box into a text box.

   ❒ choose **Item > Content > Text**

   The picture box instantly becomes a text box.

   ❒ select the **Text Content Tool**, click in the box, and type your name

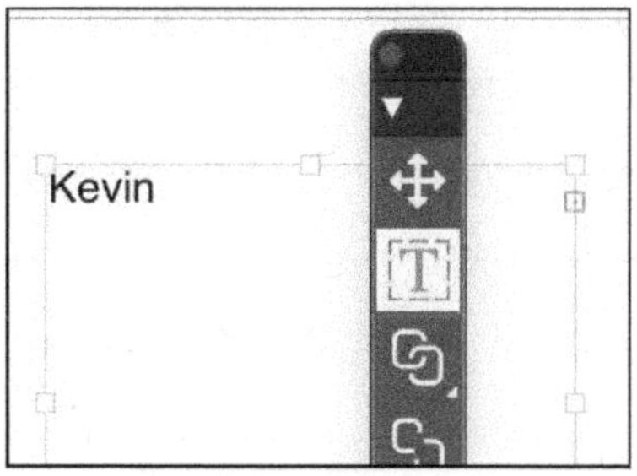

3. Change the text box into a picture box.

   ❒ choose **Item > Content > Picture**

   Because you can't have text in a picture box, you will be warned that the text will be deleted.

   ❒ click **OK**

4. Save and close the project.

NOTES

Notes

ICONLOGIC

"Skills and Drills" Learning

Lab 1

Create a Birthday Poster

Skill Level: **Basic**

Open the project called **Vonnie** from the **QuarkXPress 2025 Book Assets** folder.

Your goal is to recreate the layout. Before beginning, complete the following:

- ❒ "An Introduction to QuarkXPress" module which begins on page 1,
- ❒ The "Text Basics" module which begins on page 25,
- ❒ The "Image Basics" module which begins on page 47

Here are some project guidelines.

1. Project and Layout Name: **Vonnie Birthday Party**.
2. Graphic (**vonnieParty**) location: **images** folder.
3. Text (**vonnieText**) location: **textFiles** folder.

NOTES

Page Specs: Layout Type: Print. Size: Letter, Portrait, All margins: one-half inch, no Automatic Text Box

Picture: Draw a picture content box and import the picture named **vonnieParty.jpg** from the **Images** folder or search for a stock photo that you like better.

Resize and crop the image as appropriate.

Text: Draw a text box.

Import the vonnieParty text. (Format the text using any fonts/sizes that you like.)

Use the Measurements window to rotate the text box just a bit match the "1" image in the background.

ICONLOGIC
"Skills and Drills" Learning

Module 5: Tabs, Frames and Insets

In This Module You Will Learn About:

And You Will Learn To:

NOTES

Tabs

Tabs are most commonly used when creating lists where you want multiple paragraph alignments (i.e. both left- and right-aligned paragraphs). You can have only one type of paragraph alignment at any one time. However, by setting tab stops, you can give the illusion of multiple paragraph alignments. For instance, most tables of contents you see in books, newspapers and magazines use tab stops that allow text to appear both flush left and right. In a typical table of contents, there is text at the left of the page and page numbers lined up at the right. And there are typically fill characters (such as dots) between the text and the page number.

Guided Activity 46: Set and Move a Tab Stop

1. Create a new project with an automatic text box.

- ❒ choose **File > New > Project** (or press [**command**] [**n**])
- ❒ ensure the Layout Type is **Print**
- ❒ ensure **Single Layout Mode** is selected
- ❒ ensure the Page Size is **Letter**
- ❒ if necessary, change the margins to **0.5**" (one-half inch)
- ❒ ensure the Orientation is **Portrait**
- ❒ ensure that Facing Pages is **not selected**
- ❒ if necessary, select **Automatic Text Box** (put a check mark in the box)
- ❒ ensure the Column Guides are set to **1** column and the Gutter Width is **.167"**

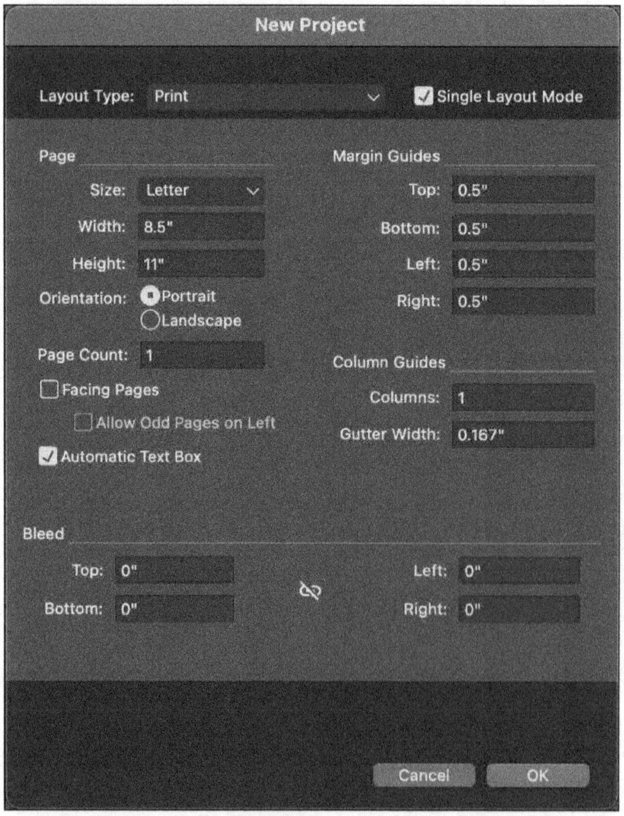

- ❒ click **OK**

2. Save the project to the **QuarkXPress 2025 Book Assets** folder as **myTabStops**.

3. If necessary, zoom away from the page just a bit so you can see the entire width of the page. (Viewing by 75% works well on a PC; on a Macintosh, Actual Size may be fine.)

4. Type text into the text box.

   ❒ using the T**ext Content Tool**, click on the page

   ❒ type **Shoes**

   ❒ press [**tab**] and type **Red**

   ❒ press [**tab**] and type **9000.72**

   ❒ press [**return**]

   ❒ type **Hats**

   ❒ press [**tab**] and type **Green**

   ❒ press [**tab**] and type **500.777**

   You have typed two rows of data into three columns.

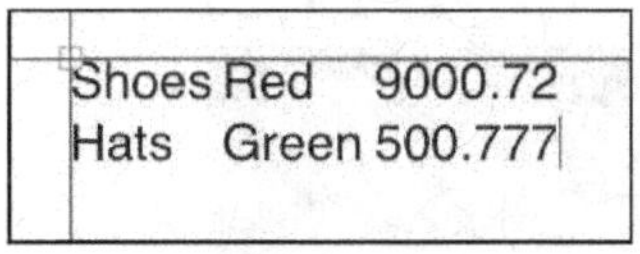

5. Show invisibles.

   ❒ choose **View > Invisibles**

   Your text should look like the picture below. The tab character you typed between the text displays as right arrows.

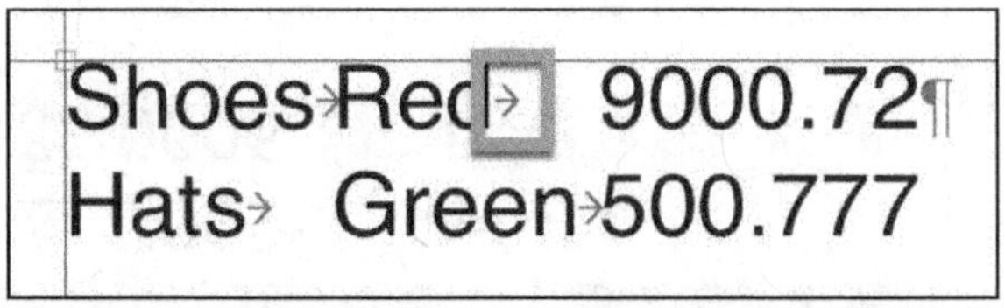

NOTES

NOTES

6. Set a Center tab stop.

❒ using the **Text Content Tool**, select all of the text that you typed

❒ on the **Measurements** window, click the **Tabs** tab

❒ from the cluster of tab stops at the left, select the **Center** tab stop

❒ position your pointer on the tab ruler (the ruler is just above the selected text)

❒ click **once** at about the 2-inch mark on the ruler to add a Center tab

Notice a few things. First, a center tab stop appears on the ruler. Second, a number appears in the Position field. And, the text to the right of the tab stop is centered.

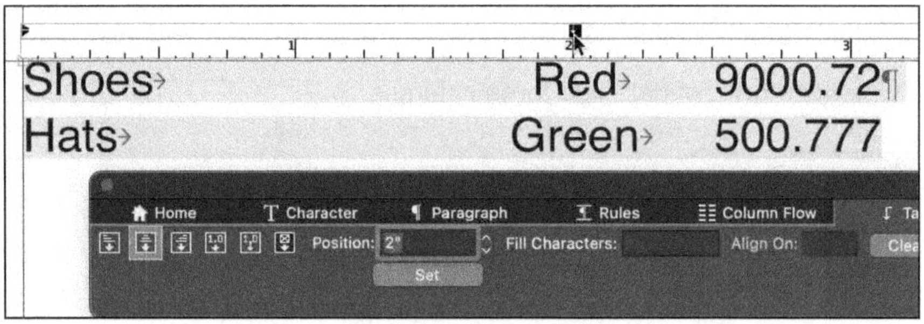

❒ with the tab stop on the ruler selected, change the Position number to **2.5**

❒ click **Set**

Notice that the colors (Red and Green) are now centered at 2.5 inches.

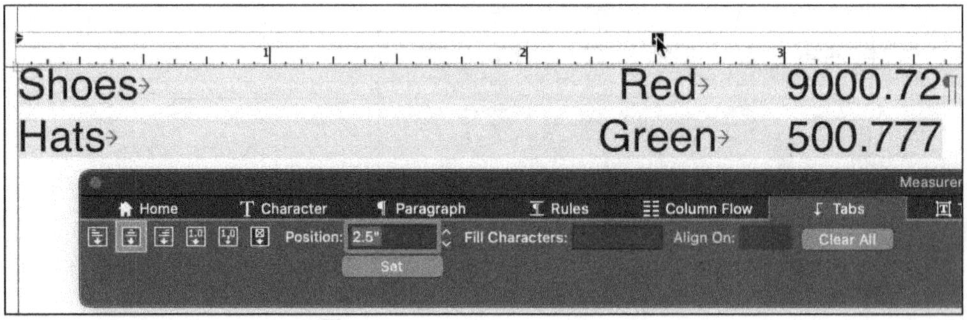

7. Drag the tab stop to a new stop position.

   ❒ carefully **drag** the tab stop that you put on the ruler **right** until the Position field reads **3**

   The second column of your text should now be centered at 3 inches.

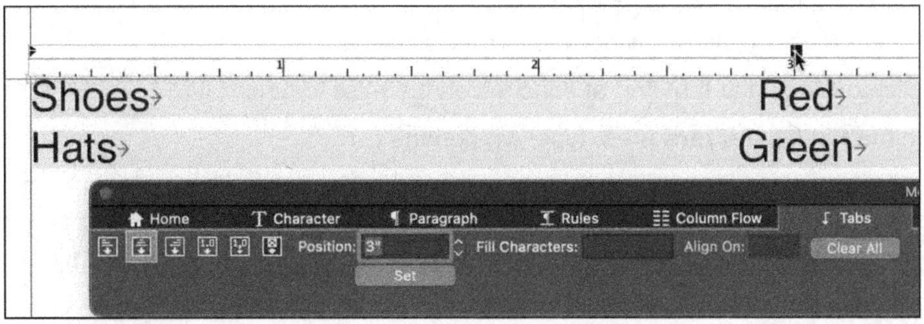

   Note: If you missed the tab stop even a little, you may end up with extra tab stops on the ruler. No worries. To remove an extra tab stop from the ruler, select the unwanted tab stop and drag it **up** or **down** off the ruler, or select the unwanted tab stop and press [**delete**] on your keyboard.

8. Save the project.

NOTES

NOTES

Guided Activity 47: Add a Tab Stop Fill Character

1. The **myTabStops** project should still be open.

2. Add a tab stop fill character.

   ❒ ensure that the text on the page is still selected

   ❒ on the **Measurements** window, click the **Tabs** tab

   ❒ click **once** on the tab stop at 3 inches on the ruler to **select** it

   ❒ in the **Fill Characters** area, type two periods (..)

   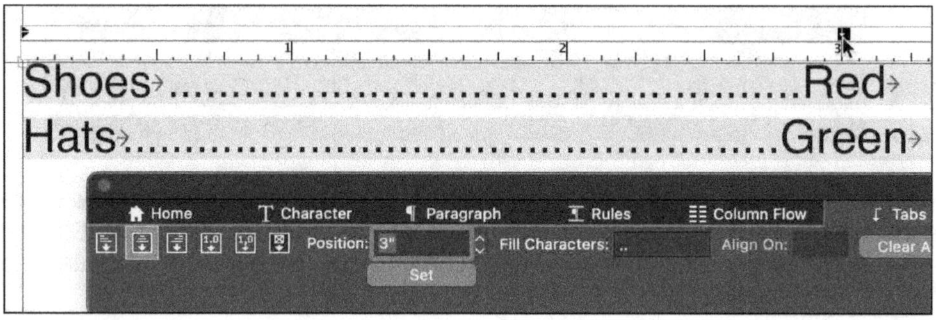

   ❒ click **Set**

   Your selected text is still centered at 3 inches and now, thanks to the Fill Characters, has dots between the entries in the first and second column.

3. Set a decimal tab with a dash Fill Character.

   ❒ select the **Decimal** tab stop from group of available tab stops

   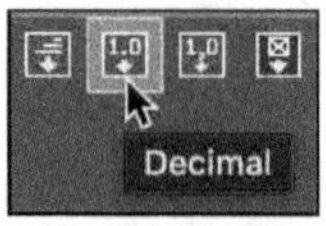

   ❒ type **5.5** into the Position field

   ❒ replace the dots in the Fill Character field with two dashes (--)

   ❒ click **Set**

   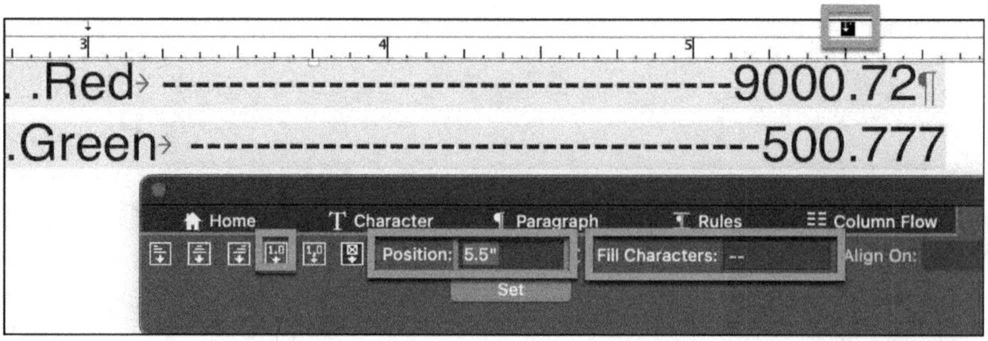

Confidence Check

1. The MyTabStops project should still be open.
2. Select all of the text and set tab stops to the following specifications:

   Set the first tab as a Left tab at **2** inches with dots for fill characters.

   Set the second tab as a Left at **4** inches with dots for fill characters.

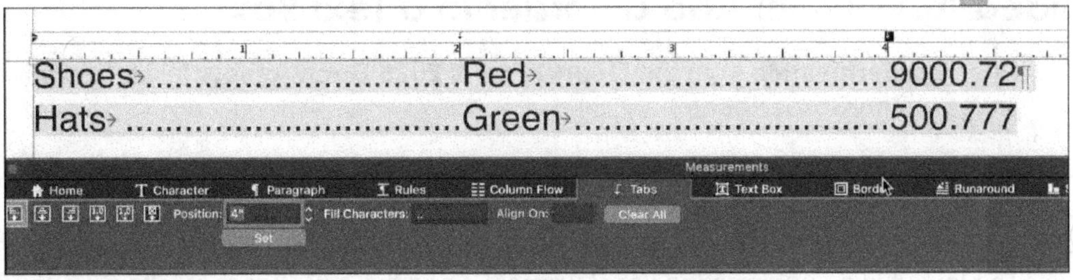

3. Save the project.
4. Edit the tab stops so that there are no fill characters.
5. Save and close the project.
6. Create a new project with an Automatic Text Box and save it as **myTabStops2**.
7. Type the following text and set a **right** tab with dot tab stop leaders.

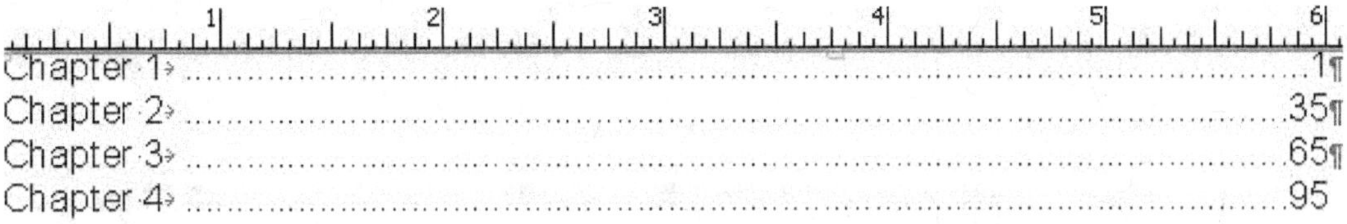

8. Save and close the project.
9. Create a new project with an Automatic Text Box and save it as **myTabStops3**.
10. Type the text and format the tab stops as shown in the image below.

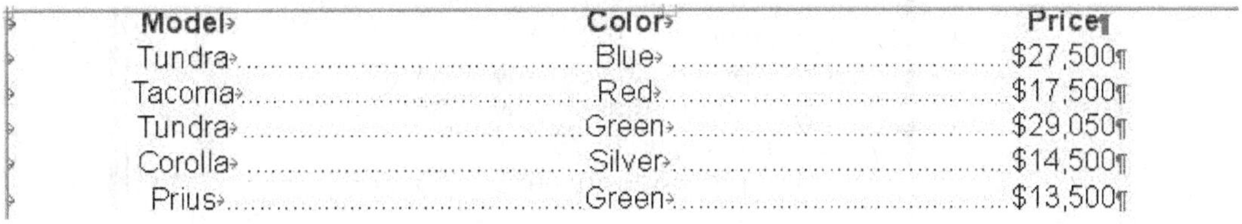

11. Save and close all projects.

NOTES

Borders and Insets

You can apply a border (also known as a frame) to any selected item. You can use the **Border** tab on the **Measurements** window to control several frame options including border thickness and type. If applying a border to a text box, you should add white space between the border and text. This is known as inset spacing and you will learn how to do this during the activity that follows.

Guided Activity 48: Add a Border to a Text Box

1. Open **borderInsetMe** from the **QuarkXPress 2025 Book Assets** folder and save the project as **myBorderInset**.

2. If necessary, zoom closer to the page so that you can more easily read the text in the text box.

   The layout is an unformatted list of wines. During the activities that follow, you will add a **border** to the text box, control the space that appears between the frame and the text, and then set a Right tab stop.

3. Use the **Measurements** window to add a border to the box.

   ❒ using the **Item Tool**, select the text box

   ❒ on the **Measurements** window, select the **Border** tab

   ❒ on the **Measurements** window, type **8** into the Weight area and press **[enter]**

   ❒ with the text box still selected, choose **Thick-Thin** from the **Frame Type** drop-down menu

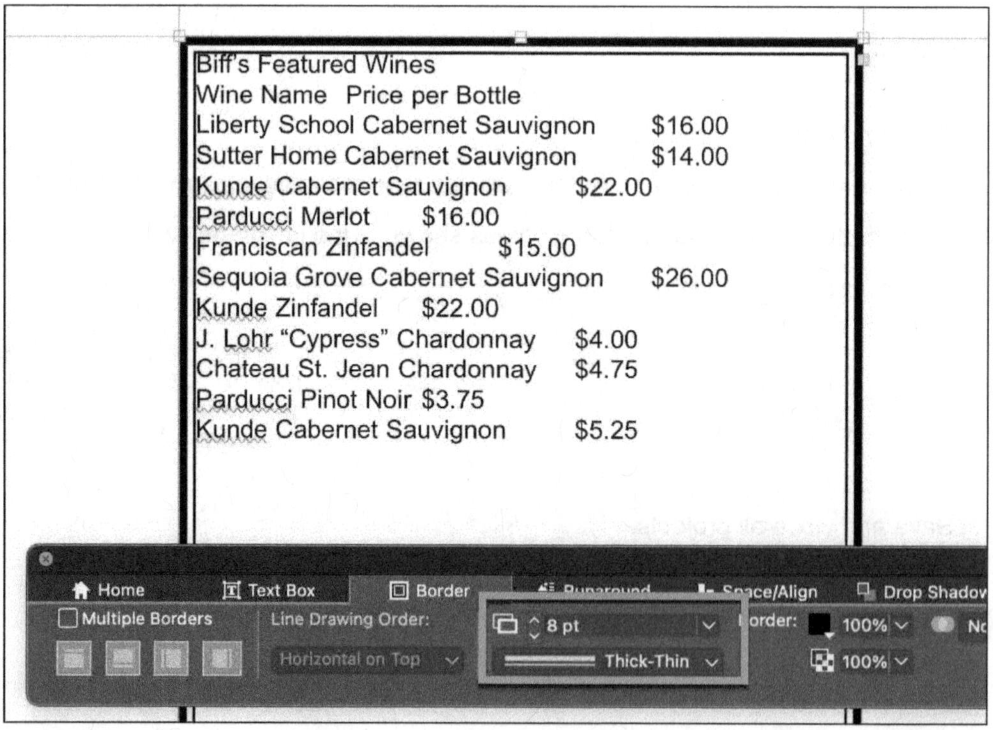

Now that the text box has a border, notice that the text inside the box is too close to the border. You will fix that next.

Guided Activity 49: Inset Text and Vertically Justify

1. The **myBorderInset** project should still be open.

2. Add white space between the border and the text.

   ❒ on the **Measurements** window, select the **Text Box** tab

   ❒ change the **Inset Text** to **12**

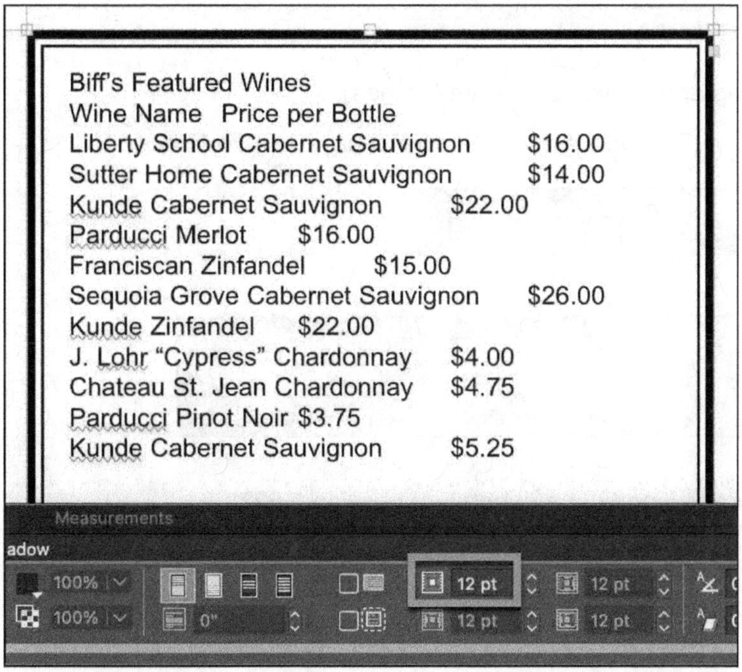

   Notice that there is white space between the border and the text inside the text box.

3. Save the project.

4. Vertically justify text within a text box.

   ❒ with the text box still selected, on the **Measurements** window, click **Justified Alignment**

   The text inside the text box has been pulled vertically and now takes up the whole text box.

Confidence Check

1. Change the Font for all of the text to **Verdana** and the Font Size to **10 pts**.

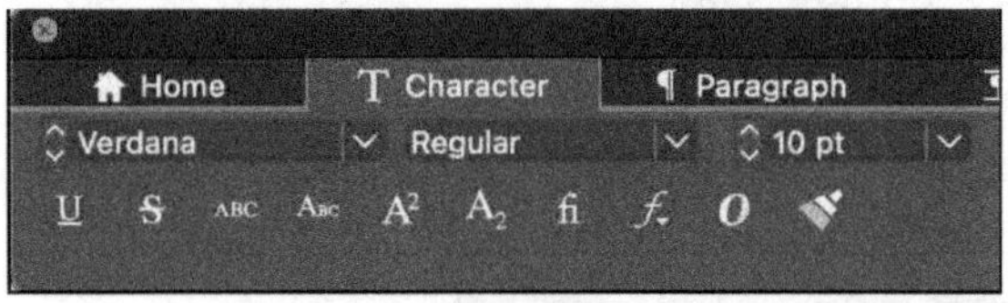

2. Select the first paragraph (Kevbo's Featured Wines).
3. Change the Font Style to **Bold** and the paragraph alignment to **Center**.

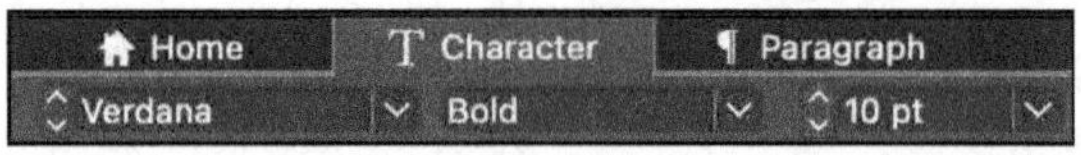

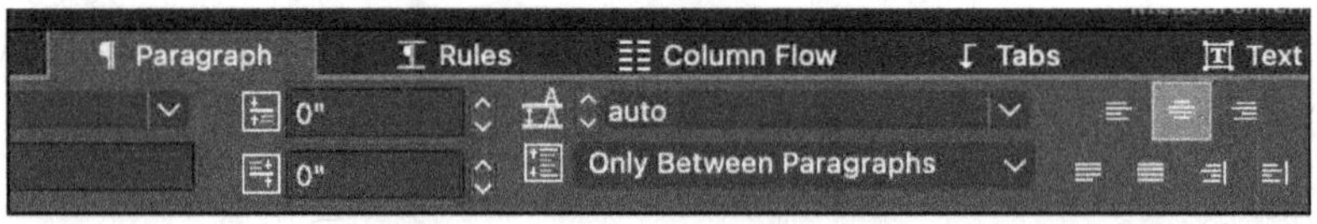

4. Select all of the wine text and set a right tab at position **3.927"**.

5. Save and close the project.

ICONLOGIC
"Skills and Drills" Learning

Module 6: Text Links

In This Module You Will Learn About:

And You Will Learn To:

Automatic Text Boxes

When you create a new layout, you are given an opportunity to create an Automatic Text Box in the New Project dialog box.

Selecting Automatic Text Box does more than automatically give you a text box. Automatic text boxes are, by default, linked—importing text into it automatically gives the overflow text a place to go. If you have a one-page layout that contains an Automatic Text Box and you import a text file into the text box, QuarkXPress automatically inserts enough pages to accommodate the text.

Guided Activity 50: Work With an Automatic Text Box

1. Create a new project that matches the following specifications (in particular, notice that Automatic Text Box is selected).

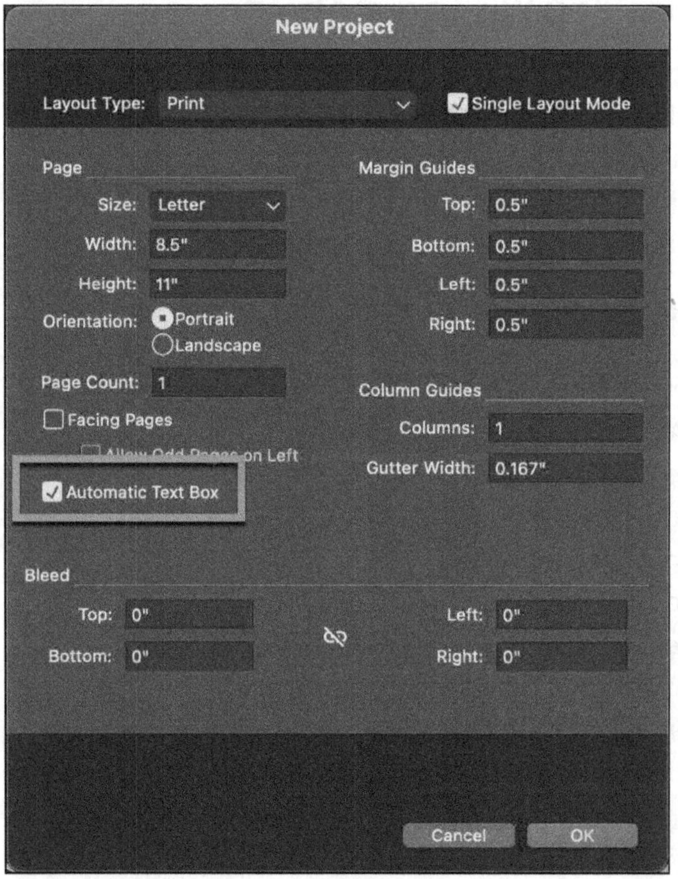

2. Save the project to the **QuarkXPress 2025 Book Assets** folder as **myAutomaticTextBox**.

3. Change your view to Fit in Window.

4. Import Text.

   ❒ using the **Text Content Tool**, click in the middle of the page (to activate the Automatic Text Box)

   ❒ choose **File > Import**

   ❒ from **QuarkXPress 2025 Book Assets** > **textFiles**, open **winerText**

There was enough text in the document to add 4 more pages to your document. QuarkXPress automatically adds the pages and takes you to page 5. Notice the page count at the bottom left of the screen now says "5."

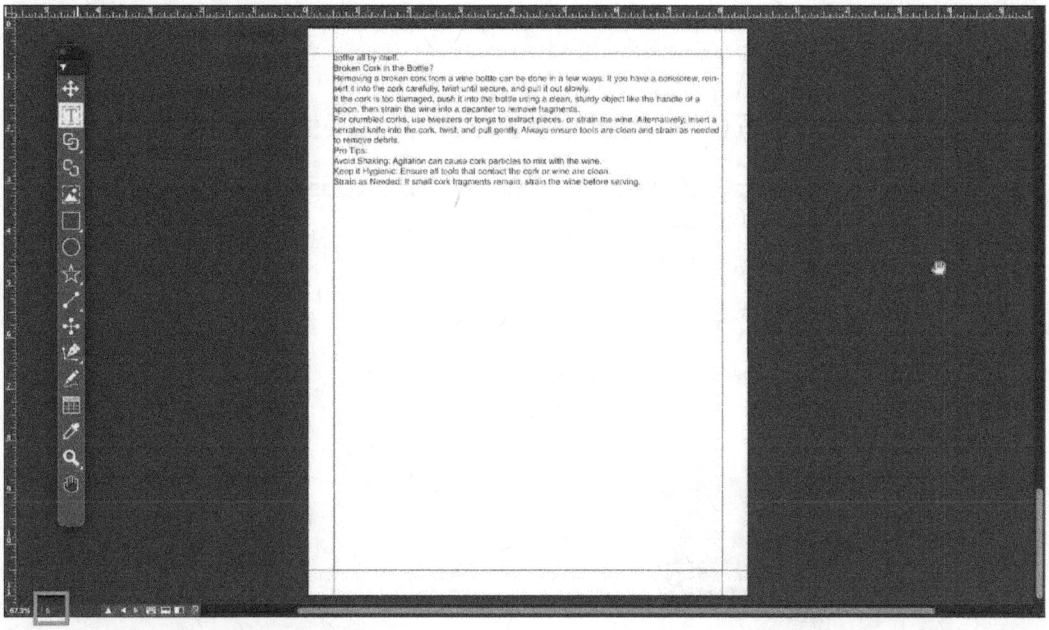

Multi-Page Documents

Now that you have a multi-page document, you need to learn how to navigate through the layout. You could use the scroll bars to scroll from page to page, but you'll often find the scroll bars to be an inefficient way to move around. Instead, consider using the Go To command or the Page Layout palette.

Guided Activity 51: Jump Between Pages

1. The **myAutomaticTextBox** project should still be open.

2. Go to a page using a menu command.

   ❒ choose **Page > Go to**

   The Go to Page dialog box opens.

   ❒ type **3**

   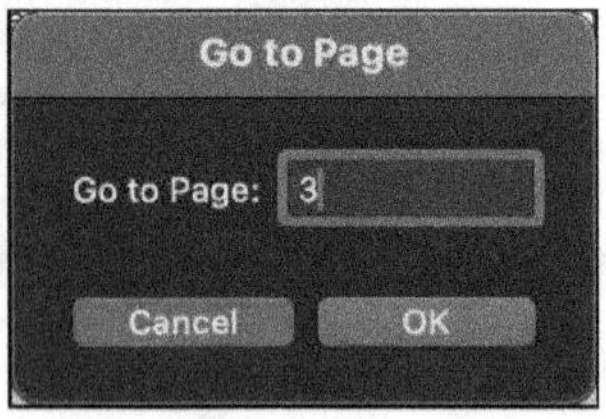

   ❒ click **OK**

3. Go to a page using a keyboard shortcut.

   ❒ press [**command**] [**j**]

   The Go to Page dialog box opens again.

   ❒ type **2**

   ❒ click **OK**

4. Jump between pages using the Next and Previous buttons.

   ❒ at the **bottom left** of the window, click the Previous and then Next Page buttons

5. Jump between pages using the navigation panel.

   ❒ click the arrow in the page navigation area and select page **5** to jump to the last page in the layout

   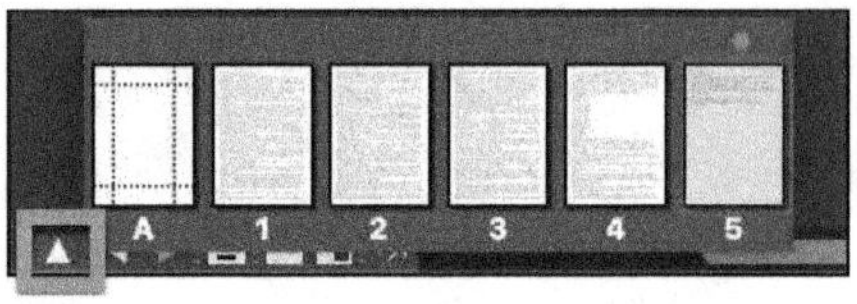

Guided Activity 52: Use the Page Layout Palette

1. The **myAutomaticTextBox** project should still be open.

2. Show the Page Layout palette.

   ❒ choose **Window > Page Layout**

3. Go to page 3 using the Page Layout palette.

   ❒ double-click the **little picture** of page **3** in the Page Layout palette

   You jump to page 3, just as if you had used the Go To command.

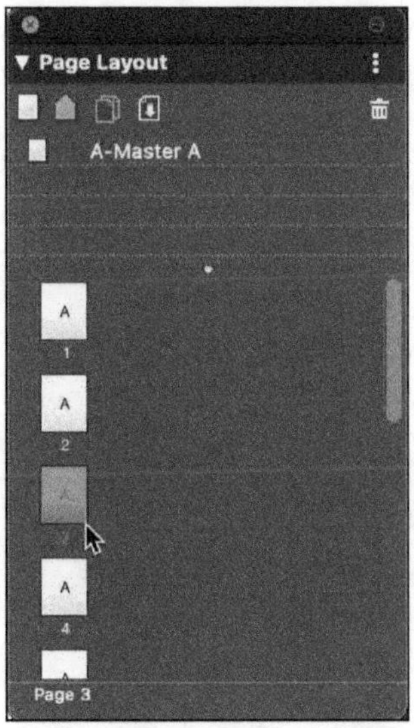

4. Use the Page Layout palette to insert one blank page.

   ❒ on the Page Layout palette, locate the **Blank Single Page** icon (it's in the upper left of the Page Layout palette)

   ❒ drag the Blank Single Page icon just below page **3** on the Page Layout palette

   A single blank page has been added to the document between pages 3 and 5. Notice that your project now consists of 6 pages.

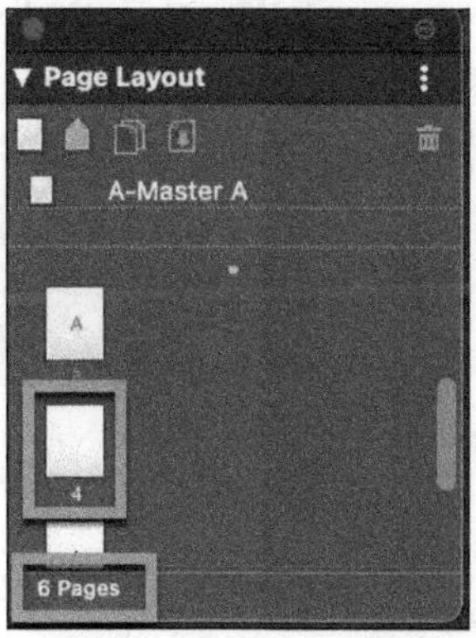

NOTES

NOTES

5. Use the Page Layout palette to insert multiple blank pages.

   ❒ on the Page Layout palette, locate the **Blank Single Page** icon again

   ❒ press [**alt**] on your keyboard and, while pressing the [alt] key, **drag** the Blank Single Page icon below page **4** on the Page Layout palette

   ❒ when you get below page 4 on the Page Layout palette, release the mouse and then release the [alt] key

   The Insert Pages dialog box opens. You can also get this dialog box to appear by choosing **Page > Insert**.

   ❒ type **3** into the Insert field

   ❒ if necessary, select **after page**

   ❒ if necessary, type **4** into the after page field

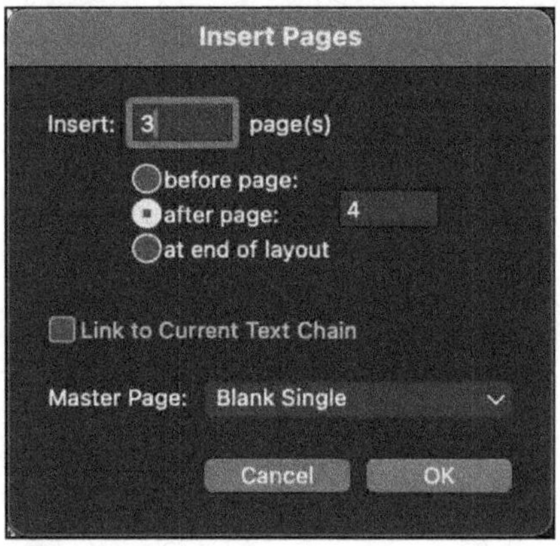

   ❒ click **OK**

   On the Page Layout palette, notice that there are now three more pages. 

6. Delete pages.

   ❒ choose **Page > Delete**

   The Delete Pages dialog box opens.

   ❒ type **4** into the Delete page(s) field

   ❒ type **7** into the thru field

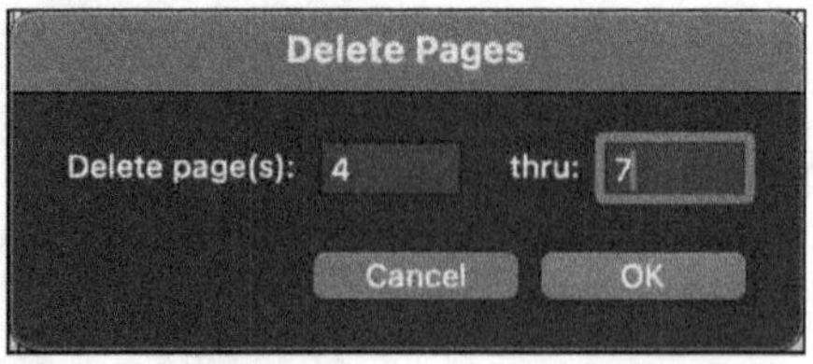

   ❒ click **OK**

   Pages 4 through 7 have been deleted. The document should once again contain 5 pages.

Confidence Check

1. Insert a blank page at the end of the myAutomaticTextBox layout. (You learned how to insert blank pages on page 93.)
2. Go to the last page of the layout and, using the Text Content Tool, draw a text box that fills the entire page (the text box should stretch from margin to margin).
3. Type **The Weekly Winer** into the text box.
4. Using the **Measurements** window, format the text as **Times New Roman, 80 pt, Italic.**

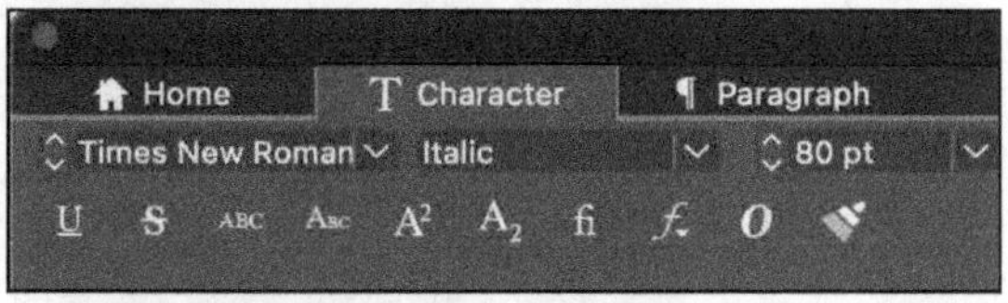

5. Change the paragraph **alignment** to **centered** alignment and **leading** to 80 pts.

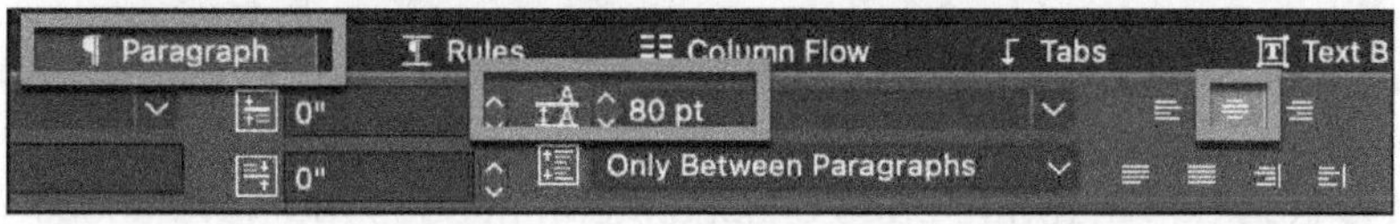

6. Using the **Measurements** window, switch to Paragraph Attributes mode and change the leading to **80 pt**.
7. Using the **Measurements** window, select the **Text Box** tab and change the vertical alignment to Center Alignment.

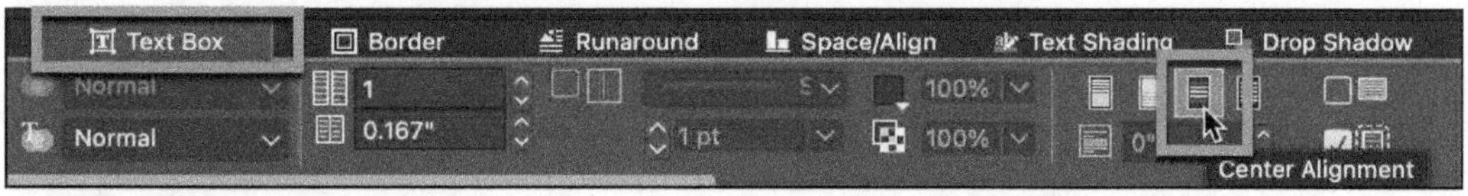

The page should look like this:

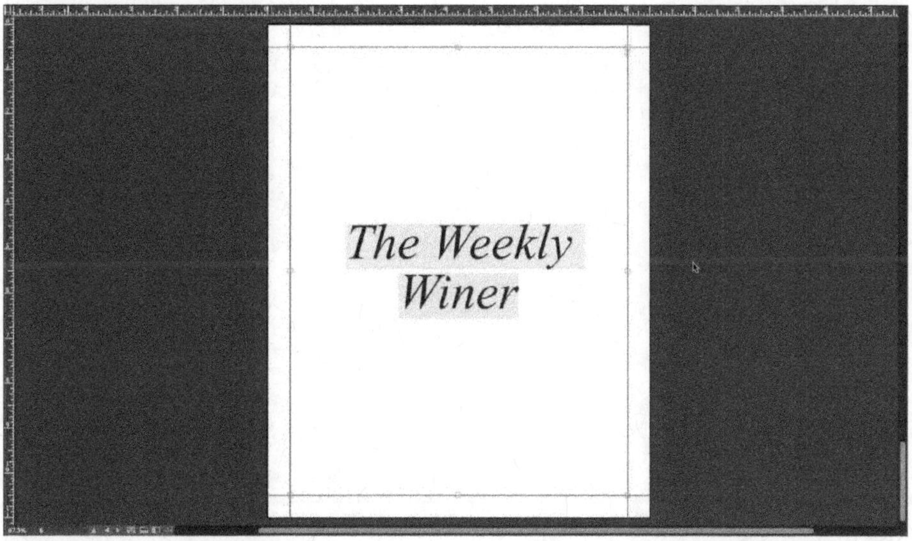

NOTES

NOTES

8. On the Page Layout palette, drag page 6 up and just above page 1.
9. On the Page Layout palette, double-click page 1 (to jump to the page).

Notice that this is the page that was page 6 just a moment ago. You have successfully *repaginated* the document with a quick flick of your wrist.

10. Save and close the project.

Numbering Pages

If you have a layout containing more than one page, you will likely want the pages numbered. To add page numbers, you can manually draw a text content box to every page of the layout and type the appropriate page number. That approach will work, but it is problematic. First, assuming there are more than just a few layout pages, it will take time to draw the text content box on the layout pages. Second, when you add or remove pages, your manually typed page numbers will be inaccurate.

In the following activity, you will learn how to add a current box page number to a master page. The advantage to adding a current box page to a master page is two-fold: speed and efficiency. You can add the current box page in seconds. And since pages in your layout can be assigned to a master page, a page number will instantly appear on the layout pages, and the numbers will update as you add or remove layout pages.

Guided Activity 53: Add a Current Box Page Number

1. Open **numberMyPages.qxp** from the **QuarkXPress 2025 Book Assets** and save the project as **myNumberedPages**.

2. Scroll through the document. There are 6 pages and none of them contain page physical numbers.

3. Display the master page using the Page menu.

   ❒ choose **Page > Display > A-Master A**

   QuarkXPress documents can contain multiple master pages. By default, you will always have one called **A-Master A** in every new project.

4. Display the layout using the Page menu.

   ❒ choose **Page > Display > Layout**

   Because you did not change the master page in any way, there are no changes to your layout pages.

5. Display the master page using the Page Layout palette.

   ❒ at the top of the Page Layout palette, double-click the little page to the left of the words **A-Master A** to open the master page

   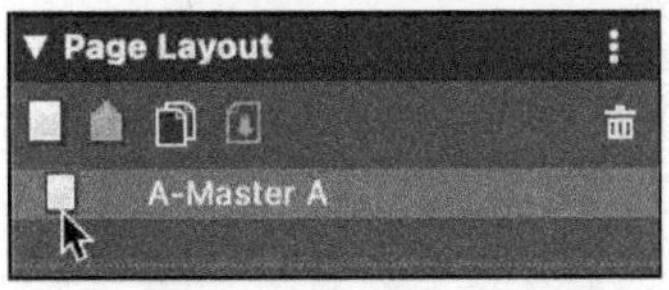

   You can confirm you are working on the master page by observing the page indicator at the lower left of the window.

   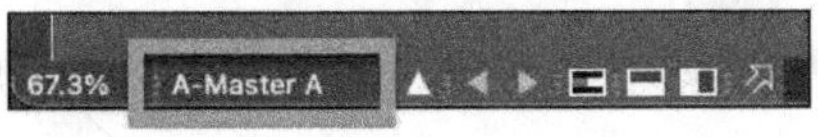

NOTES

6. Draw a text content box on a master page.

❒ using the **Text Content Tool**, draw a text box near the bottom of the master page (the exact size of the box is not important)

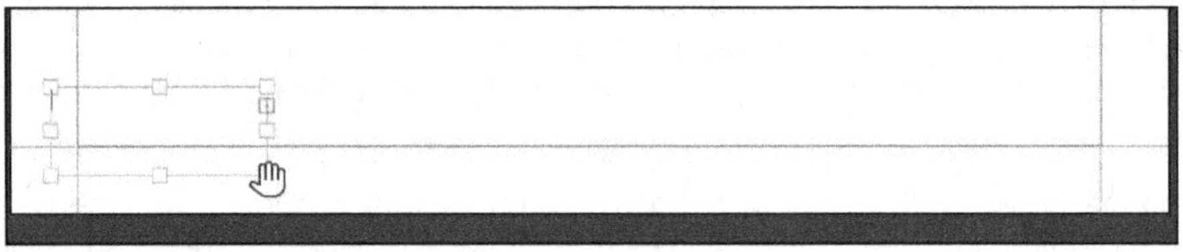

7. Use the **Measurements** window to resize and reposition the text box.

❒ with the text box you just drew selected, use the **Measurements** window to change the X value to **.5**

❒ change the Y value to **10.25**

❒ change the W value to **7.5**

❒ change the H value to **.25**

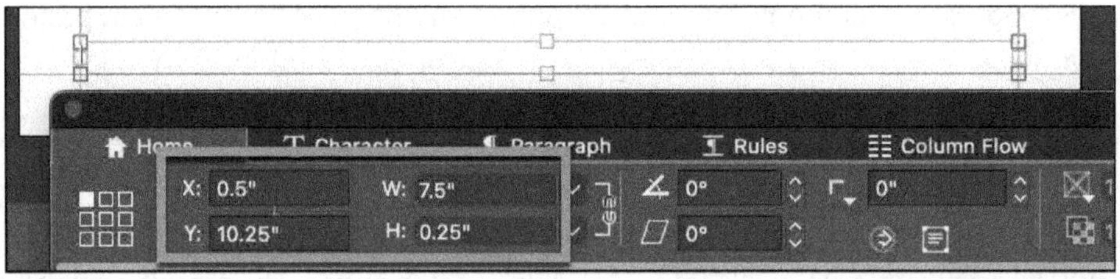

Note: Press [**return**] on you keyboard after typing the final value—simply clicking outside of the H field does not necessarily mean you have made the value stick. Prior to pressing [return], ensure you are still within the H field.

Your new text box should now be located at the bottom of the master page. The page should now contain two text boxes—the large, automatic text box, and a smaller one at the bottom of the page.

8. Add the current text box page number to the text box.

❒ using the **Text Content Tool**, click inside the text box at the bottom of the page

❒ choose **Utilities > Insert Character > Special > Current Box Page #**

The placeholder for the current box page # appears inside the text box. When you return to your layout, every page in the layout that is using the A-Master A page will display the current page number.

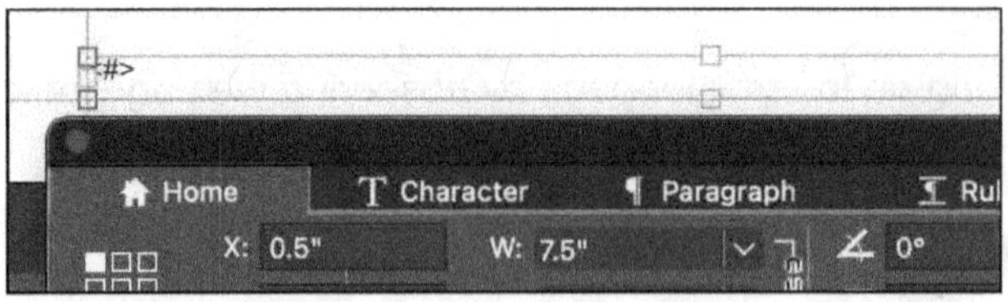

Confidence Check

1. Using the **Measurements** window, center the current box page # inside the text box horizontally.
2. Using the Page Layout palette, double-click page 2 to display the page.

   At the bottom of the page, notice that the page number appears. However, there's a problem. The box containing the page number is overlapping the layout text. You'll fix that next.

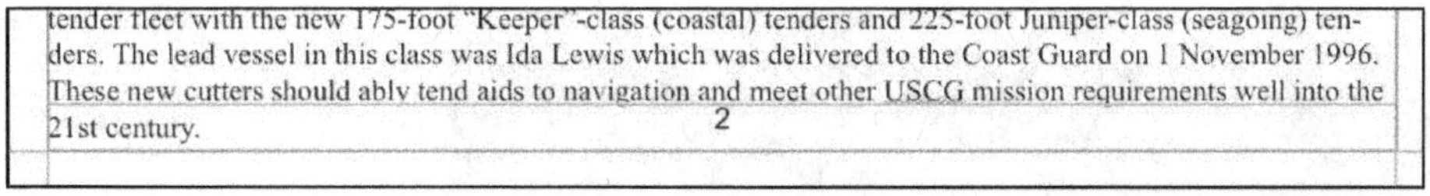

3. Display the Master-A Master page.
4. Using the **Item Tool**, select the text box containing the current box page #.
5. On the Measurements window, select the **Runaround** tab.
6. Choose **Item** from the first drop-down menu.
7. Change the **Top Runaround Outset** value to **6 pt**.

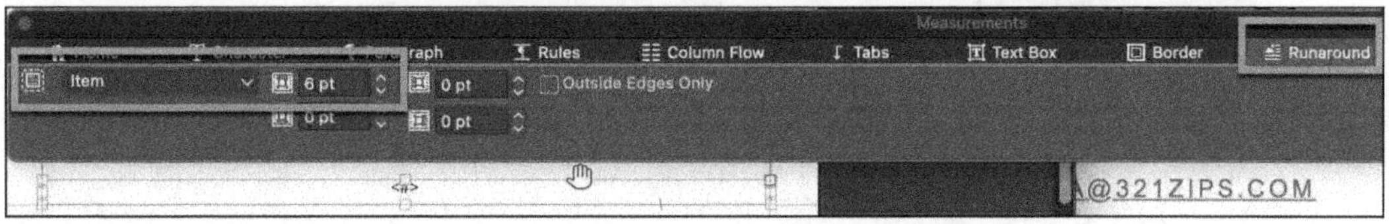

8. Return to the layout and go to the bottom of any page except page 1.

   Now that every text box containing the current box page # has an **Item Runaround** of 6 points **from the top** of the text box, the text in the story is being pushed away from the page number on every page that is using the A-Master A master page (only page 1, the cover page, isn't using the A-Master A master page).

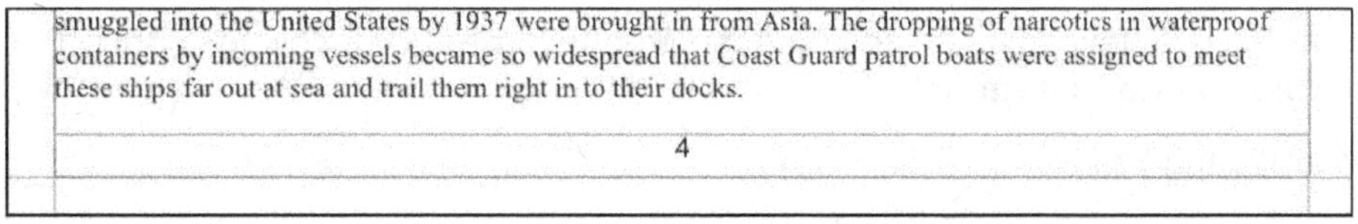

9. Save your work and close the project.

NOTES

NOTES

Guides

For perfect positioning of items, you can add non-printing **ruler guides** to the page. You can drag ruler guides from either the vertical or horizontal ruler. Once a guide is on the page, it can be repositioned or, if no longer needed, easily deleted.

Guided Activity 54: Super Step and Repeat an Item

1. Create a new project with the following specifications (in particular, notice that Automatic Text Box is **not selected** and the margins are one-half inch).

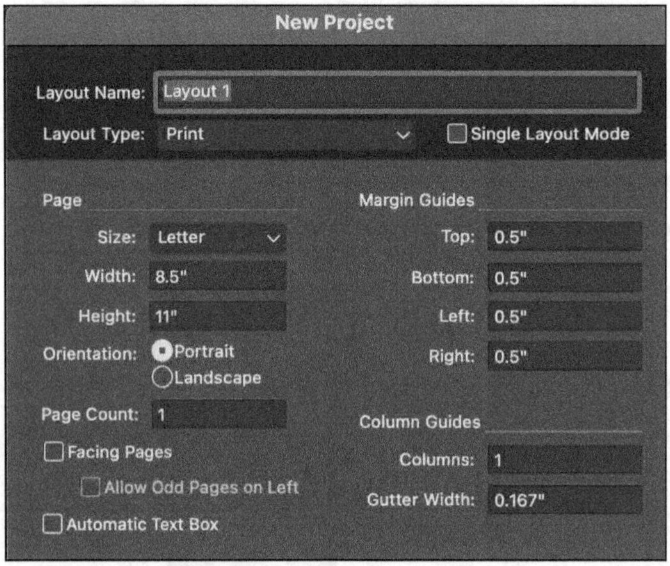

2. Save the project to the **QuarkXPress 2025 Book Assets** folder as **myManualTextLinks**.

3. Change your view to Fit in Window.

4. Draw and modify a text box.

   ❒ using the **Text Content Tool**, draw a text box anywhere on the page

   ❒ with the new text box selected, use the **Measurements** window to change the X and Y values to **one-half inch**

   ❒ change the W value to **3.5**

   ❒ change the H value to **6.5** and press [**return**]

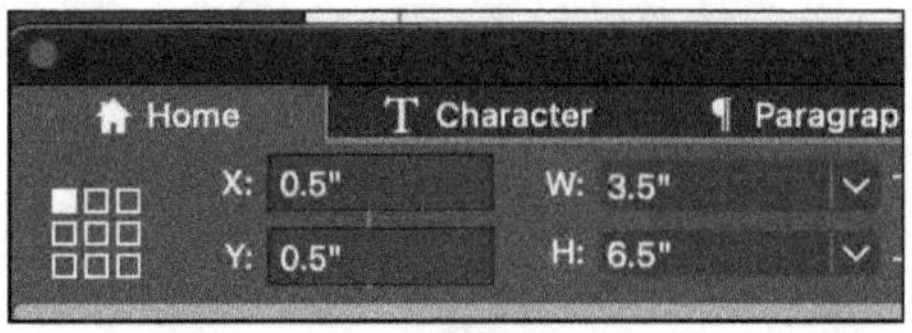

The text box should be located in the upper left of the layout.

5. Step and Repeat the text box.

   ❐ ensure that the text box is still selected

   ❐ choose **Item > Super Step and Repeat**

   ❐ ensure that the **Repeat Count** is **1**

   ❐ change the **Horizontal Offset** to **4"**

   ❐ change the **Vertical Offset** to **0"**

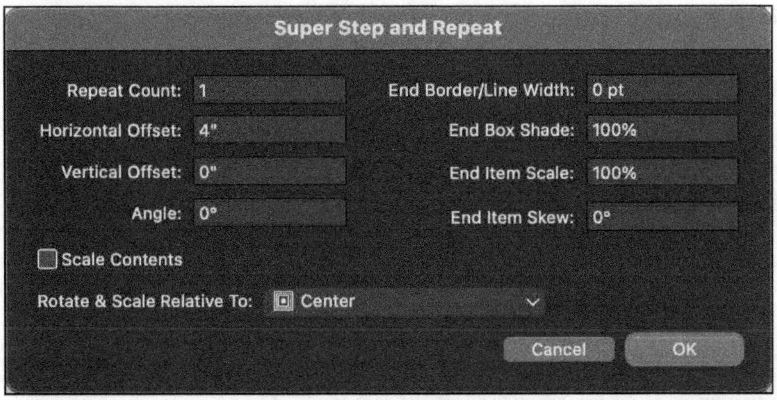

   ❐ click **OK**

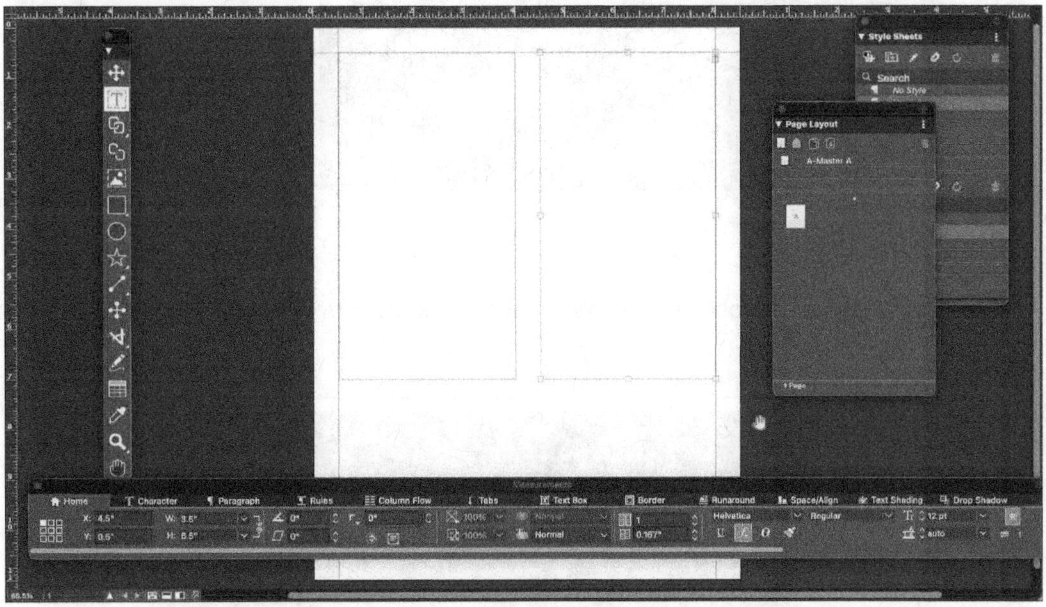

NOTES

Guided Activity 55: Add Guides to the Page

1. The **MyManualTextLinks** project should still be open.

2. Show the Guides palette.

   ❐ if necessary, change your view to Fit in Window

   ❐ choose **Window > Guides**

   The Guides palette opens.

3. Add a horizontal guide to the page.

   ❐ from the left of the Guides palette, click the **New** icon

   The Guide Attributes dialog box opens.

   ❐ change the **Location** to **7**

   ❐ change the **Direction** to **Horizontal**

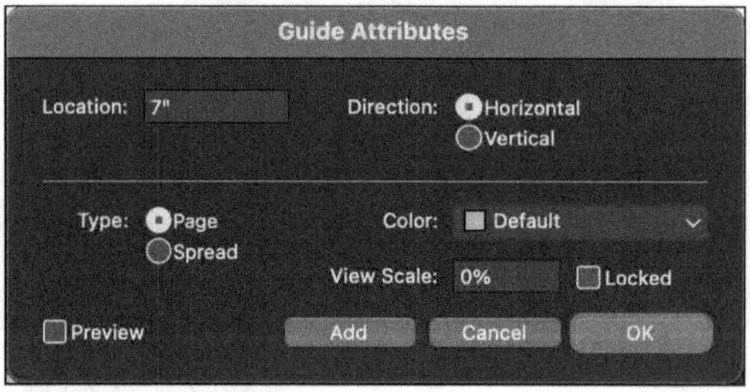

   ❐ click **OK**

   A green guide is positioned at the 7-inch mark on your page. The guide also appears on the Guides palette.

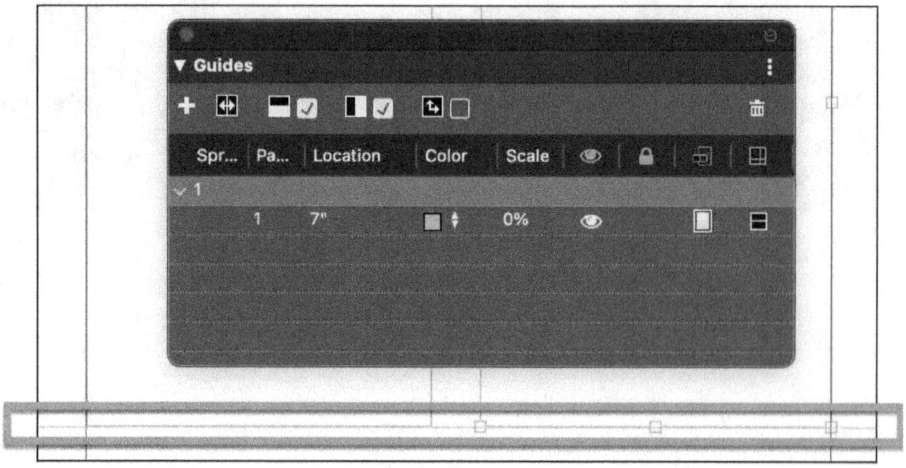

4. Reposition a guide using your mouse.

   ❒ using the **Item Tool** , position your mouse pointer over the guide

   ❒ when the mouse pointer changes to a double-headed arrow , **drag** the guide up or down a bit to change its page location

5. Reposition a guide using Guide Attributes.

   ❒ on the page, click one time on the guide

   The Guide Attributes open.

   ❒ change the **Location** to **7**

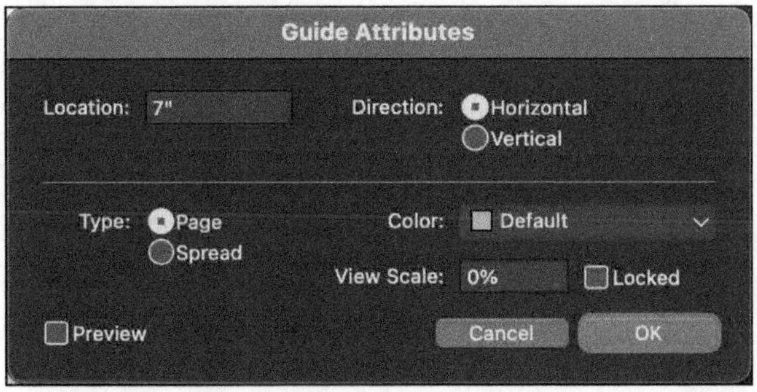

   ❒ click **OK**

6. Delete a guide.

   ❒ on the **Guides** palette, select the guide

   ❒ in the upper right of the Guides palette, click the **Delete** icon

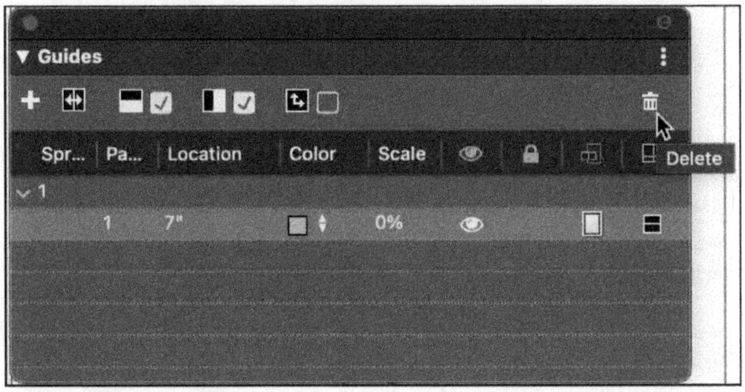

NOTES

NOTES

Confidence Check

1. Add a new **Horizontal** guide to the page at page location **7**.
2. Add another **Horizontal** guide to the page at page location **7.25**.
3. Draw a text box on the page that begins at the **7.25** guide, down to the margin guide at the bottom of the page.

   Your page should look like the picture below.

4. Close the Guides palette.
5. Save the project.

Manually Linking Text Boxes

You learned during the activity beginning on page 90 that creating layouts with an automatic text box is perfect if your layout is relatively simple and you want QuarkXPress to automatically control where overflow text goes.

However, using text boxes that you can manually link together allows you to create more complex layouts than those you get with automatic text boxes. If your layout did not start with an automatic text box, you'll need to draw text boxes before you can import text into the layout. The text boxes that you draw will not be linked like automatic text boxes. If you import text into a text box and there is more text than will fit, you'll see an overflow marker in the lower right corner of the text box. To make the text flow from text box to text box, you'll need to use the Linking tool and jump the text overflow from text box to text box.

Guided Activity 56: Use the Text Linking Tool

1. The **myManualTextLinks** project should still be open.

2. Import Text.

   - ❒ on the **Tools** window, select the **Text Content Tool** 
   - ❒ using the **Text Content Tool**, click in the text box in the upper left of the layout
   - ❒ choose **File > Import**
   - ❒ from **QuarkXPress 2025 Book Assets > textFiles**, open **CoastGuardHistory.doc**

   The text flows into the text box. Because there is more text than will fit in the text box, an overflow marker appears at the bottom of the text box.

   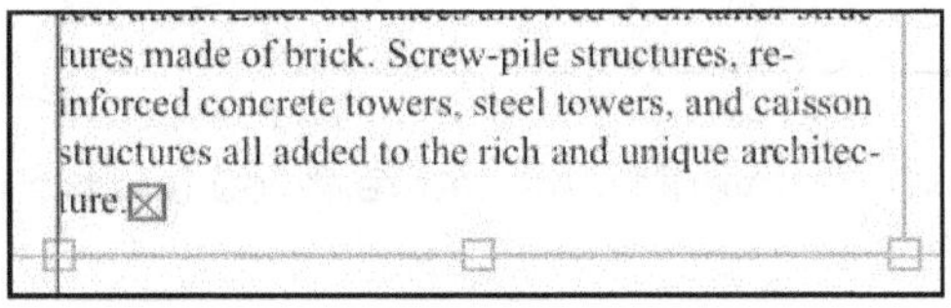

3. Jump the overflow text into a second text box.

   - ❒ on the **Tools** window, select the **Text Linking Tool** 
   - ❒ click in the first text box containing the text you imported

   Notice that "marching ants" surround the text box.

   - ❒ click anywhere in the second text box (the one in the upper right)

   The overflow text from the first text box jumps into the second text box.

   - ❒ with the Text Linking Tool still selected, click anywhere in the third text box (the one at the bottom of the page)

   The overflow text jumps into the third text box.

   - ❒ click one more time in the third text box (the one at the bottom of the page) to stop the linking process

NOTES

NOTES

Guided Activity 57: Use the Text UnLinking Tool

1. The **myManualTextLinks** project should still be open.

2. Break the current text link.

   ❒ on the **Tools** window, select the **Text Unlinking Tool** and click in any of the three text boxes

   You will see the two text flow arrows. The first begins in the bottom right of the first text box. The second flow arrow begins in the bottom right of the second text box.

   ❒ using the Text Unlinking Tool, click the beginning of the second flow arrow

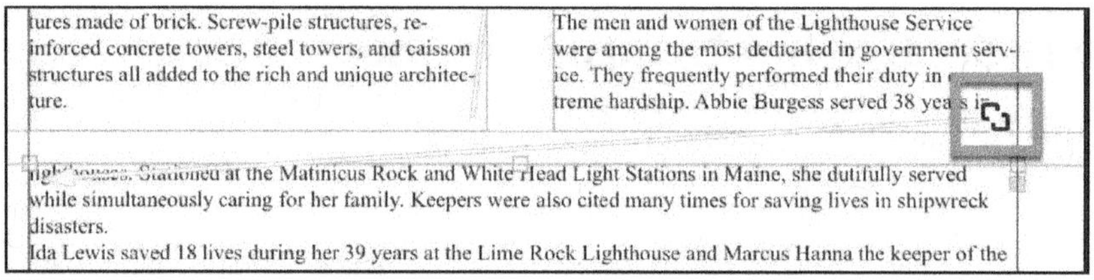

   The link is broken for the third text box. The overflow marker reappears in the second text box.

   ❒ using the Text Unlinking Tool, click the beginning of the first flow arrow

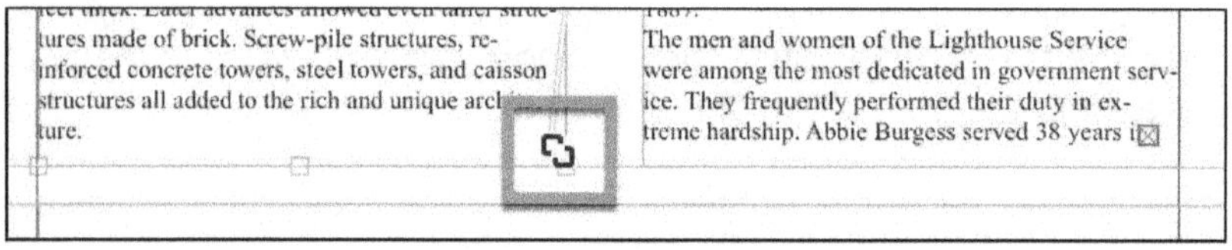

   The link is broken for the second text box. The overflow marker reappears in the first text box.

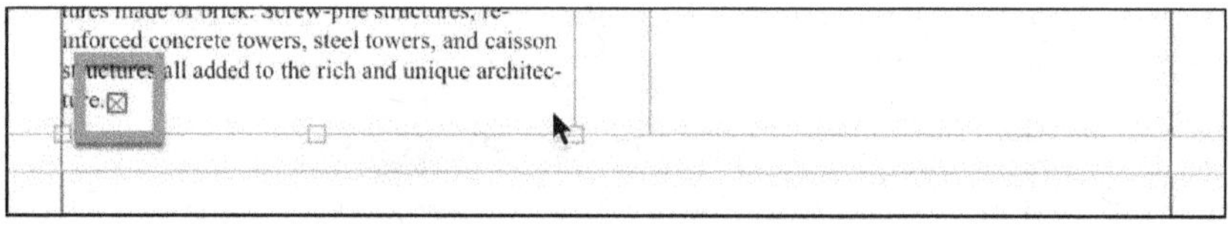

Guided Activity 58: Manually Create Page Jumps

1. The **myManualTextLinks** project should still be open.

2. Insert pages.

   ❒ choose **Page > Insert**

   ❒ type **9** into the Insert area

   ❒ ensure **after page 1** is selected

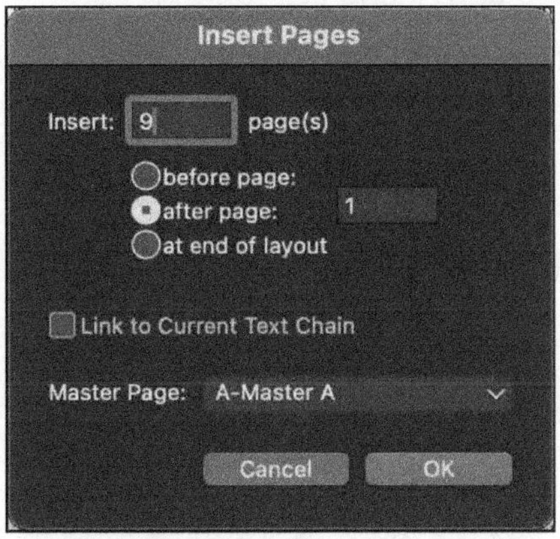

   ❒ click **OK**

   Nine pages have been added to the document.

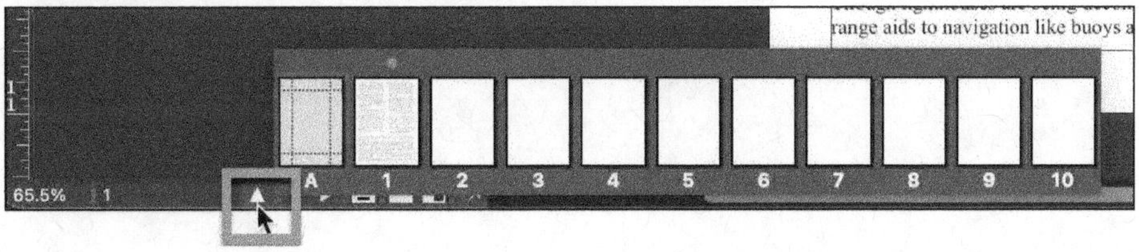

3. Create a text content box on page 3.

   ❒ press [**command**] [**j**] to display the Go to Page dialog box

   ❒ type **3**

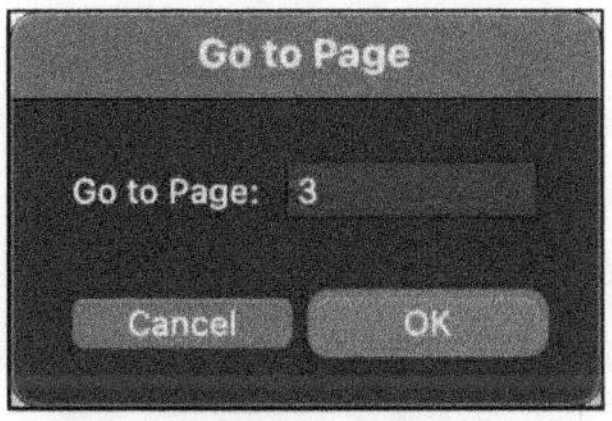

   ❒ click **OK**

   ❒ using the **Text Content Tool**, draw a text box to fill the entire page (from the top left margin to the bottom right margin)

NOTES

NOTES

Confidence Check

1. Using the Text Content Tool, draw text boxes on every odd page in the layout (pages 5, 7 and 9).
2. Go to page 1.
3. Using the Text Linking Tool, link the text from the first text box on the page to the second box on page 1 and then the third.
4. Using the Linking tool, continue linking the text from the last text box on page 1 to the text boxes you added to pages 3, 5, 7 and 9.

   There will still be overflow text after you link the text into the text box on page 9, but you should now have a good grasp of how to link text to QuarkXPress text boxes.
5. Save and close the project.

ICONLOGIC

"Skills and Drills" Learning

Module 7: Combining Text, Images, and Style Sheets

In This Module You Will Learn About:

And You Will Learn To:

NOTES

Creating a Poster (Flyer)

Up to this point in your QuarkXPress learning journey, you have been introduced to the QuarkXPress environment (page 1), worked with text (page 25), images (page 47), and items (page 61). You have even learned to control tab stops (page 79) and text links (page 89). Now it's time to combine several of your new-found skills and create a multi-column poster that includes text within a multi-column text box, an image with runaround text, and paragraph style sheets. Along the way, you will use the Find/Change feature, use the spell check feature, prepare to have the poster printed, and create a PDF.

Guided Activity 59: Preview the Completed Project

1. Review the features in a finished project.

   ❒ open **hotelFlyer** from the **QuarkXPress 2025 Book Assets** folder

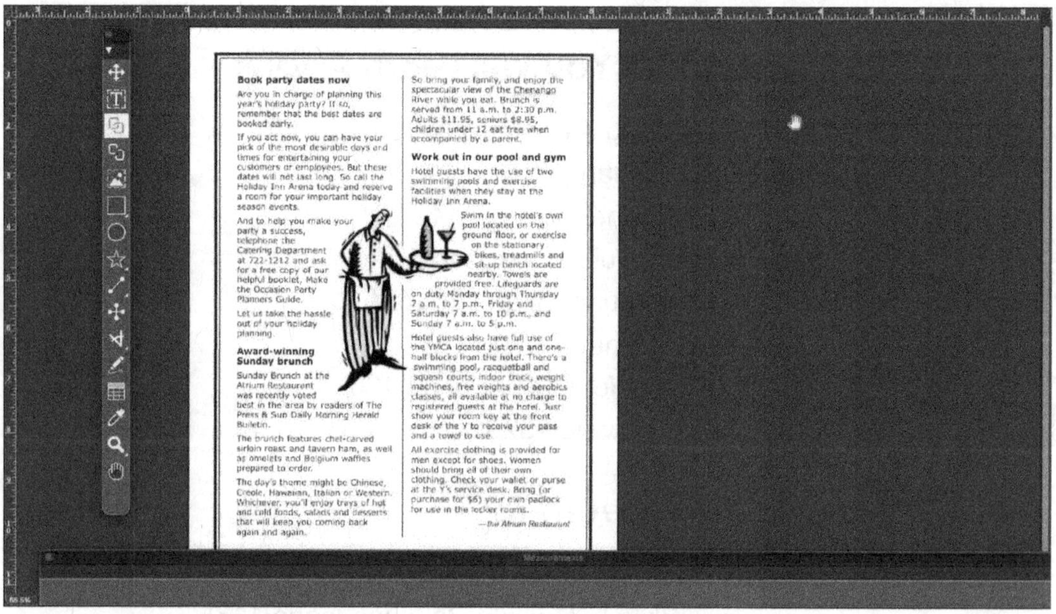

   Notice the following features (some of which you have learned how to do; you'll learn about other features soon):

   ❒ There is a frame surrounding the large text box.

   ❒ The text is flowing into two equal columns.

   ❒ The text has been is consistently formatted (there are three headlines and a significant amount of body text).

   ❒ The text is wrapping around the shape of the waiter image.

   ❒ There is a vertical line between the two columns.

   During the activities that follow, you will be recreating this project.

2. Close the project without saving changes.

Guided Activity 60: Add a Border to an Item

1. Create a new project with specifications that match the picture below. (Specifically, notice that Facing Pages and Automatic Text Box are both deselected.)

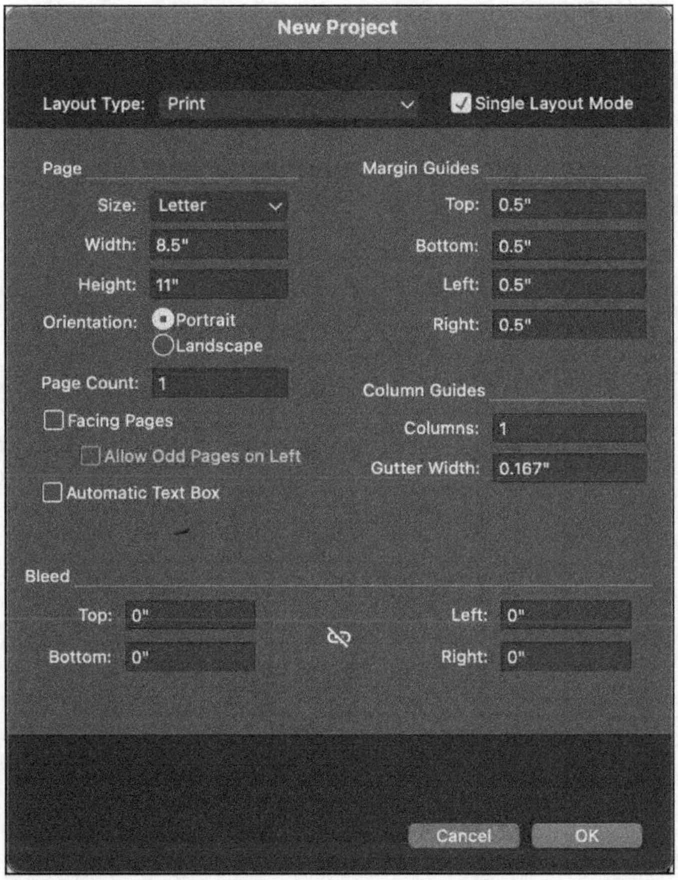

2. Save the project to the **QuarkXPress 2025 Book Assets** folder as **myHotelFlyer**.

3. Change the layout view to **Fit in Window**.

4. Use the Text Content Tool to create a page border.

   ❒ select the **Text Content Tool** and draw a text box anywhere on the page (any size is fine)

   ❒ on the **Measurements** window, **Home** tab, change the **X** value to **0.5**

   ❒ change the **Y** value to **0.5**

   ❒ change the **W** value to **7.5**

   ❒ change the **H** value to **10**

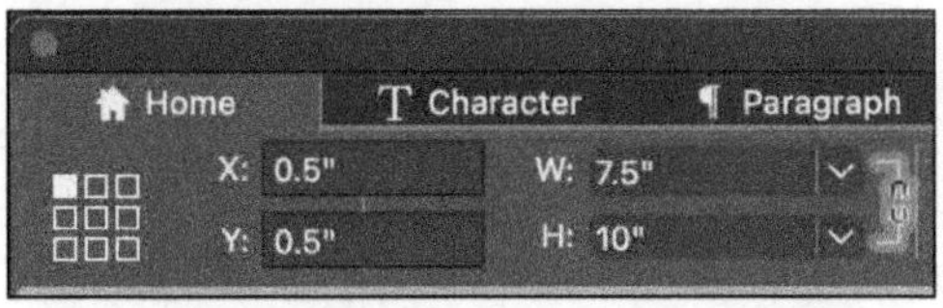

The text box should now fill the page, from margin to margin.

NOTES

5. Add a border to the text box.
    - ❒ ensure that the rectangle you drew is still selected
    - ❒ on the **Measurements** window, **Border** tab, change the **Width** to **8**
    - ❒ change the Style to **Thick-Thin**

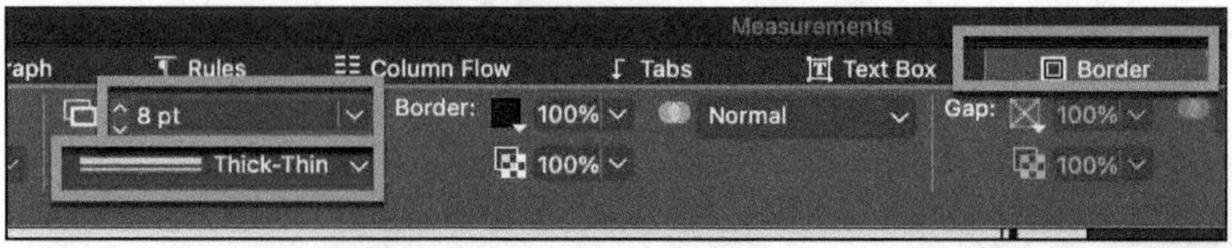

6. Save the project.

Guided Activity 61: Work with Multiple Columns

1. The **myHotelFlyer** project should still be open.

2. Import text.

   ❒ select the **Text Content Tool**  and then click in the text box

   ❒ press **[command]** **[e]** to open the Import dialog box

   ❒ from **QuarkXPress 2025 Book Assets > textFiles** folder, open **Flyer.txt**

   Notice that the text is too close to the text box frame, and there is currently only one column.

3. Change the number of columns and the gutter width.

   ❒ ensure that the text box is still selected

   ❒ on the **Measurements** window, select the **Text Box** tab

   ❒ change the number of **Columns** to **2**

   ❒ change the **Gutter Width** to **.333**

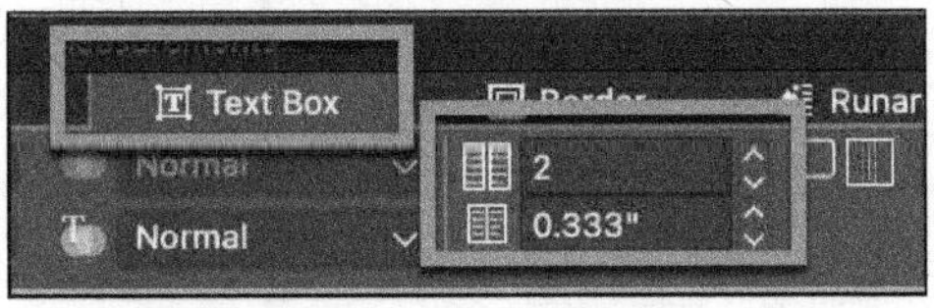

The Gutter Width is the space between two or more columns.

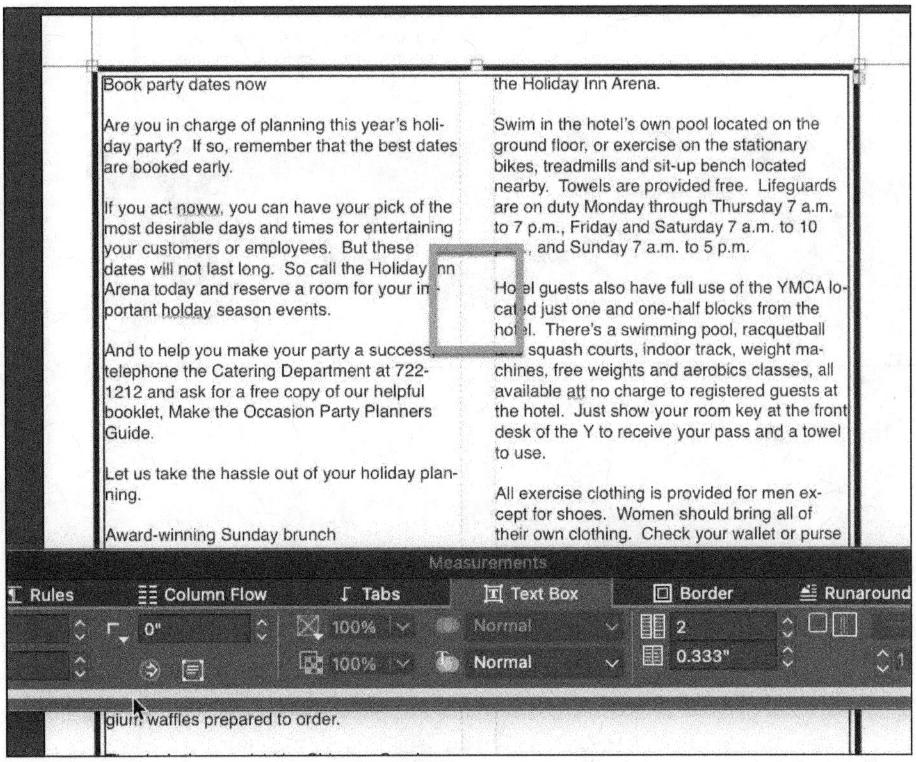

NOTES

NOTES

4. Add space between the border and the text.

   - ❒ ensure that the text box is still selected
   - ❒ on the **Measurements** window, select the **Text Box** tab
   - ❒ change the **Text Inset on All Edges** to **24**

By insetting the text, you have moved the text away from the text box border.

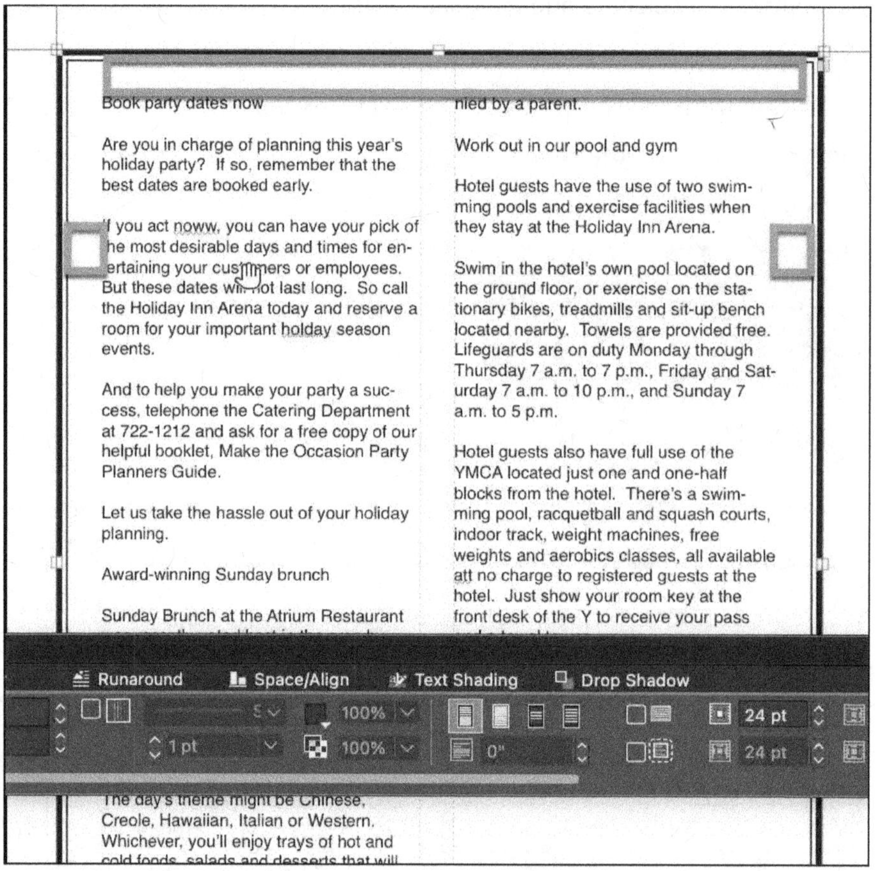

5. Save the project.

Find/Change

You will find dozens of uses for the Find/Change command. By way of illustration, suppose you are working with an article about dogs. Each occurrence of the word dog—and there could be thousands of occurrences—is bold. You decide to change the focus of the article to cats. You can use Find/Change to locate all occurrences of the word dog that are **bold** and replace them with the word cat set in *italics*. You can also use Find/Change to search for non-printing symbols (invisible characters) such as hard returns, tabs and multiple spaces between words.

Guided Activity 62: Use Find/Change

1. The **myHotelFlyer** project should still be open.

2. Zoom close enough to the page so that you can easily read the text.

3. Show Invisibles.

   ❒ choose **View > Invisibles**

   The text you imported was typed with two paragraph returns after every paragraph and two spaces at the end of each sentence. While this was correct on a typewriter, pressing the [return] key after every paragraph is not the proper way to control white space between paragraphs when using a computer with a word processor or QuarkXPress. Instead, adjust paragraph spacing by specifying a **Space Before** or **Space After** value on the Measurements window, Paragraph tab. Similarly, while adding two spaces at the end of every sentence was correct on a typewriter, this technique is incorrect on a computer—there should be only one space after each sentence.

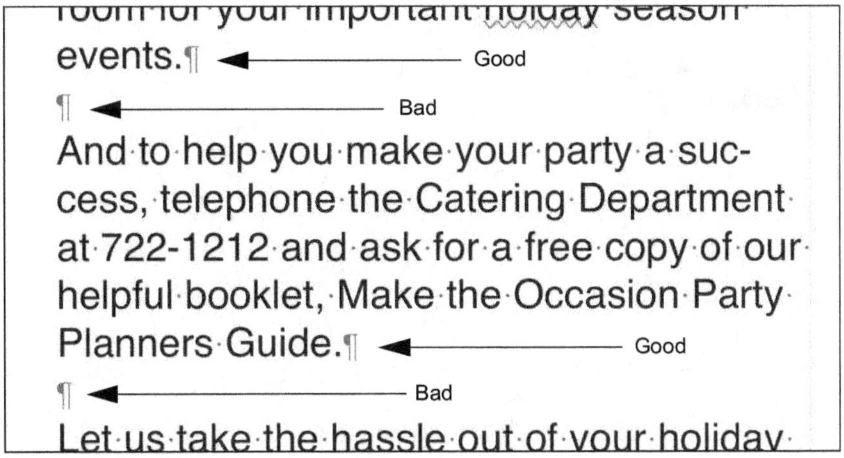

NOTES

4. Remove extra paragraph breaks.

❒ choose **Edit > Find/Change**

The Find/Change dialog box opens.

❒ from the **Query** drop-down menu, choose **Remove Extra Paragraph Breaks**

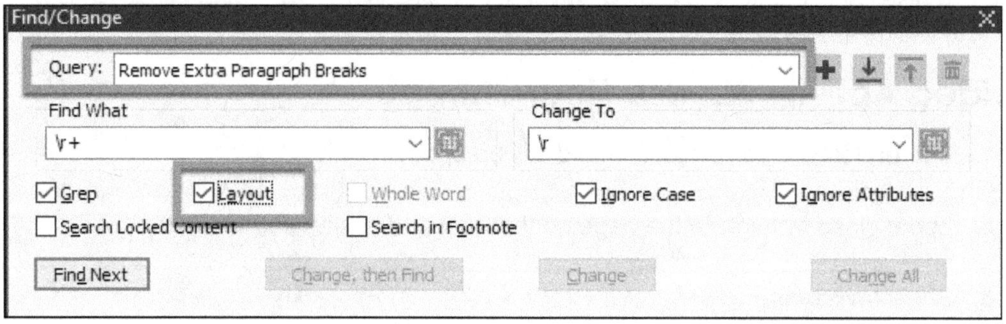

❒ from beneath the Find What area, select **Layout**

❒ press the [**alt**] key on your keyboard

Notice that with the [alt] key pressed, the Find Next button becomes **Find First**. This is a useful trick if you want to ensure that QuarkXPress searches from the top of the story.

❒ click **Find First** and then release the [**alt**] key

❒ click **Change All**

You should be alerted that several changes were made.

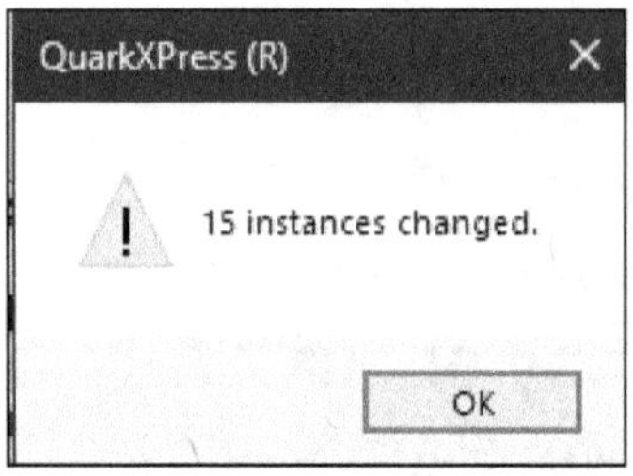

❒ click **OK**

5. Find and remove the extra spaces between sentences.

❒ the Find/Change dialog box should still be open (if not, choose **Edit > Find/Change**)

❒ remove all of the text in the Find What field

❒ press the [**spacebar**] **twice**

❒ remove all of the text in the Change To area

❒ press the [**spacebar**] **once**

❒ press the [**alt**] key on your keyboard

❒ click **Find First** and then release [**alt**]

❒ click **Change All**

You should be alerted that several changes were made.

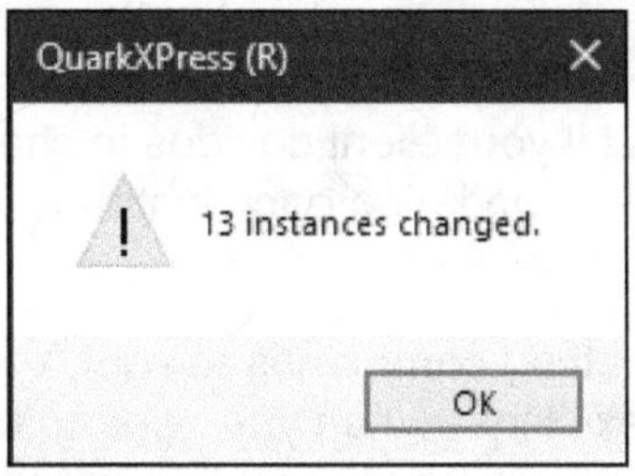

- ❒ click **OK**
- ❒ close the Find/Change dialog box

6. Save and close the project.

NOTES

NOTES

Style Sheets

Imagine all the steps in formatting a paragraph with a specific font, color, size, leading, and rules above and below. Now, consider having to repeat this process for hundreds of similar paragraphs. It could take hours to format everything. And what if your client decides to change the font or color? Without style sheets, you'd spend even more time updating each instance manually.

Style sheets provide a convenient way to apply multiple formatting commands to your text with a single action. They are easy to create and offer significant flexibility—when you need to update your text's appearance, you can edit the style sheets. Styles allows you to make hundreds of changes across your document in moments, saving time and effort.

Guided Activity 63: Create a Paragraph Style Sheet

1. Open **hotelFlyerStyleMe** from the **QuarkXPress 2025 Book Assets** folder and save the project as **myHotelFlyerStyles**.

2. Show the Style Sheets palette.

   ❐ choose **Window > Style Sheets**

   New QuarkXPress projects contain one paragraph style sheet and one character style. They are both called **Normal**, and they are both currently being used by the text throughout your layout.

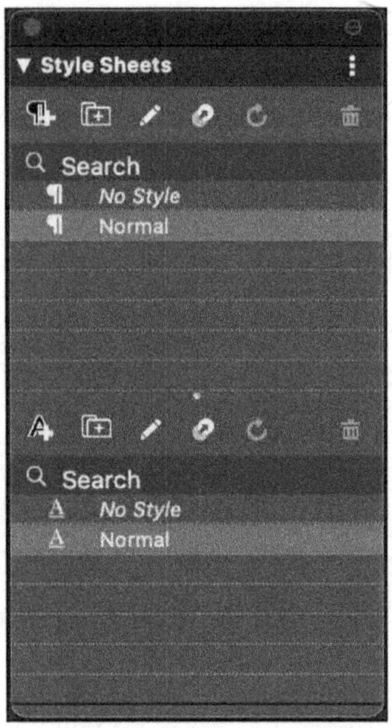

3. Create a new paragraph style sheet.

   ❐ on the top of the Styles sheet palette, click the **New** icon

   The Edit Paragraph Style Sheet dialog box opens.

   ❐ change the Name to **BodyText**

4. Set the character attributes for the BodyText style.

   ❒ at the right of the Character Style area, click the **Edit** button 

   The Character Attributes dialog box opens.

   ❒ change the Font to **Verdana**

   ❒ ensure the Font Size is **12**

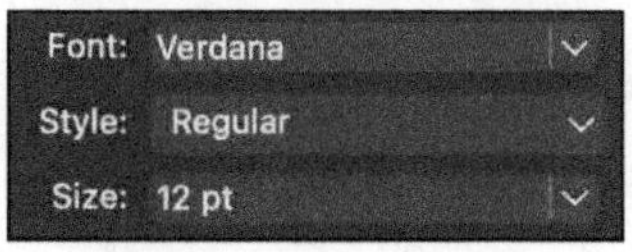

   ❒ click **OK**

   You are now back in the Edit Paragraph Style Sheet dialog box. Notice the font attribute you just changed appears in the Description area.

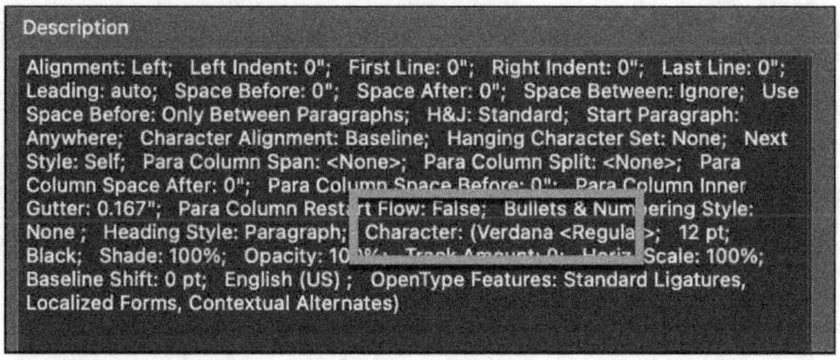

5. Set the paragraph attributes for the BodyText style.

   ❒ click the **Formats** tab

   ❒ change the Leading to **14**

   ❒ change the Space After to **.083**

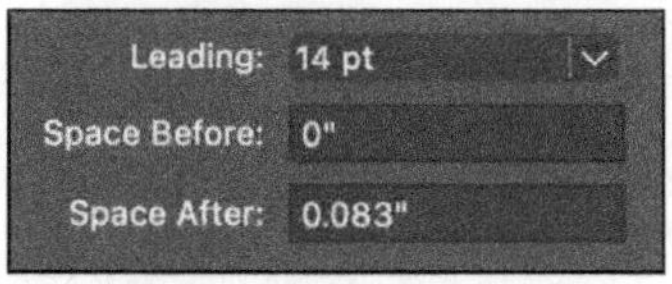

   ❒ click **OK**

   The new paragraph style appears in the Style Sheets palette. It is not currently being anywhere in the project.

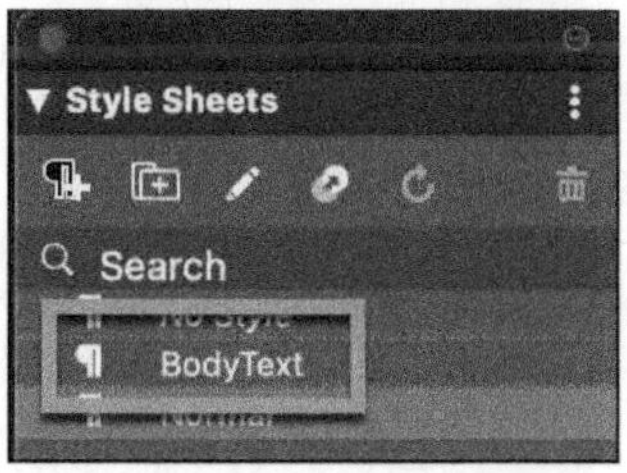

NOTES

NOTES

6. Apply the BodyText style to all of the text.
   - ❐ select the **Text Content Tool** and click anywhere in the text
   - ❐ choose **Edit > Select All** to select all of the text
   - ❐ on the Style Sheets palette, click the **BodyText** paragraph style sheet

   The entire document is formatted with the attributes of the BodyText paragraph style sheet.

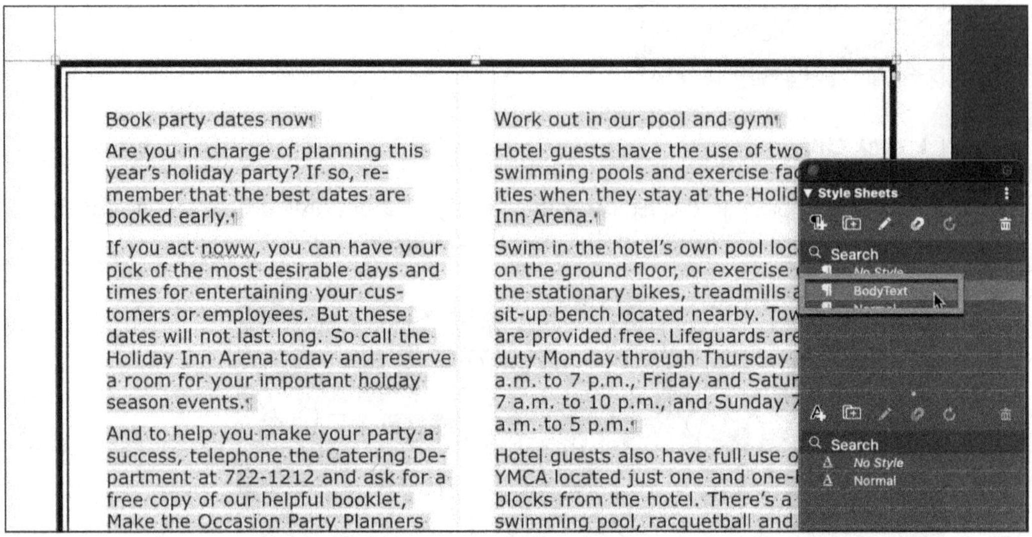

Confidence Check

1. With no next in the layout selected, create a new paragraph style named **Headlines**.
2. Format the new style as follows:

   Font: **Verdana**

   Font Size: **13 pt**

   Type Style: **Bold**

   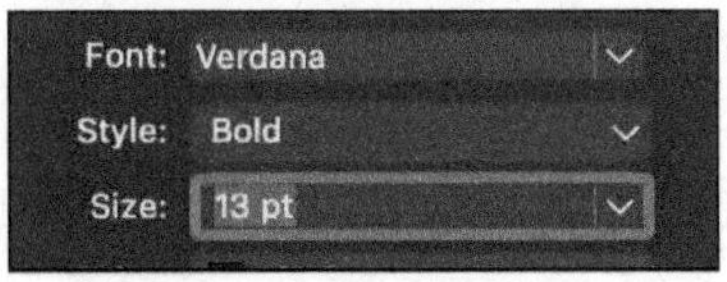

   Leading: **14**

   Space Before: **.125**

   Space After: **.083**

   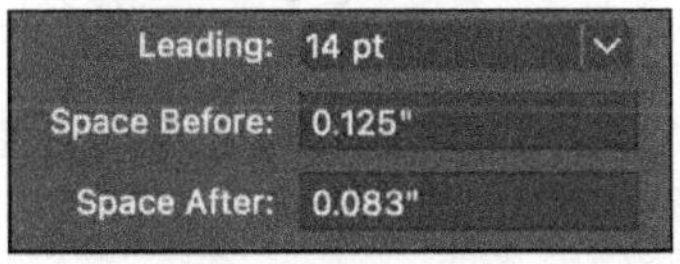

3. Apply the Headlines style to the three headlines in the project:

   Book party dates now

   Award-winning Sunday brunch

   Work out in our pool and gym
4. Choose **Edit > Style Sheets**.
5. Double-click **Headlines.**
6. On the **General** tab, **Character Styles** area, click **Edit**.
7. Change the **Font Color** to any color you like.
8. Click **OK twice** and click **Save**.
9. Notice each of the headlines in the poster has been updated with your new color.
10. Edit the Headlines style sheet again, this time changing the font color back to **Black**.
11. Save and close the project.

    Note: You will learn much more about style sheets, including character styles, during "Advanced Style Sheets" module which begins on page 167.

NOTES

NOTES

Page Guides

During the next few activities, you will add page guides to the layout using the Guides palette. The guides will help when you insert an image later.

Guided Activity 64: Add Page Guides

1. Open **imageMe** from the **QuarkXPress 2025 Book Assets** folder and save the project as **myImage**.

2. Show the Guides palette.

   ❒ choose **Window > Guides**

   The Guides palette appears. You first learned about the Guides palette on page 102.

3. Add a vertical ruler guide to the page using the Guides palette.

   ❒ from the left of the Guides palette, click the **New** icon

   The Guide Attributes dialog box opens.

   ❒ change the **Location** to **2.5**

   ❒ if necessary, change the **Direction** to **Vertical**

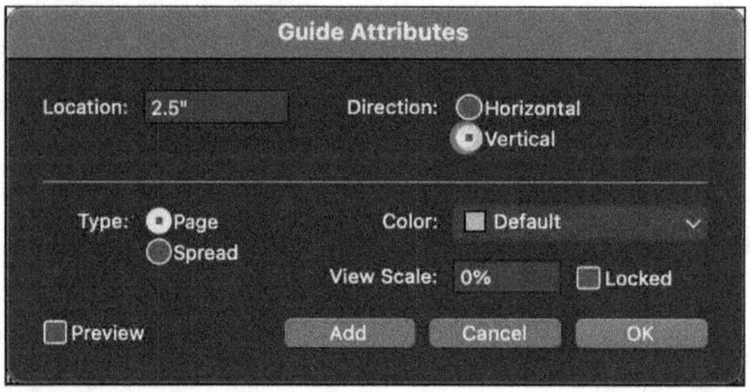

   ❒ click **OK**

   There should now be a green ruler guide on your page at position 2.5 on the ruler.

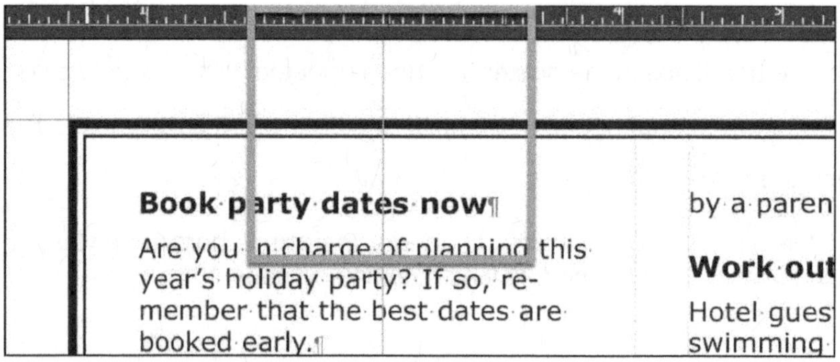

4. Drag a vertical ruler guide onto the page.

   ❒ position your mouse pointer in the **Vertical** ruler at the left of the window

- ❒ click and hold your mouse

Notice that your mouse pointer becomes a double-headed arrow. 

- ❒ drag a guide from the vertical ruler **over** to horizontal ruler position **4.25**
- ❒ drag a third guide from the vertical ruler **over** to ruler position **6**

5. Add horizontal ruler guides to the page.

- ❒ drag a ruler guide from the top (horizontal) ruler **down** to ruler position **3.5**
- ❒ drag a guide from the horizontal ruler **down** to ruler position **7.5**

You will be adding an image to the layout where the four guides intersect.

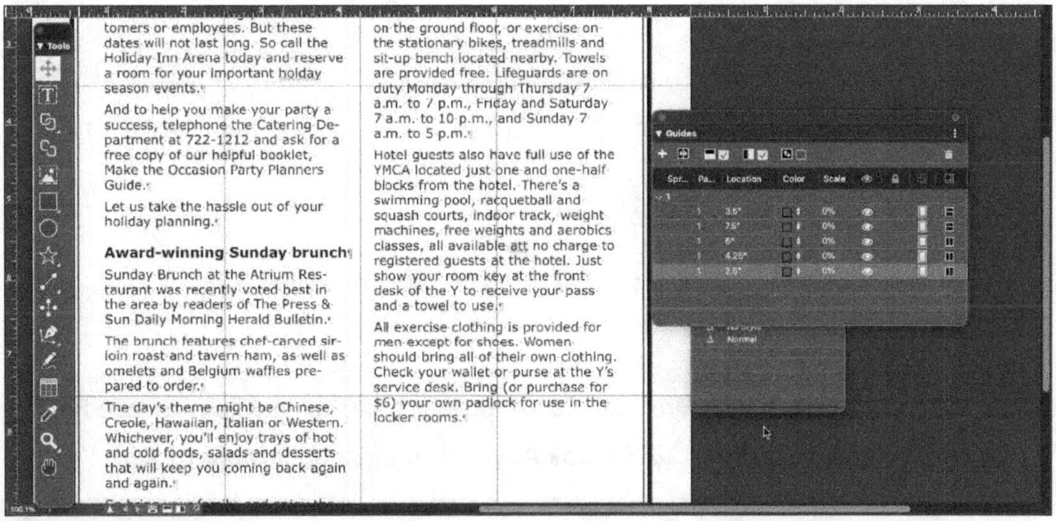

The Guides palette should look like the picture below.

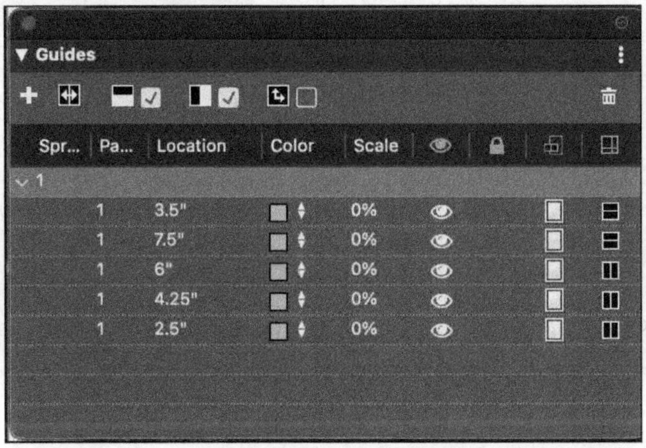

Note: You can edit the page location of any guide either by double-clicking the guide on the page, or double-clicking the guide's position value on the Guides palette. In addition, you can change the color of a guide by clicking the color you see on the Guide's palette and selecting a new color.

NOTES

NOTES

Guided Activity 65: Import an Image

1. The **myImage** project should still be open.

2. Draw a picture box.

    ❒ use the **Picture Content Tool** to draw a box that goes from the upper left intersection of your new guides to the lower right intersection

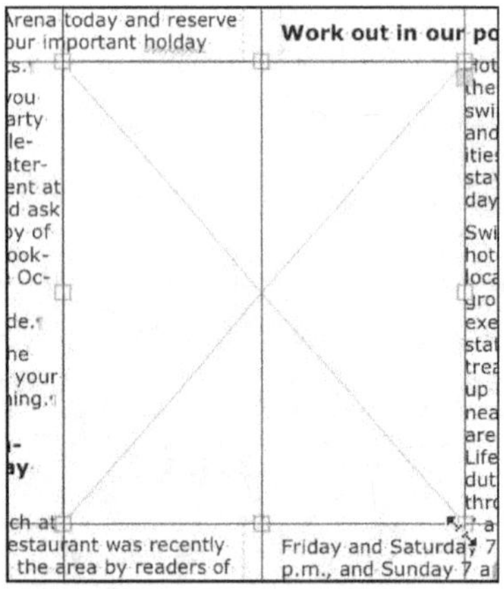

Notice that the text runs around all sides of the picture box.

3. Import a picture.

    ❒ ensure that the picture box you just drew is selected and then choose **File > Import**

    ❒ from **QuarkXPress 2025 Book Assets> images** open **waiter.jpg**

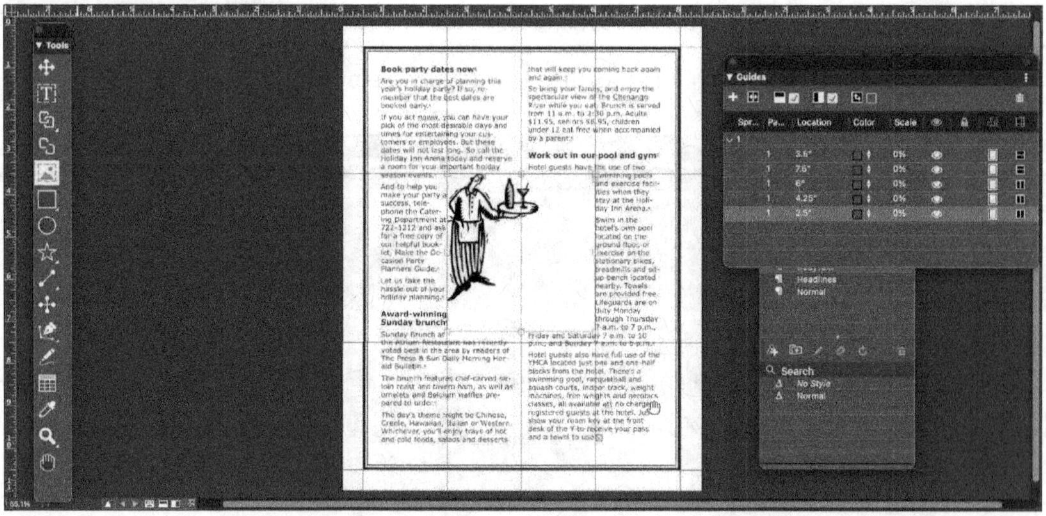

4. Center the picture in the picture box.

   ❒ ensure that the picture box is still selected

   ❒ choose **Style > Center Picture**

5. Enlarge the picture.

   ❒ ensure that the picture box still selected

   ❒ on the **Measurements** window, select the **Home** or **Picture Box** tab

   ❒ change the X% (picture width) to **115**

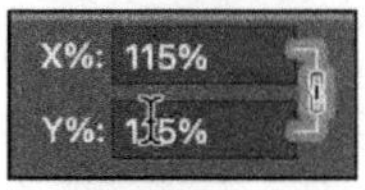

As long as the Constrain proportions icon is enabled,  the Y% should also change to 115%

Now that you have resized the picture, it is no longer centered in the picture box.

   ❒ choose **Style > Center Picture**

6. Save the project.

NOTES

Runaround

The text in the layout is, by default, wrapping around the picture box instead of the picture. You can disable the runaround so the text runs through the item, force the text to wrap around the image, and more.

Guided Activity 66: Run Text Around an Image

1. The **myImage** project should still be open.

2. Change the text wrap to Auto Image.

   ❒ ensure that the picture box is still selected

   ❒ on the **Measurements** window, select the **Runaround** tab

   ❒ from the **Type** drop-down menu, choose **Auto Image**

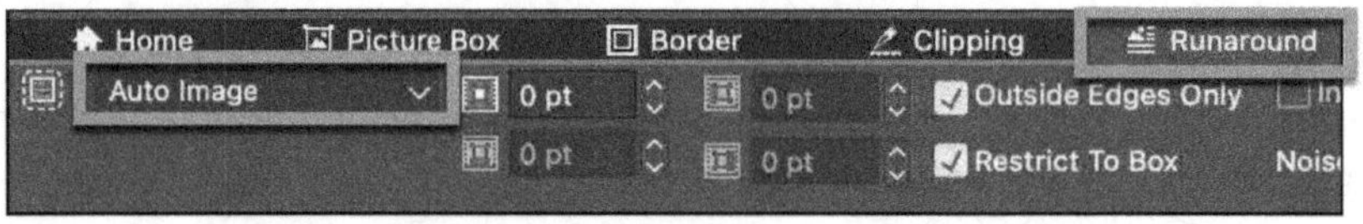

   The text is now running around the image instead of the picture box. You can increase the space between the image and the text by changing the Outset value.

3. Increase the runaround outset.

   ❒ on the **Runaround** tab of the **Measurements** window, change the **Outset** to **4**

   The space between the image and the text has been increased.

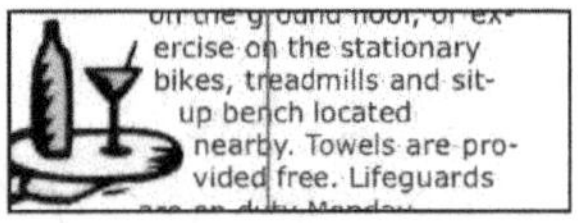

Confidence Check

1. Change the Runaround Outset to **8 pt**.

2. Increase the size of the picture to **120%** .

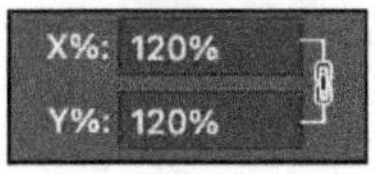

3. Center the picture in the picture box. (Style > Center Picture)
4. Select the text box.
5. On the Measurements window, select the **Text Box** tab.
6. At the right of the Measurements window, select **Multiple Insets** and change the Bottom Text Inset to **12**.

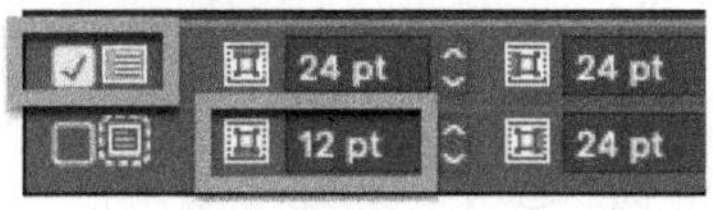

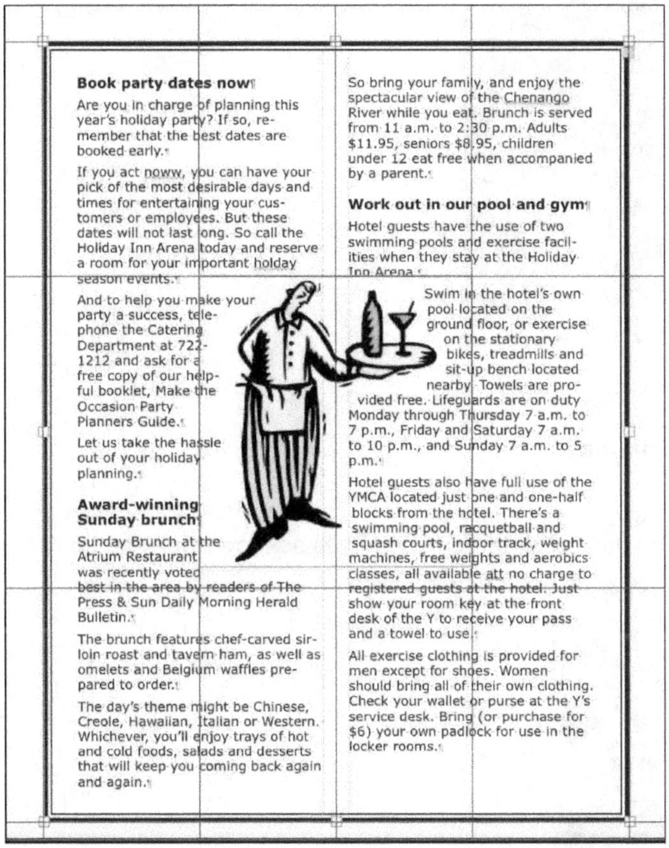

Book party dates now

Are you in charge of planning this year's holiday party? If so, remember that the best dates are booked early.

If you act noww, you can have your pick of the most desirable days and times for entertaining your customers or employees. But these dates will not last long. So call the Holiday Inn Arena today and reserve a room for your important holday season events.

And to help you make your party a success, telephone the Catering Department at 722-1212 and ask for a free copy of our helpful booklet, Make the Occasion Party Planners Guide.

Let us take the hassle out of your holiday planning.

Award-winning Sunday brunch

Sunday Brunch at the Atrium Restaurant was recently voted best in the area by readers of The Press & Sun Daily Morning Herald Bulletin.

The brunch features chef-carved sirloin roast and tavern ham, as well as omelets and Belgium waffles prepared to order.

The day's theme might be Chinese, Creole, Hawaiian, Italian or Western. Whichever, you'll enjoy trays of hot and cold foods, salads and desserts that will keep you coming back again and again.

So bring your family, and enjoy the spectacular view of the Chenango River while you eat. Brunch is served from 11 a.m. to 2:30 p.m. Adults $11.95, seniors $8.95, children under 12 eat free when accompanied by a parent.

Work out in our pool and gym

Hotel guests have the use of two swimming pools and exercise facilities when they stay at the Holiday Inn Arena.

Swim in the hotel's own pool located on the ground floor, or exercise on the stationary bikes, treadmills and sit-up bench located nearby. Towels are provided free. Lifeguards are on duty Monday through Thursday 7 a.m. to 7 p.m., Friday and Saturday 7 a.m. to 10 p.m., and Sunday 7 a.m. to 5 p.m.

Hotel guests also have full use of the YMCA located just one and one-half blocks from the hotel. There's a swimming pool, racquetball and squash courts, indoor track, weight machines, free weights and aerobics classes, all available att no charge to registered guests at the hotel. Just show your room key at the front desk of the Y to receive your pass and a towel to use.

All exercise clothing is provided for men except for shoes. Women should bring all of their own clothing. Check your wallet or purse at the Y's service desk. Bring (or purchase for $6) your own padlock for use in the locker rooms.

7. Save the project.

NOTES

Spell Check

You can check the spelling of a single word, a story or an entire layout. QuarkXPress highlights misspelled or unknown words and offers possible corrections.

Guided Activity 67: Spell Check a Layout

1. The **myImage** project should still be open.

2. Spell check the entire project.

   ❒ using the **Text Content Tool**, click in the story

   ❒ choose **Utilities > Check Spelling > Layout**

   The first suspect word is "noww."

   ❒ select **now** from the list of suggestions

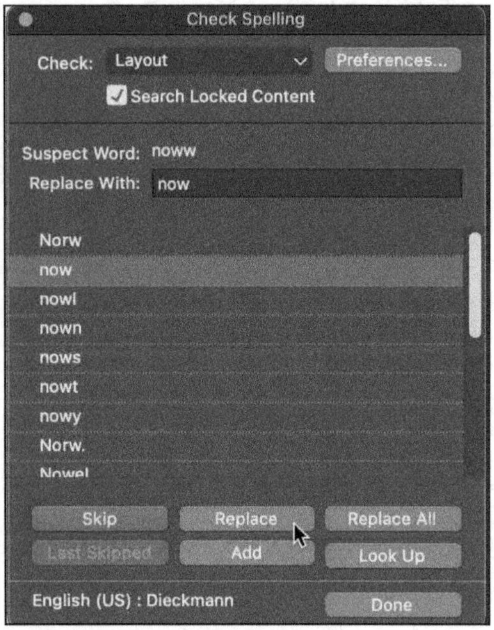

   ❒ click **Replace**

   ❒ **replace** "holday" with **holiday**

   ❒ skip **Chenango**

   ❒ replace "att" with **at** and then click the **OK** button to acknowledge the completed spellcheck

Confidence Check

1. An empty line should be at the end of the story (if not, click at the end of the story and press **[return]** to add a line.
2. Type **the Atrium Restaurant**.
3. Click at the beginning of the line you just typed and choose **Utilities > Insert Character > Special > Em Dash**

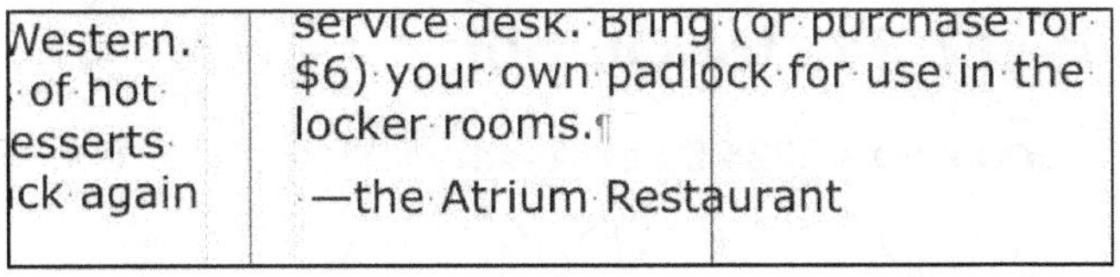

4. Create a **new paragraph style** named **Byline**.
5. Format the paragraph style with an **italic** character style and **right** paragraph alignment.
6. Apply the **Byline** style to the text that you typed.

7. Select the text box.
8. On the Measurements window, select the **Text Box** tab.
9. Select **Line Between**.

10. Choose **View > Guides** to hide the page guides.
11. Choose **View > Invisibles** to hide the paragraph symbols.

    The is essentially a print preview of your poster.
12. Save and close the project.

NOTES

NOTES

Collect for Output

Your poster is finished. If you intend to have the poster printed commercially, your printer may require that you fill out a lengthy report about your layout that details the fonts you have used, your pictures and other project details. QuarkXPress comes with a handy utility called Collect for Output that will place a copy of your layout, all of the pictures you used and even a copy of the fonts into a folder. You can then send the folder to your printer, confident that your printer has everything needed to print your layout without problems.

Guided Activity 68: Collect a File for Output

1. Open **collectMe** from the **QuarkXPress 2025 Book Assets** folder and save the project as **myCollect**.

2. Check the Font and Picture usage in the project.

   ❒ choose **Utilities > Usage** to display the Usage dialog box.

   ❒ on the **Fonts** category, notice that Verdana is the only font used in the layout

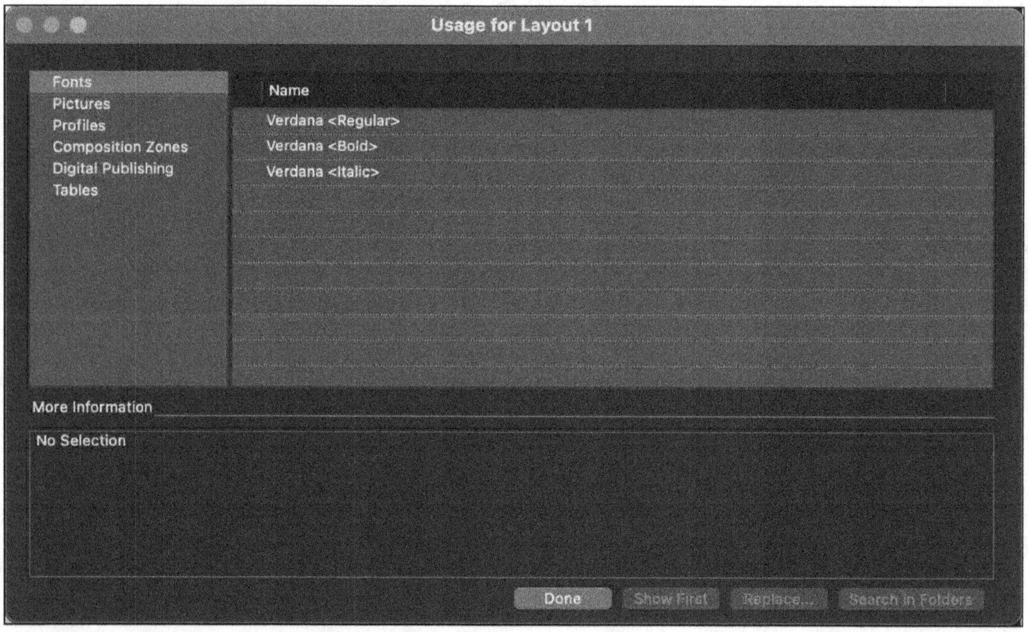

   ❒ select the **Pictures** category

The project's waiter image is listed. The Status column reads OK—an ideal situation because you intend to both print the poster and create a PDF. You should always check the status of your pictures prior to printing or creating a PDF. If the status had been anything other than OK—you might see "Missing" or "Updated"—you can use the **Update** relink to the image

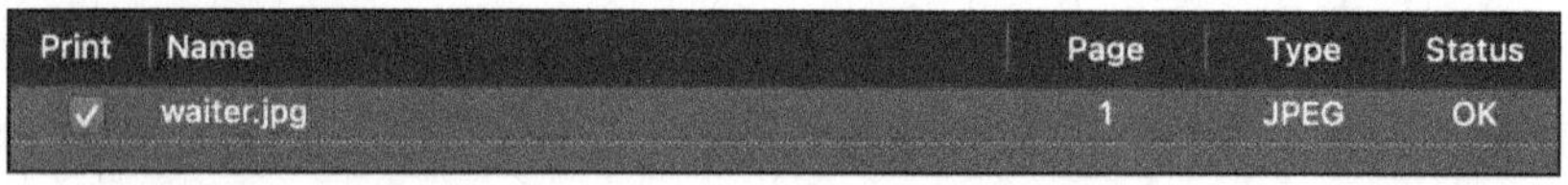

   ❒ click the **Done** button

3. Collect for Output.

❒ choose **File > Collect for Output**

The Collect for Output options appear.

❒ from **QuarkXPress 2025 Book Assets**, open the **giveToThePrinter** folder

❒ from the Collect area, select **Layout as Project** and **Linked Pictures**

❒ select **Fonts** (PC users) or **Printer Fonts** (Mac users)

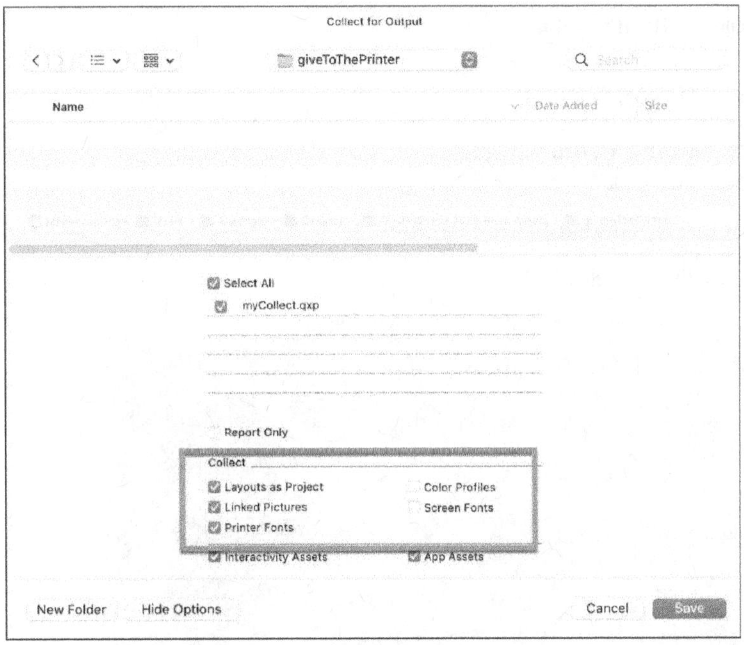

❒ click **Save**

If prompted, acknowledge the font alert.

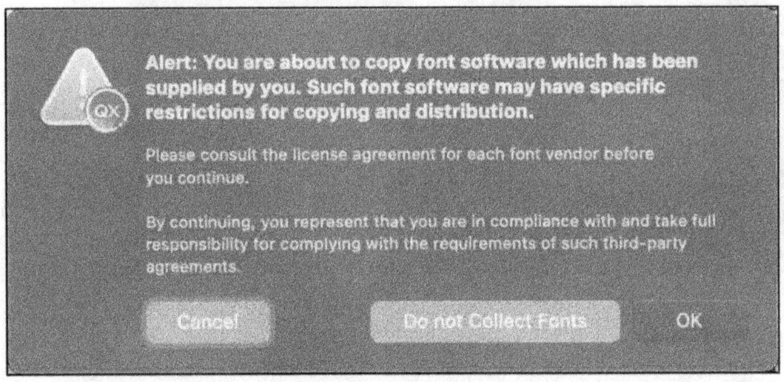

Your document is collected and copies of the file, fonts and pictures have been placed in the **QuarkXPress 2025 Book Assets** folder in the Give To Printer folder. Minimize or hide QuarkXPress and review the output files in the Give To Printer folder. When finished, return to QuarkXPress.

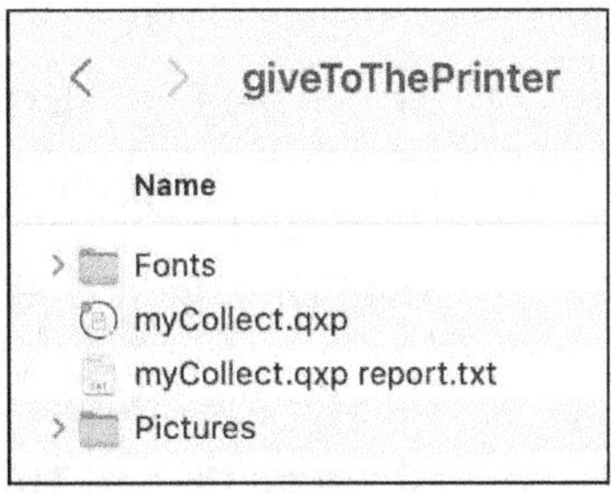

NOTES

NOTES

PDFs

You can export your QuarkXPress layouts into Portable Document Format (PDF) files. Providing PDF files to the printer or a customer has many advantages: PDFs can be opened and printed by just about anyone who has a PDF reader installed on their computer (Mac or PC) or mobile device. PDFs are widely accepted at service bureaus and prepress operations. And PDFs can be uploaded to a web server and easily downloaded and opened by users who have a PDF Reader.

Guided Activity 69: Create a PDF

1. The **myCollect** project should still be open.

2. Check the PDF Export preferences.

   ❒ PC users, choose **Edit > Preferences**;
   Mac users, choose **QuarkXPress > Settings**

   ❒ select **PDF** from the Application Preferences

   ❒ ensure **Direct to PDF** is selected

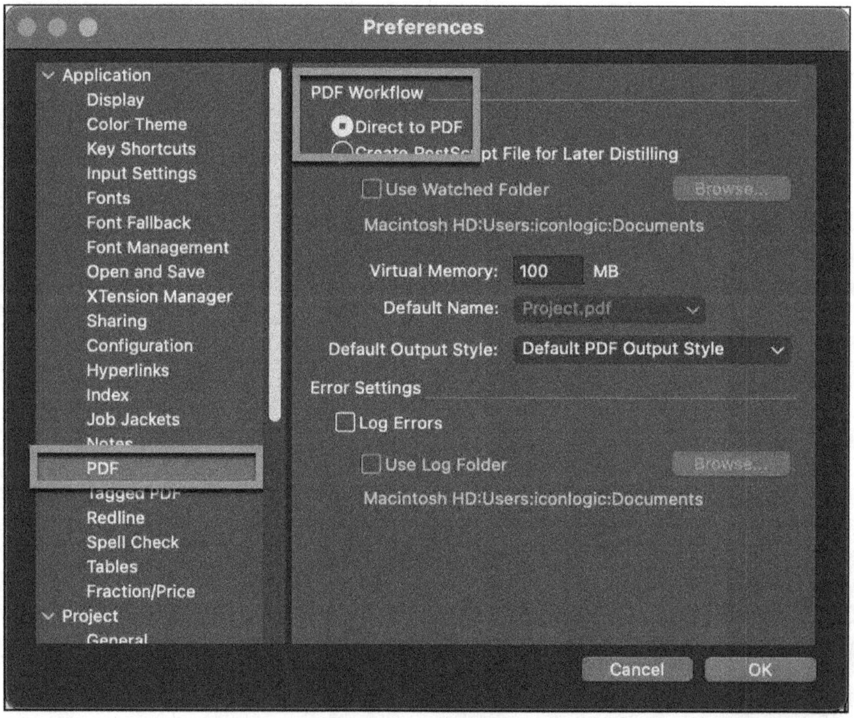

   ❒ click **OK**

3. Export the project as a PDF.

   ❒ choose **File > Export as > PDF**

   ❒ click the **Options** button

   The PDF Export Options dialog box opens.

   ❒ select the **Pages** category

   ❒ select **Embed Thumbnail** and ensure **Color Thumbnail** is selected in the menu

With this option selected, you will see a small preview of the PDF should you import the PDF back into a QuarkXPress layout.

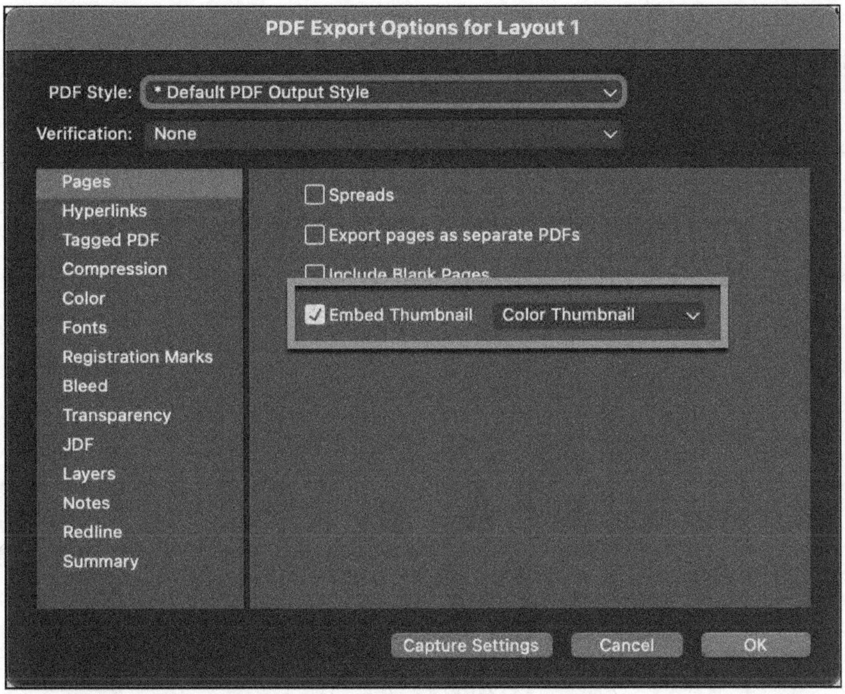

❒ click **OK**

❒ change the File name to **hotelPoster**

❒ ensure you are saving to the **giveToThePrinter** folder

❒ click **Save**

The PDF is created and saved to the giveToThePrinter folder.

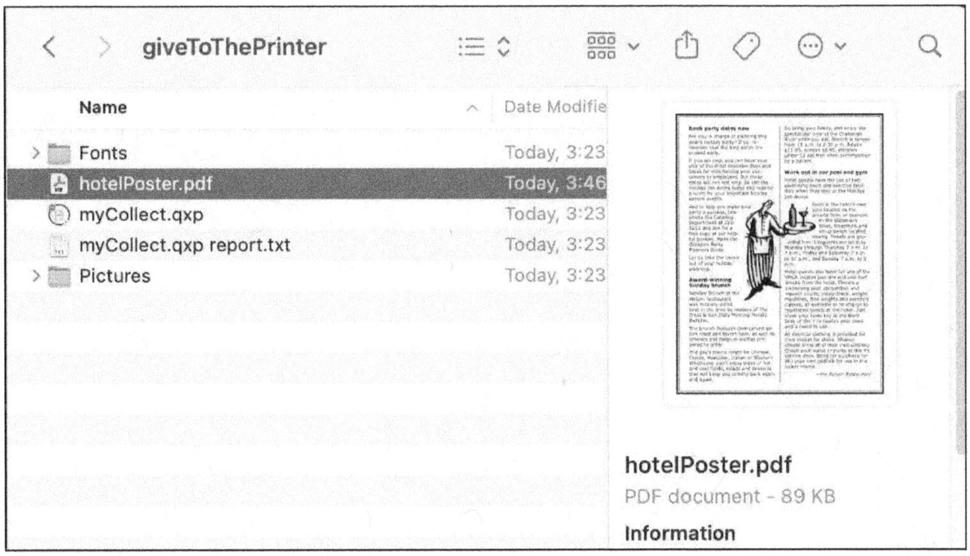

4. Hide (Minimize) QuarkXPress.

NOTES

5. Open the **QuarkXPress 2025 Book Assets** folder.

6. Open the **giveToThePrinter** folder.

7. Open **hotelPoster.pdf**.

8. Close the PDF.

9. Return to QuarkXPress.

10. Save the close all projects.

ICONLOGIC

"Skills and Drills" Learning

Module 8: Measurements, Colors, and Libraries

In This Module You Will Learn About:

- Points and Picas vs Inches, page 136
- Working With Colors, page 139
- Libraries, page 143

And You Will Learn To:

- Change Measurements, page 136
- Work with Process Color, page 139
- Add and Format Text, page 142
- Create and Use a Library, page 143

Points and Picas vs Inches

Up until now, you have created QuarkXPress projects using inches as the measurement system. As mentioned on page 11, new QuarkXPress users often feel more comfortable using inches as the measurement system instead of points or picas. Don't look now, but you're not a newbie anymore. Working with inches has two significant drawbacks:

Complex Calculations: Performing arithmetic with fractional inches can be challenging. For instance, finding half of 1 5/8 inches requires converting to a mixed fraction and then dividing—a task that can be cumbersome without AI or a smartphone.

Industry Standards: Most commercial printers use points or picas, not inches. Calculations in these units are much simpler. For example, determining half of 36 points or half of 6 picas is straightforward: 18 points and 3 picas, respectively.

Becoming proficient with points and picas will not only streamline your work but also make collaboration with other print professionals easier. Here is a table that provides a quick method for memorizing point/pica/inch conversions.

12 points = 1 pica	6 picas = 1 inch	36 points = 1/2 inch	72 points = 1 inch

Guided Activity 70: Change Measurements

1. Ensure that QuarkXPress is running and that no projects are open.

2. Change the measurement system from inches to picas.

   ❒ PC users, choose **Edit > Preferences**;
   Mac users, choose **QuarkXPress > Settings**

   The Preferences dialog box opens.

   ❒ from the **Default Print Layout** category, select **Measurements**

   ❒ from the **Horizontal** drop-down menu, choose **Picas**

   ❒ from the **Vertical** drop-down menu, choose **Picas**

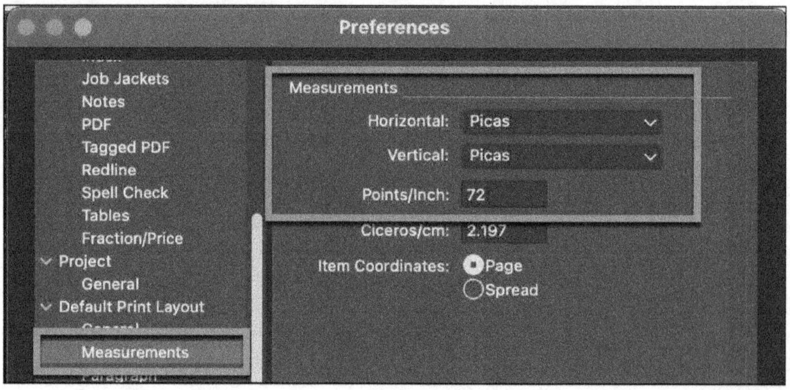

   ❒ click **OK**

   Because you changed the preferences with no projects open, only new projects will be measured using picas. Had you changed the preferences with a project open, the change would have affected only the active project. Note that existing projects will continue to use the inch measurement system. You can easily change the measurements from picas back to inches by returning the Preferences dialog box.

3. Create a new project.

   Notice that the Page Size, Width and Margin Guides read in picas (the letter "p" after a number indicates picas).

   ❒ ensure the Layout Type is **Print** and Single Layout Mode is enabled

   ❒ ensure the Page size is **Letter** and the Orientation is **Portrait**

   ❒ if necessary, turn **off** Facing Pages and Automatic Text Box

   ❒ if necessary, set all of the Margins to **3p** (3p stands for 3 picas, the same as one-half inch

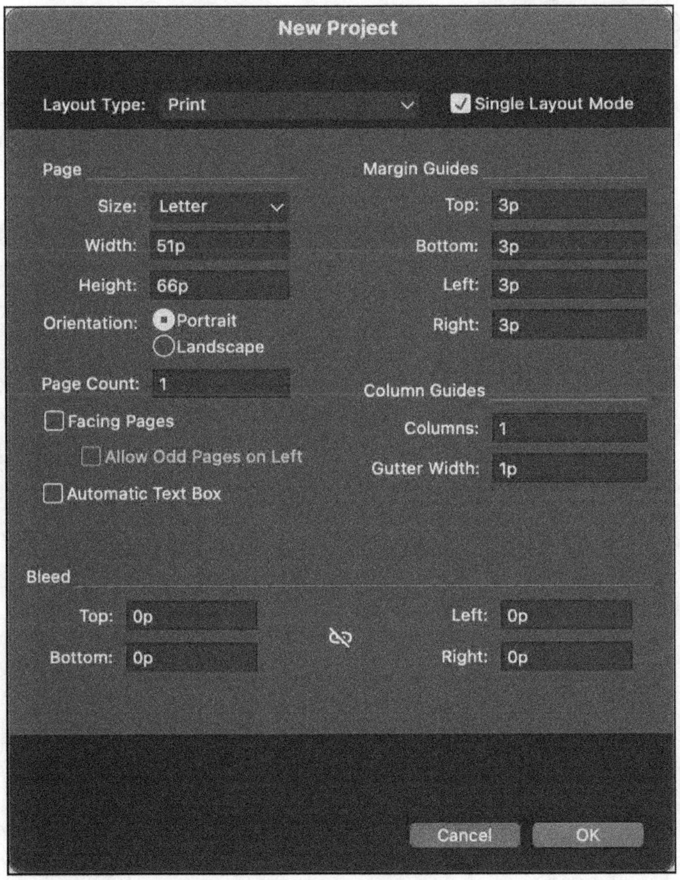

   ❒ click **OK**

4. Change the view to **Fit in Window**.

5. Draw a rectangle.

   ❒ on the **Tools** window, use the **Rectangle Box Tool**  to draw a rectangle anywhere on the page

6. Using the **Measurements** window, change the size and page position of the rectangle.

   ❒ with the box you just drew selected, on the **Measurements** window, **Home** tab, change the **X** value to **13p**

   ❒ change the **Y** value to **-1p**

NOTES

NOTES

❒ change the **W** value to **13p6**

Note: The position of the "p" is important when working with the pica measurement system. Numbers to the left of the "p" indicate picas. Numbers to the right of the "p" indicate points. By typing **13p6** you are specifying 13 picas and 6 points. If you had typed **136p**, you'd be asking for **136 picas**. If you had typed **p136** and you are asking for 136 points.

❒ change the **H** value to **69p** and then press [**return**]

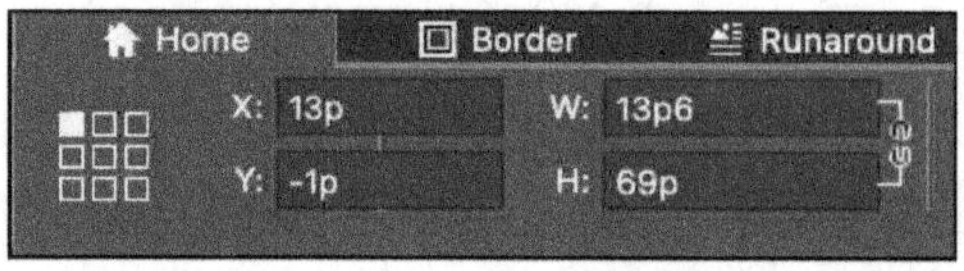

Your page should now contain one very tall rectangle. The top and bottom of the rectangle should be **bleeding** off the page (the edges of the rectangle should be hanging over the page margins).

7. Save the project to the **QuarkXPress 2025 Book Assets** folder as **myLibraryStuff**.

Working With Colors

Adding color in QuarkXPress is straightforward. Open the Colors window, select an item, and click a color swatch—that's it! But hold on. While making text blue is easy, which blue are you actually using? When you print your project or export it as a PDF, the outcome depends on the type of blue you've chosen. QuarkXPress offers spot colors and process colors. Additionally, colors may come from two sources: those you apply directly to elements within QuarkXPress and those embedded in imported images. There's also a difference between print colors and web colors.

While managing colors can seem complex, QuarkXPress simplifies the process. You can create virtually any color you need, either on-the-fly—which isn't recommended unless you know the exact "recipe"—or by choosing from existing color models. These models allow you to select and apply colors to boxes, lines, text, and even certain images. Once a color is added to your project, you can fine-tune it by adjusting its shade, blend, or opacity.

Spot and Process Colors

Colors intended for commercial printing are typically created using four inks: cyan, magenta, yellow, and black (CMYK). If your layout contains three or fewer colors, consider using spot colors. With spot colors, only the specific inks you need are added to the press, and you're charged solely for those inks.

For layouts with four or more colors, opt for process colors. In this case, the individual CMYK inks are applied to the press one at a time, and you're charged for all four inks. If your layout includes a photograph, it likely contains thousands of colors. However, because these colors are created by blending CMYK inks, you're still only charged for four inks—not thousands.

You can also combine spot and process colors in the same layout. While this approach can be more expensive, it can yield stunning results. For example, you might design a layout with color photographs (which require CMYK process inks) alongside a logo that uses one or two spot colors.

Guided Activity 71: Work with Process Color

1. The **MyLibraryStuff** project you created during the last activity should still be open.

2. Change an item's color using the **Colors** window.

   ❐ choose **Window > Colors**

3. Use the **Colors** window to change an item's background color.

   ❐ with the rectangle on the page selected, select the **Background Color** icon on the Colors window

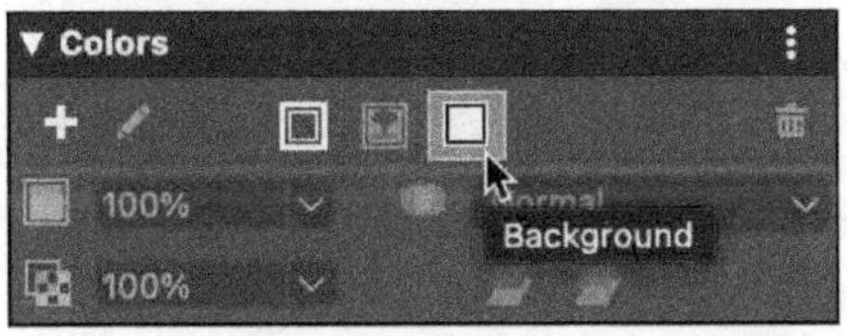

   ❐ on the **Colors** window, **Swatches** tab, click **Magenta**

NOTES

The item's background color changes to magenta.

❒ on the **Colors** window, click **Cyan**

The item's background changes to cyan.

4. Add a process color to the project.

❒ on the **Colors** window, click the **New** icon

The **Add Color** dialog box opens.

❒ from the **Model** drop-down menu, select **Pantone process coated**

Color swatches appear at the right of the dialog box.

❒ in the **Pantone DS** area (bottom right of the dialog box), type **185-7**

The number you typed corresponds to a specific Pantone process coated color.

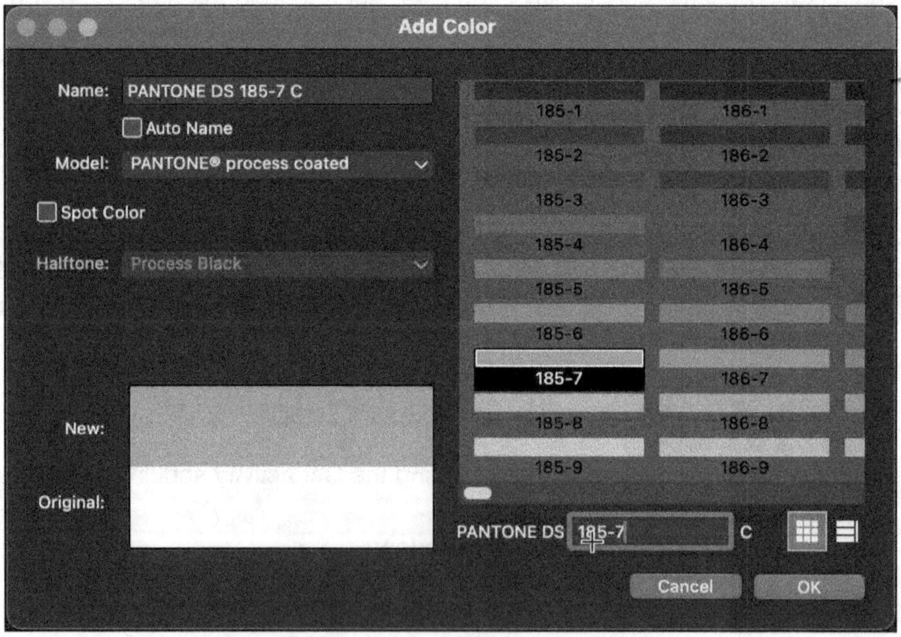

❒ click **OK**

The new color is available for use in the **Colors** window.

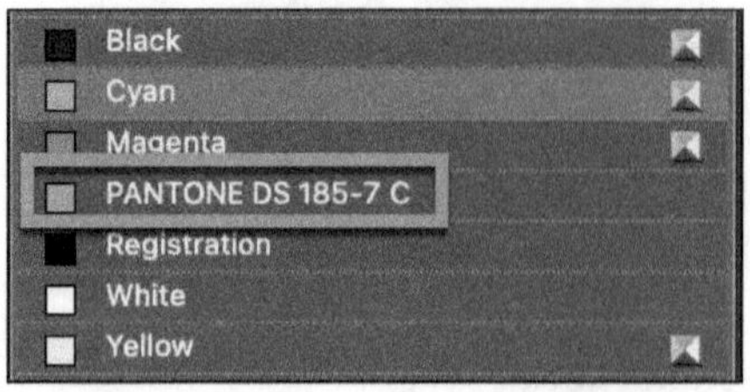

Confidence Check

1. Change the rectangle's Background color from **Cyan** to **Pantone DS 185-7 C**.
2. With the rectangle still selected, find the **Shade** area of the **Colors** window and drag the slider down to 35%.

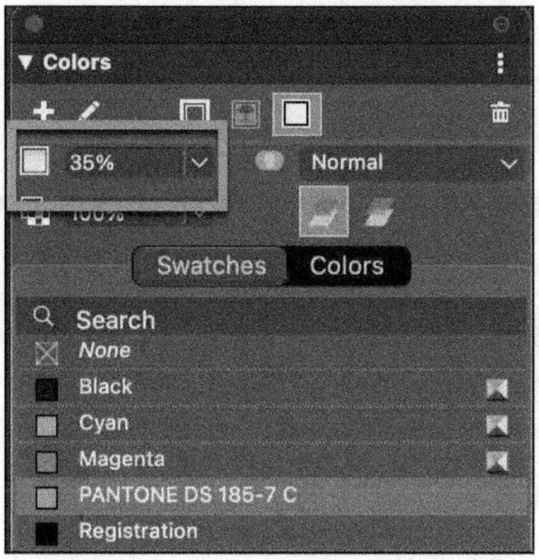

   Your rectangle should now have a light periwinkle background color.

3. Save the project.

NOTES

Guided Activity 72: Add and Format Text

1. Add text to the page.

   ❒ change your view to **Actual Size**

   ❒ using the **Text Content Tool**, draw a text box anywhere on the page

   ❒ type **The Weekly Winer** into your new text box

2. Use the **Measurements** window to format text.

   ❒ using the **Text Content Tool**, select the text you just typed

   ❒ using the **Measurements** window, **Character** tab, change the Font to **Verdana**

   ❒ change the Font size to **11 pt**

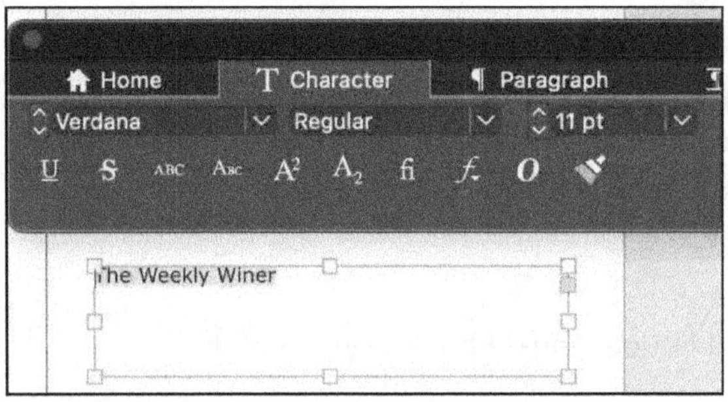

   ❒ using the **Measurements** window, **Paragraph** tab, click the **Centered** tool to center the text horizontally in the text box

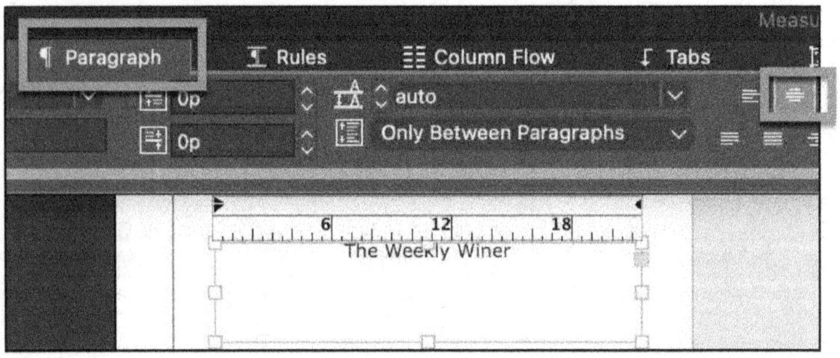

3. Use the **Measurements** window to change the width of an item.

   ❒ using the **Measurements** window, **Home** tab, change the **W** value to **9p**

   ❒ change the **H** value to **2p**

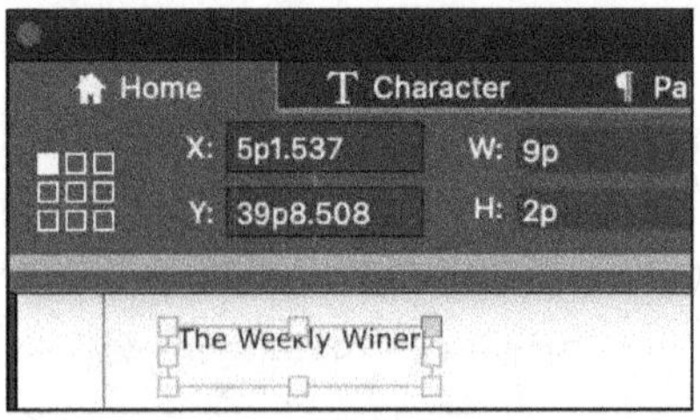

There should now be two items on your page: the tall rectangle with the periwinkle background color and the text box containing the text "**The Weekly Winer**."

Libraries

You can use libraries to store commonly used graphics and text that you can pull onto your page anytime you need them. There's really no limit to the number of items that you can add to a library, and there is no limit to the number of libraries you can create. As you are about to see, creating effective libraries will make quick work out of adding common objects to layouts.

Guided Activity 73: Create and Use a Library

1. Create a new library.

   ❒ choose **File > New > Library**

   The New Library dialog box opens.

   ❒ name the library **winerLibrary** and save it to the **QuarkXPress 2025 Book Assets** folder

   ❒ click **Create**

   The new library appears on your screen.

2. Add the tall rectangle to the library.

   ❒ using the **Item** tool, drag (move) the tall rectangle into the library

   A miniature of the item appears in the library. You'll be using the item later when you learn to create master pages.

Note: By default, QuarkXPress automatically saves the library every time you add a new item.

NOTES

NOTES

3. Use the Library.

❒ from the Library, drag the item drag onto the page

You should now have two rectangles on your page. There is no limit to how many times you can use library elements.

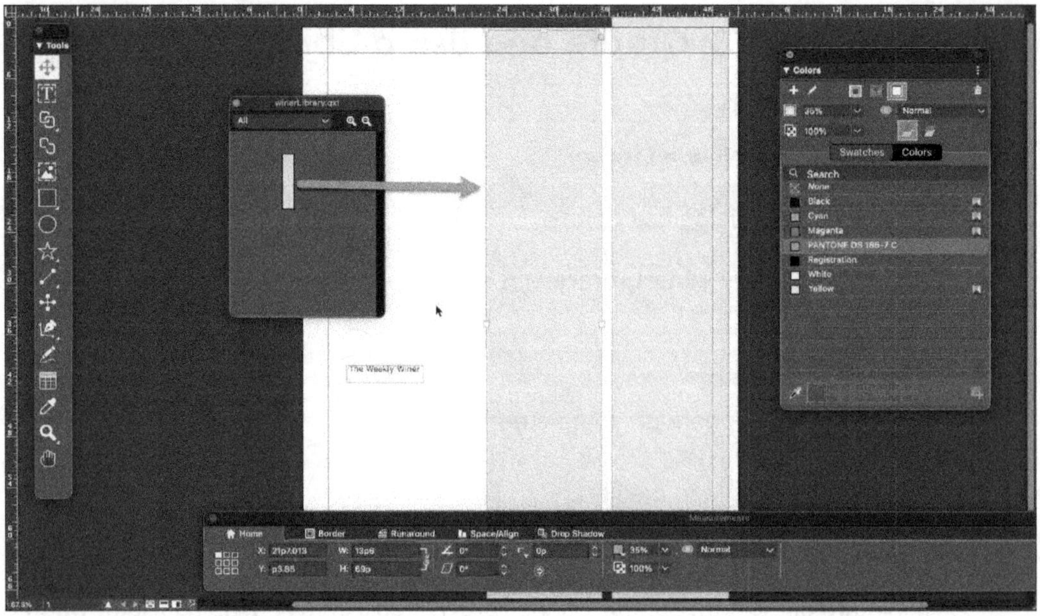

4. Label the library entry.

❒ on the Library, double-click item you added earlier

The Library Entry dialog box opens.

❒ type **sideBar** into the Label area

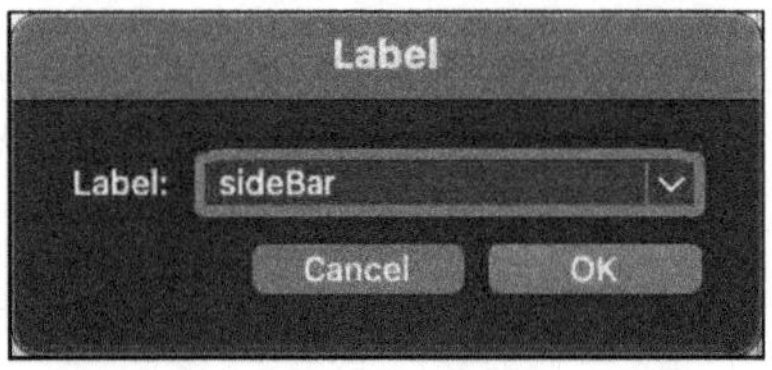

❒ click **OK**

It does not appear that you have done anything since the label does not appear. Not to worry, you will see and use the label soon.

Confidence Check

1. Using the Item tool, drag the text box containing "The Weekly Winer" into the library.

   Give the new library entry the Label **weeklyWiner**.

   Note: If you need to remove library items from the library, select the item and press [**command**] [**x**].

2. Drag both library items from the library and onto your layout.
3. Save and then close the project.

   Notice that the library remain open, independent of the project.

4. Open the **moreStuffForTheLibrary** project from the **QuarkXPress 2025 Book Assets**.

5. Add all of the layout items to your library, label each item as indicated in the picture below.

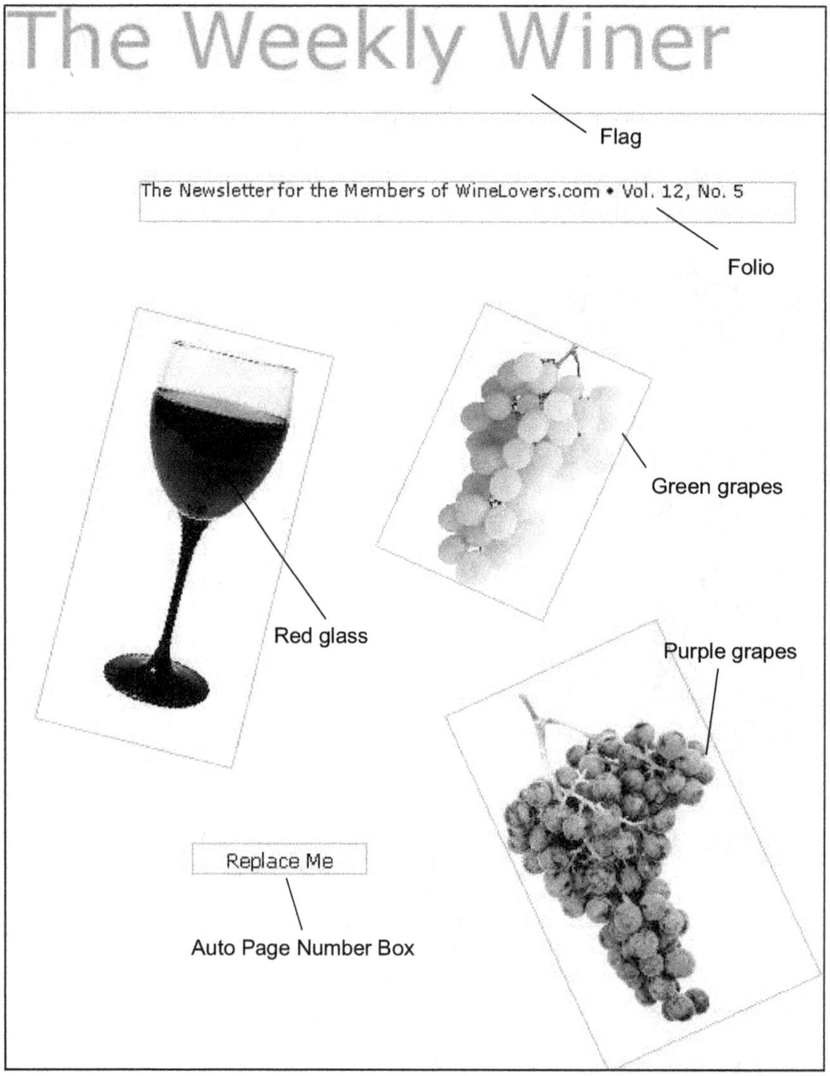

The library should now contain eight items. You will be using the library during the next module.

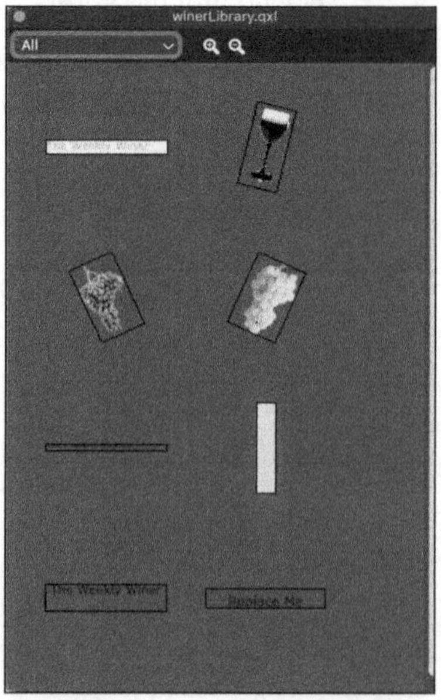

6. Save and close all projects.

ICONLOGIC

"Skills and Drills" Learning

Module 9: Master Pages

In This Module You Will Learn About:

And You Will Learn To:

NOTES

Master Pages

Master pages in QuarkXPress are invaluable for streamlining workflows and ensuring design consistency across a project. Master pages allow you to maintain uniformity for elements like headers, footers, logos, page numbers, and backgrounds across multiple pages.

For instance, in a multi-page document, a master page ensures that headers or footers appear in the same position. This consistency not only enhances the professionalism of your design but also reduces errors by minimizing the chance of misaligned or inconsistent elements.

Using master pages also saves significant time. Instead of updating repetitive elements on each page, you can make changes once on the master page, which will automatically apply throughout the document. This efficiency is particularly valuable in large projects where manual updates would be tedious and error-prone. Additionally, QuarkXPress supports creating multiple master pages for different project sections, such as a unique master for a book cover, chapter openings, or main body text.

Guided Activity 74: Create a Multi-Column Master Page

1. Create a new project with an Automatic Text Box, Facing pages, and a large outside margin.

   ❒ choose **File > New Project**

   ❒ change the Layout Type to **Print**

   ❒ select **Single Layout Mode**

   ❒ ensure that the page size is **Letter**

   ❒ ensure that the Orientation is **Portrait**

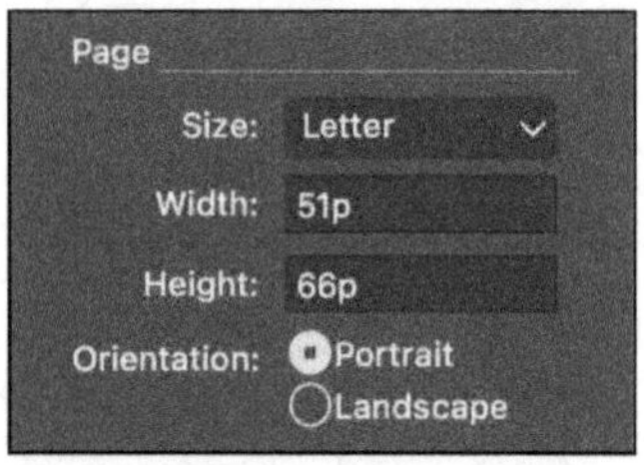

   ❒ select **Facing Pages**

   When two pages are displayed side by side, resembling an open book, magazine, or other bound publication, they are called facing pages. This layout ensures continuity and alignment across the open left and right page (known as a spread). In a facing pages setup, the left-hand page is called the verso (even-numbered pages), while the right is the recto (odd-numbered pages). The central area where the pages meet is the spine, and designers typically adjust the inner margins near the spine to be wider than the outer margins to account for the binding. You were not instructed to **Allow Odd Pages on Left** because in a typical layout, even number pages are positioned at the left of a spread.

❒ select **Automatic Text Box**

You have already learned about Automatic Text Boxes. With this option selected, overflow will automatically move to a new page.

❒ ensure the top and bottom margins are **3p**

Notice that the left and right margins have changed and how are shown as **Inside** and Outside. Inside and outside margins define the spacing between the edge of a page and the content within a document, particularly in a facing pages layout. Inside margins are located closest to the document's spine, where the pages are bound together.

In a facing pages layout, the inside margins of both pages in a spread face each other. In larger layouts, the inside margins are often made wider than the outside margins to ensure that text or important content is not obscured by the binding.

Outside margins, on the other hand, are the margins on the outer edges of the page, farthest from the spine. They are typically narrower than the inside margins, providing a clean, balanced border for content on the page's outer edge. These settings are crucial when designing multi-page documents such as books or magazines, as they ensure proper alignment and readability after printing and binding. The layout you are creating isn't going to be very large so you'll side the inside margin to 3p. To account for items placed on the outside of the spread, you'll leave lots of white space by setting a large outside margin.

❒ change the **Inside** to **3p** and the **Outside** to **13p6**

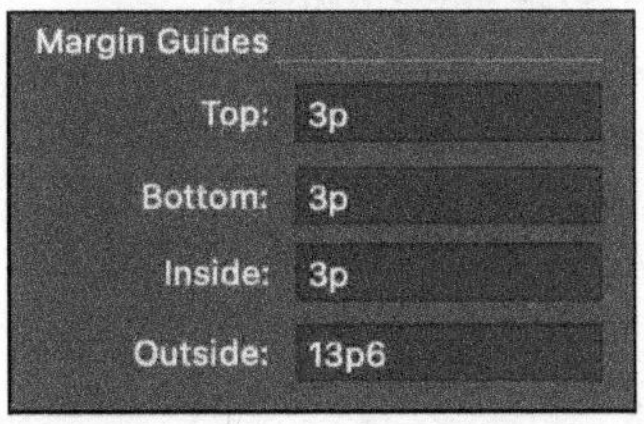

❒ ensure **Columns** is set to **1**

❒ click **OK**

2. Save the project to the **QuarkXPress 2025 Book Assets** folder as **myMasterPages**.

3. Display the master page.

   ❒ choose **Page > Display > A-Master A**

   You can tell that you are displaying a master page in two ways. First, there is a link symbol in the upper left of each master page (the left and the right). In addition, the page number indicator at the bottom of your window always indicates the active master page.

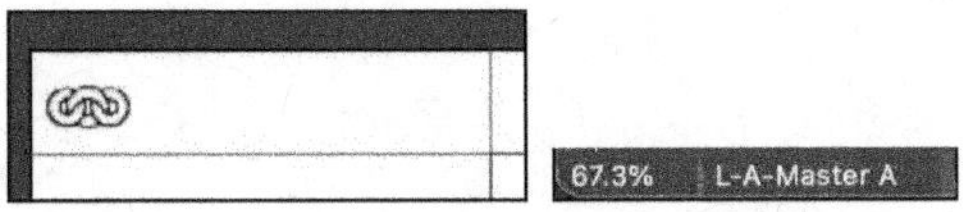

NOTES

NOTES

4. Change your view to Fit in Window.

5. Change Master Guides.

   ❒ choose **Page > Master Guides & Grid**

   The Master Guides & Grid dialog box opens.

   ❒ from the **Column Guides** area, change the number of **Columns** to **3**

   ❒ change the **Gutter Width** to **1p6**

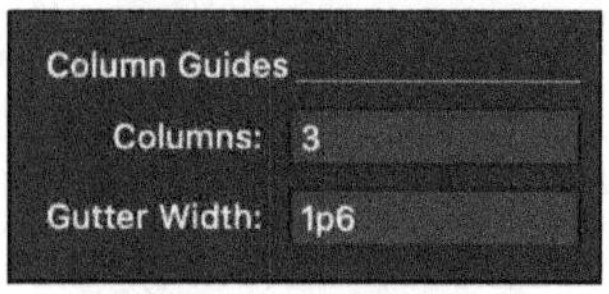

   ❒ click **OK**

   The automatic text boxes on both facing pages now have three columns, and the gutter—the space between the columns—is a pica and a half.

6. Save the project.

Guided Activity 75: Add Guides to a Master Page

1. The **myMasterPages** project should still be open.

2. Ensure you are still displaying the master page (**Page > Display > Master Page**).

3. Add ruler guides to the left master page.

   ❒ scroll left so you can see the left pasteboard

   ❒ position your pointer in the vertical ruler (the ruler at the left of your window) and drag a guide from the ruler and onto the area to the left of the page (this area is known as the pasteboard)

   ❒ click once on the guide

   The Guide Attributes dialog box opens.

   ❒ change the **Location** to **-1p6**

   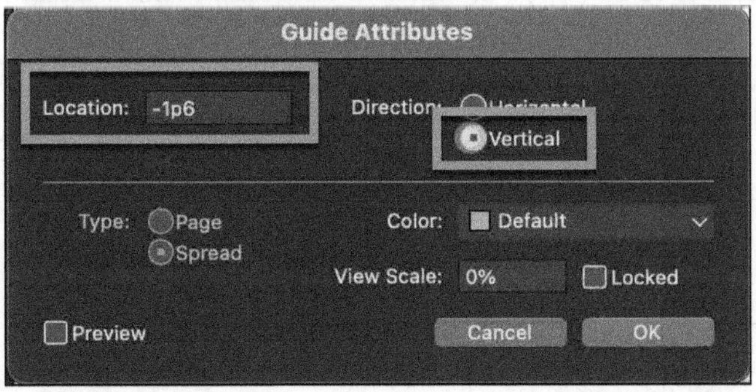

   ❒ click **OK**

   The guide is positioned exactly one and a half picas off the left edge of the left page.

   ❒ position the mouse pointer in the horizontal ruler above the left page (the ruler at the **top** of the window) and drag a guide down to the pasteboard

   ❒ click once on the guide to open the Guide Attributes again

   ❒ change the **Location** to **-1p6** (negative 1p6)

   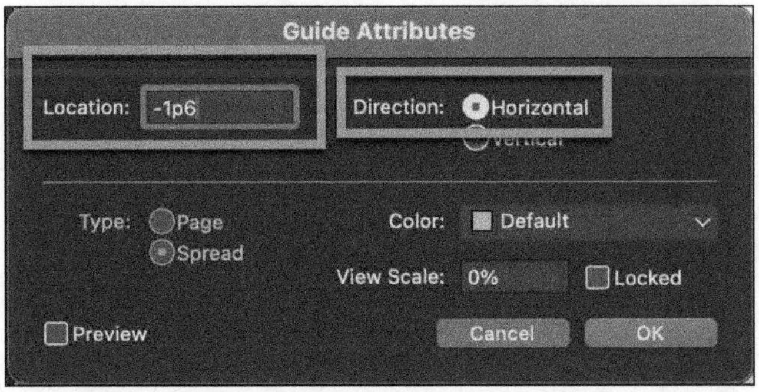

NOTES

❐ click **OK**

There are two ruler guides on the master page. Both guides are one and one-half picas off the page: one guide is on the left, one above.

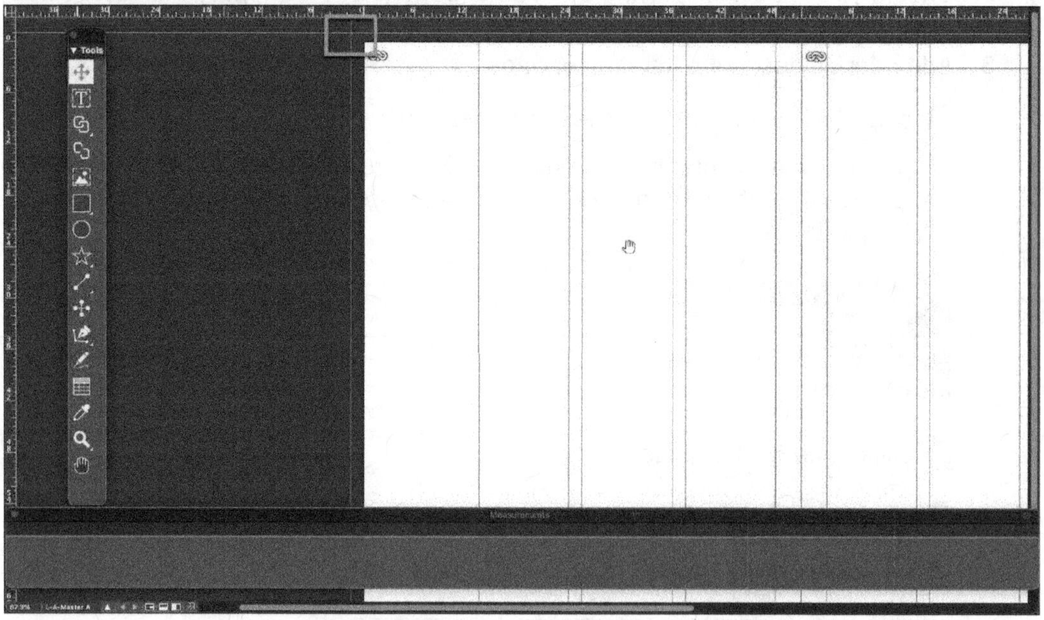

4. Save the project.

Guided Activity 76: Add Library Assets to a Master Page

1. The **myMasterPages** project should still be open.

2. Ensure you are still working on the master page (**Page > Display > Master Page**).

3. Ensure the **winerLibrary** you began working with beginning on page 143 is open.

   Note: If you accidentally closed the library, you can re-open it by choosing **File > Open**. If you did not create the library during the "Libraries" activity that begins on page 143, you can open the **doneLibraryMac or doneLibraryPC** as appropriate and use that library instead.)

4. Add a library image to the left master page.

   ❒ PC users, on the library, choose **Labels > sideBar**
   Mac users, on the library, choose **All > sideBar**

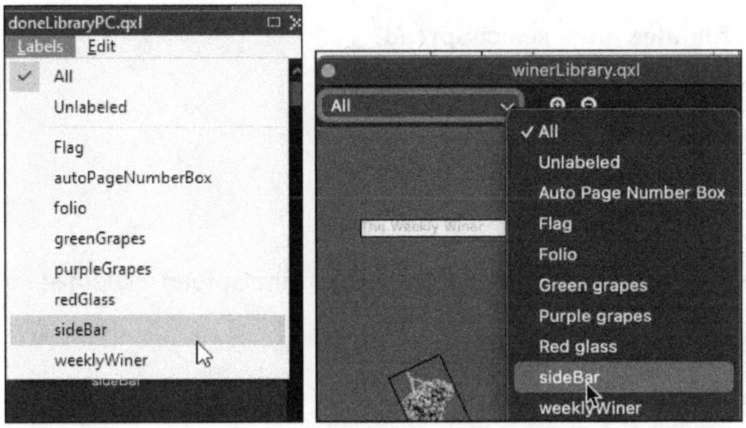

   All library items disappear from the library except the one you labeled sideBar during the activity on page 143.

   ❒ drag the **SideBar** library element from the library and over to the upper **left** of the left master page (drop the item where the green guides you drew intersect)

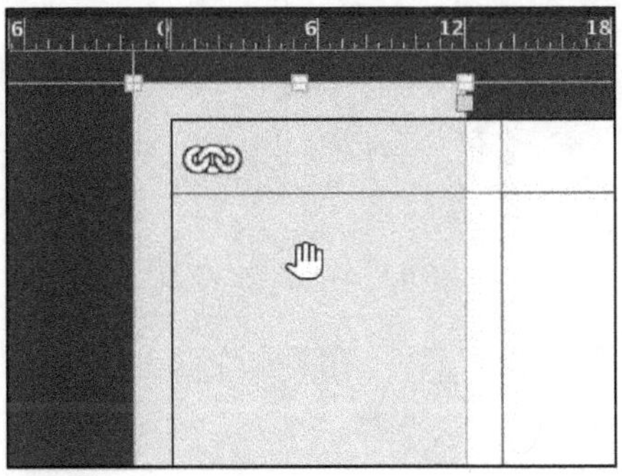

5. Save the project.

NOTES

Confidence Check

1. Still working on the master page, scroll right so you can see the right master page.

   Notice that the ruler at the top of the page starts over again.

   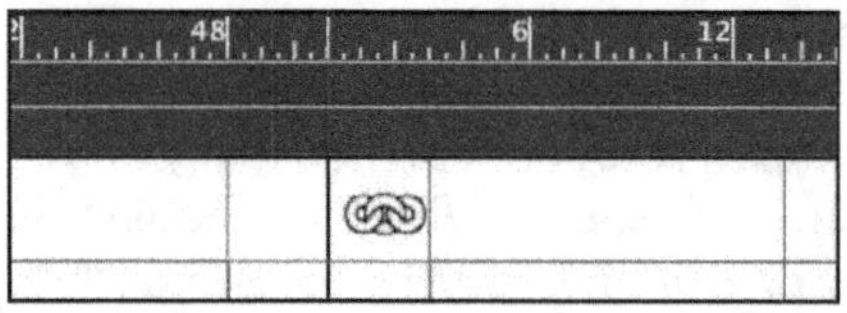

   QuarkXPress is treating each master page as a unique page instead of a spread. Let's edit the Preferences so that QuarkXPress uses one continuous ruler for both pages.

2. PC users, choose **Edit > Preferences**; Mac Users, choose **QuarkXPress > Settings**.
3. Select **Measurements** from the Print Layout category.
4. From the **Item Coordinates** area, select **Spread**.

5. Click **OK**.

   The ruler starts on the left master page and goes across the spread without starting over.

   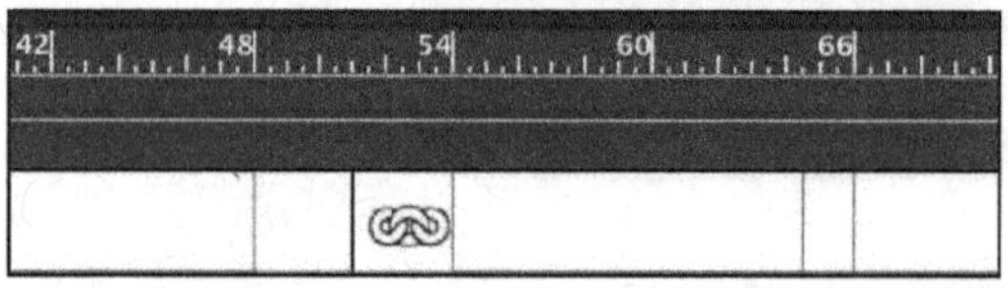

6. Choose **Window > Guides** to display the Guides window.
7. On the **Guides** palette, click the **New** icon. 
8. Type **103p6** into the **Location** field.
9. From the **Direction** area, ensure **Vertical** is selected.
10. From the **Type** area, select **Spread**.

11. Click the **Add** button and then click **OK**.

    The newest guide is positioned 1p6 off the right side of the right master page.

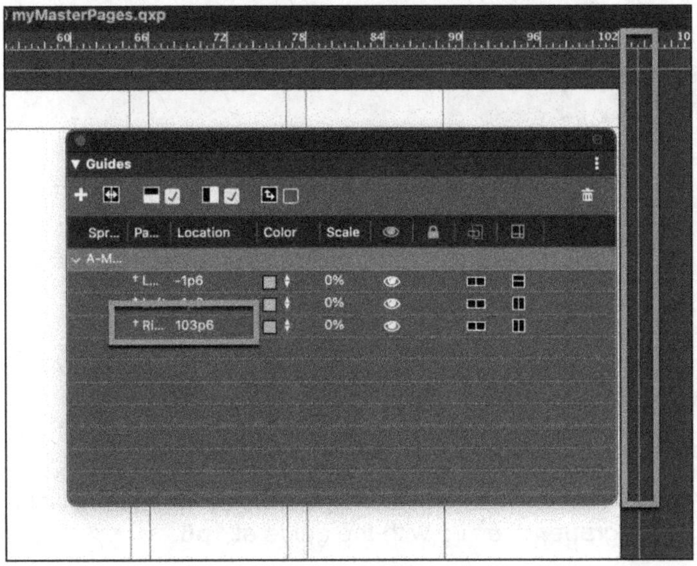

12. Drag the **sideBar** element from the library and position it where the guides intersect on the right side of the master page.

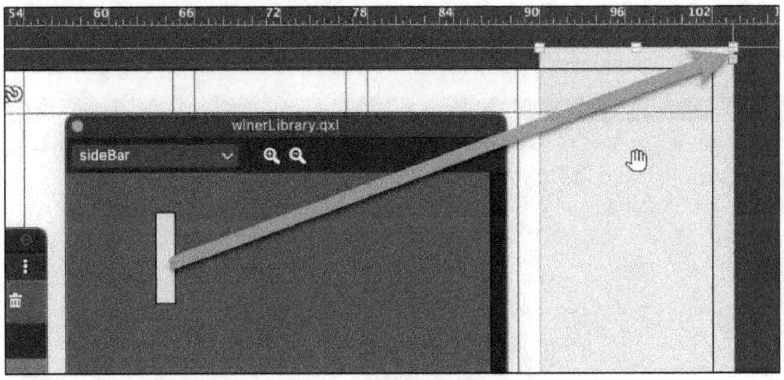

13. Add a vertical page guide at position **1p6**.
14. PC users: On the library, choose **Labels > All** to display all of the library items, then choose **Labels > WeeklyWiner**

    Mac users: choose **sideBar > All**, then choose **All > WeeklyWiner**.
15. Drag the **WeeklyWiner** library element onto the **left** master page.
16. Position the item so that its left edge lines up with your newest guide, and the top of the text box lines up with the page margin guide.

NOTES

NOTES

17. Add a vertical page guide at position **100p9**.
18. Drag the WeeklyWiner library element onto the **right** master page and position it so that its right edge lines up with your newest guide, and the top of the text box lines up with the page margin guide.

19. Add a horizontal spread guide at **4p6**.
20. Drag the **purpleGrapes** from the library over to the left master page.
21. Position the grapes image so that the stem in the image lines up with the newest guide at **4p6** and the **left edge** of the grapes lines up with the guide at **1p6**.
22. Drag the **greenGrapes** from the library over to the right master page.
23. Position the green grapes so that the stem lines up with your **4p6** guide and the right edge lines up with the guide at **100p9**.

    The spread should look like the image below.

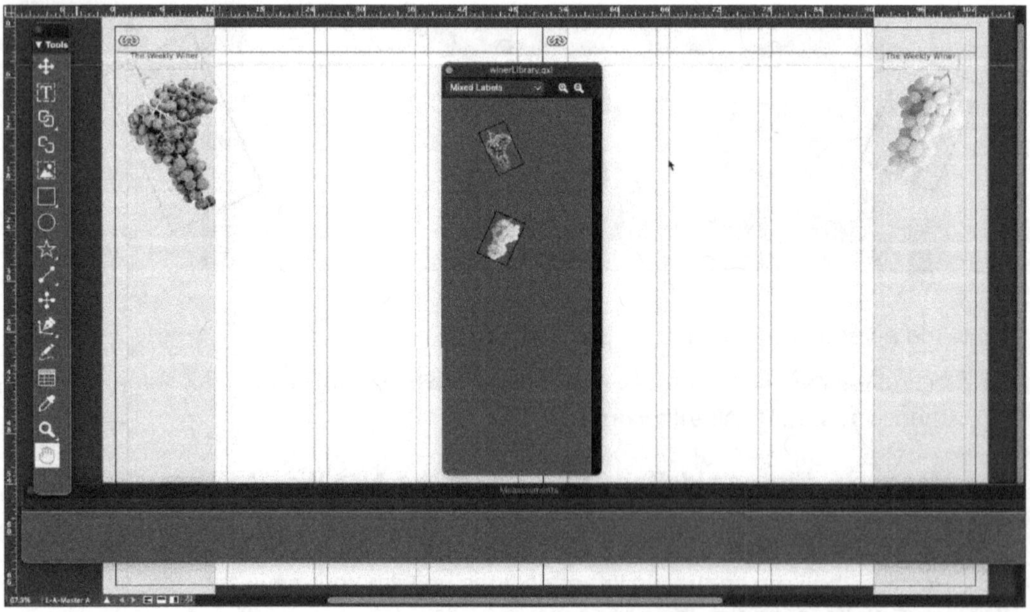

24. Save the project.

Automatic Page Numbers

QuarkXPress lets you easily add automatic page numbers by selecting the Text Content Tool, clicking in the box and pressing a few keys on your keyboard. The result is an embedded code that tells you instantly what page you are on. On a document page, the code looks like a number; on a master page, the code looks like <#>.

Guided Activity 77: Add an Automatic Page Number

1. The **myMasterPages** project should still be open.

2. Ensure you are still working on the master page (**Page > Display > Master Page**).

3. Add a library item to the left master page.

   - ❒ scroll to the **bottom left** of the master page
   - ❒ in the library, display the **autoPageNumber** item
   - ❒ drag the **autoPageNumber** element from the library and position it at the bottom of the left master page (line its left edge up with the **green page guide** and the bottom edge with the **blue margin guide**)

   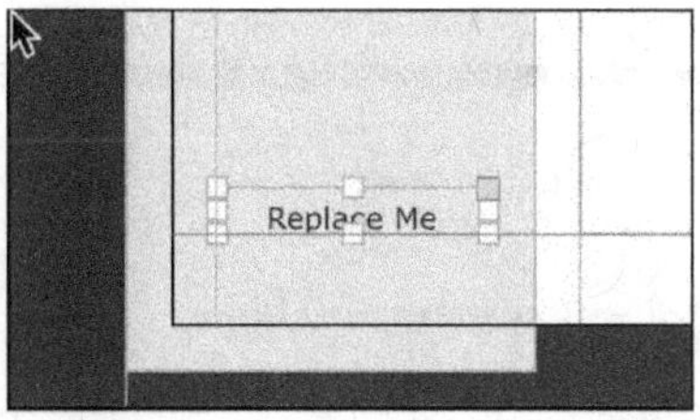

4. Add an automatic page number.

   - ❒ using the **Text Content Tool** , select the words **Replace Me**
   - ❒ choose **Utilities > Insert Character > Special > Current Box Page #**

   The tag for an automatic page number appears (<#>). The tag does not look like a page number because you are on a master page. You will see the actual page number when you view the layout.

   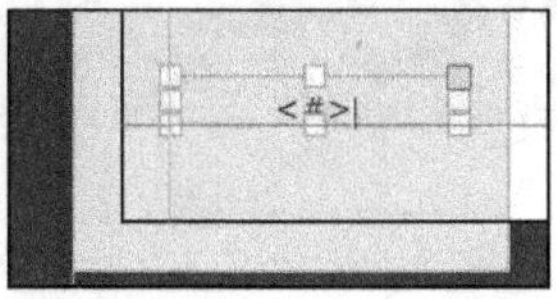

5. Close the library. (You can also close all other palettes except for the Tools and Measurement windows.)

NOTES

NOTES

6. Duplicate an item.

   ❒ ensure the text box with the automatic page number tag is selected

   ❒ choose **Item > Duplicate**

   There should now be two items contains page number tags.

7. Move the duplicate item to the right master page.

   ❒ on the Tools window, select the **Item Tool**

   ❒ using the Item tool, drag the duplicate text box over to the bottom of the right master page (line its right edge up with the ruler guide and the bottom edge with the page margin guide)

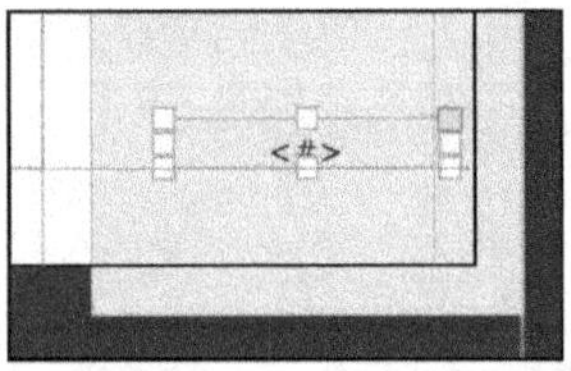

   Your master pages should look like the picture below.

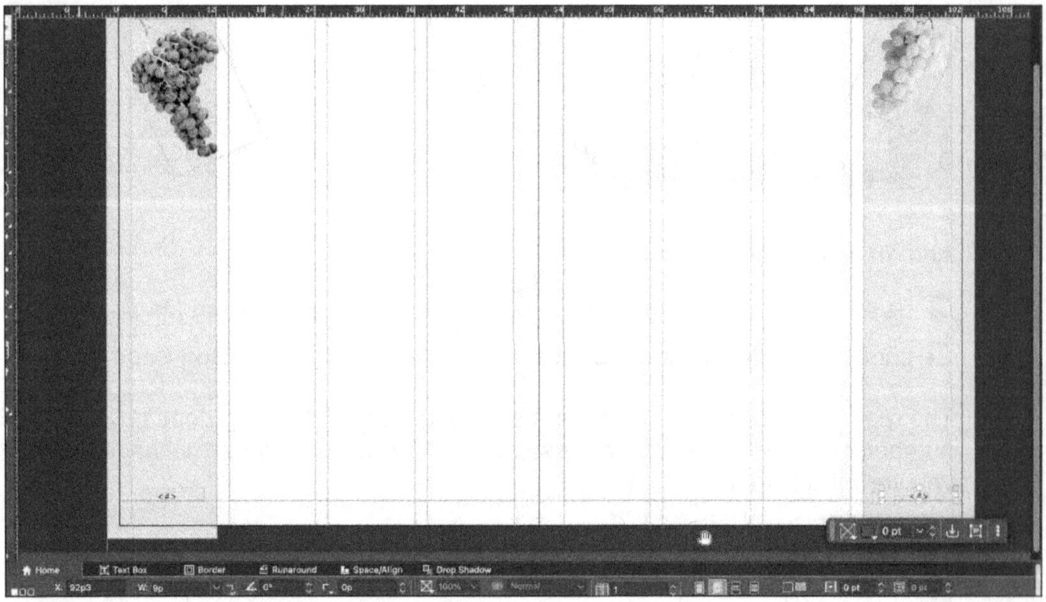

8. View the page numbers.

   ❒ choose **Page > Display > Layout**

   Notice that there is a page number in the lower right of page one instead of the <#> tag.

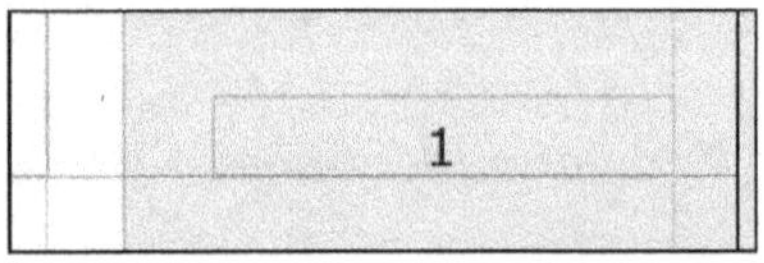

9. Save your work and close the project.

Guided Activity 78: Duplicate and Rename Master Pages

1. Open **duplicateMasterPages.qxp** and save the project as **myMasterPages2**.

   This project is identical to the project you were working on during the past activity.

2. Show the Page Layout palette.

   ❒ choose **Window > Page Layout**

3. Use the Page Layout palette to duplicate a master page.

   ❒ click the little page **icon** to the left of the words **A-Master A** (to select the A-Master A master page)

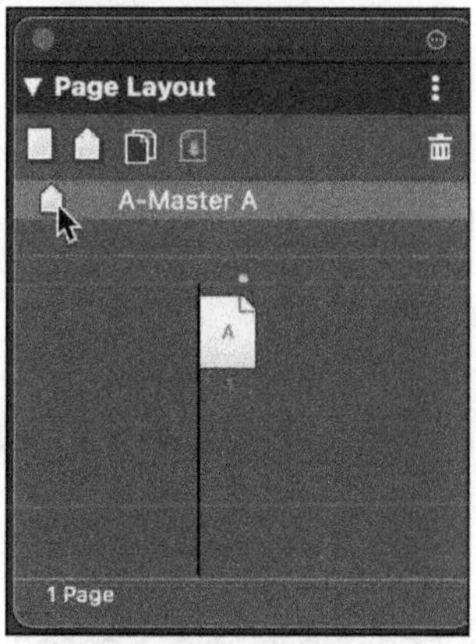

   ❒ click the **Duplicate** icon  at the top of the Page Layout palette

   There should be two master pages: **A-Master A** and **B-Master B**.

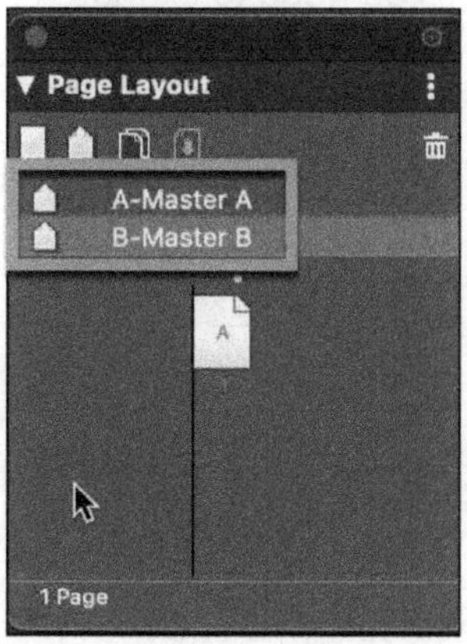

NOTES

NOTES

4. Rename master pages.

   ❒ on the **Page Layout** palette, double-click the name **A-Master A**, rename the master page **ThreeColumns**, and press [**return**]

   ❒ on the **Page Layout** palette, select the name **B-Master B**

   ❒ type **TwoColumns** and press [**return**]

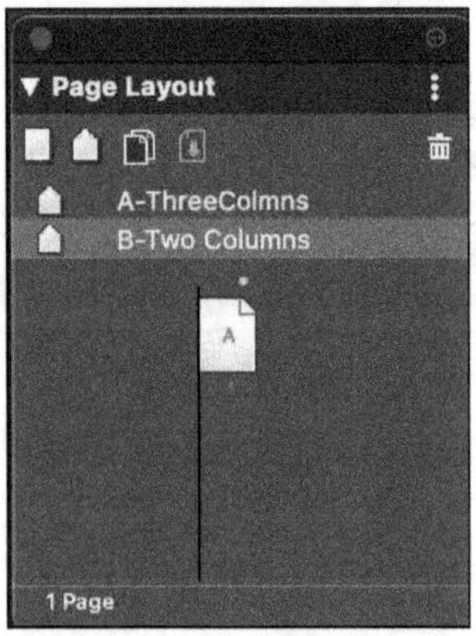

5. Change the number of columns used on the B-Two Columns master page.

   ❒ on the **Page Layout** window, double-click the icon next to the name **B-TwoColumns** to display the master page

   Note: You can tell which master page you are on in a couple of different ways. First, notice the name B-TwoColumns on the Page Layout palette is bold. Second, notice the name L-B-TwoColumns appears in the current page area at the bottom left of the window.

   On the B-TwoColumns master page, notice that even though the name of the master page is TwoColumns, the actual layout is three columns. You need to fix that.

   ❒ choose **Page > Master Guides & Grid**

   ❒ in the **Column guides** area, **Columns** field, change the number of Columns to **2**

   ❒ click **OK**

   The B-TwoColumns master pages should now contain two columns each.

6. Save the project.

Guided Activity 79: Assign a Master Page to a Layout Page

1. Go to page one.

   ❒ on the Page Layout palette, double-click the page 1 icon 

   ❒ change your view to **Fit in Window**

   Notice that page 1 is currently following the **A-ThreeColumns** master page.

2. Import text.

   ❒ select the **Text Content Tool**  and click in the large text box on the page

   ❒ choose **File > Import** (or press [**command**] [**e**])

   ❒ from the **textFiles folder**, open **winerText**

   The text flows into the document.

3. Scroll through and review the document.

   Because there was more text in the winerText file than could fit onto just a single page, additional pages were automatically inserted into the layout. Notice that all of the pages follow the same master page (A-ThreeColumns).

4. Save the project.

5. Assign the TwoColumns master page to page 1.

   ❒ on the Page Layout palette, drag master page **B-TwoColumns** directly on top of the thumbnail for page 1 (on the Page Layout palette)

   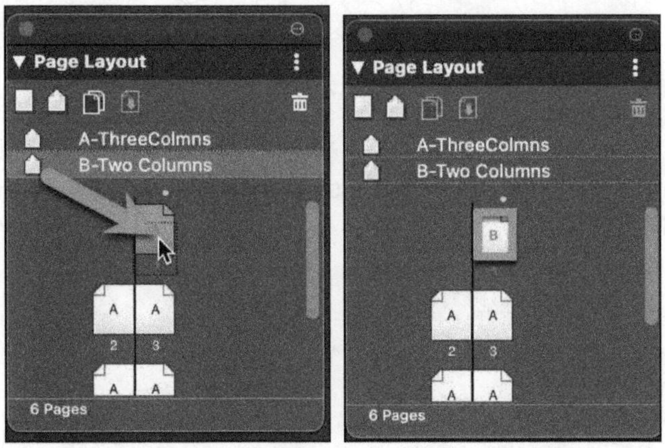

   ❒ on the Page Layout palette, double-click the page 1 icon to open the page

   Page 1 now looks like and follows the TwoColumns master. The text automatically flows into the new column grid. Also notice that on the Page Layout palette, there is a large **"B"** in the middle of page one. The letter corresponds to the **B-TwoColumns** master page. Whenever you apply master pages to document pages, the document pages get the letter of the master page they're following.

6. Apply a master page to multiple, non-contiguous document pages at one time.

   ❒ press [**command**] on your keyboard

NOTES

- ❒ on the Page Layout palette, click one time on page **3**
- ❒ with [**command**] still pressed, click one time on page **5**

Pages 3 and 5 should be selected on the Page Layout palette.

- ❒ release [**command**]
- ❒ press the [**alt**] key on your keyboard and click the little page to the left of the words **B-TwoColumns** (on the Page Layout palette)
- ❒ release [**alt**]

Because they were both selected, pages 3 and 5 are now following the B-TwoColumns master page.

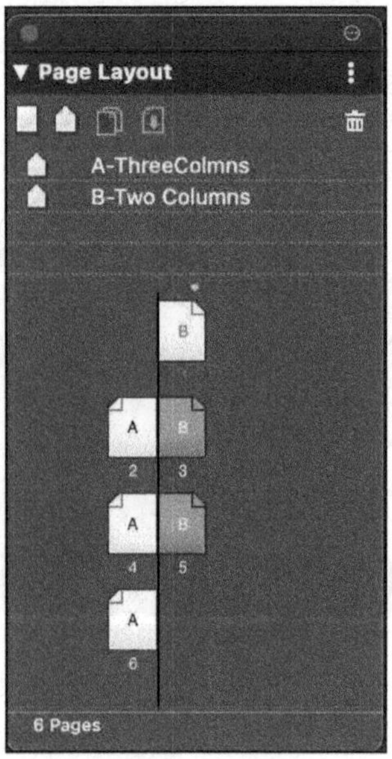

- ❒ scroll through the document

Pages 1, 3 and 5 are following the B-TwoColumns master page; pages 2 and 4 are following the A-ThreeColumns master.

7. Save the project.

Confidence Check

1. In the upper right of the Page Layout palette, click the three vertical dots and choose **New Single Page Master**.

2. Change the name of the new master page to **Cover**. (You learned how to rename master pages on page 160.)

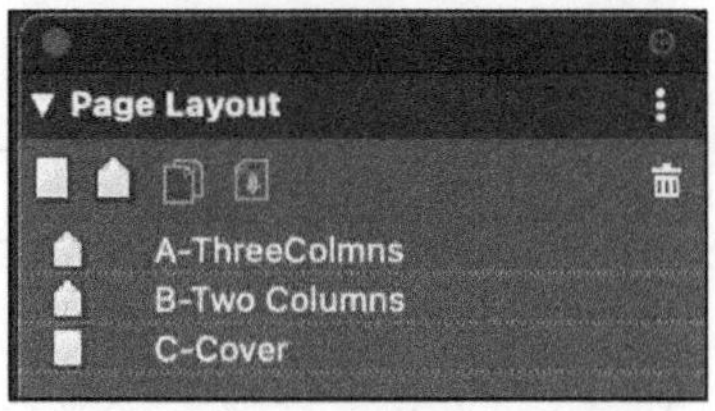

3. Open the **C-Cover** master page open the **Master Guides and Grids** dialog box (you learned how on page 160).
4. Change the guides as follows:

   Top Margin Guide: **10p6**

   All other Margin Guides: **3p**

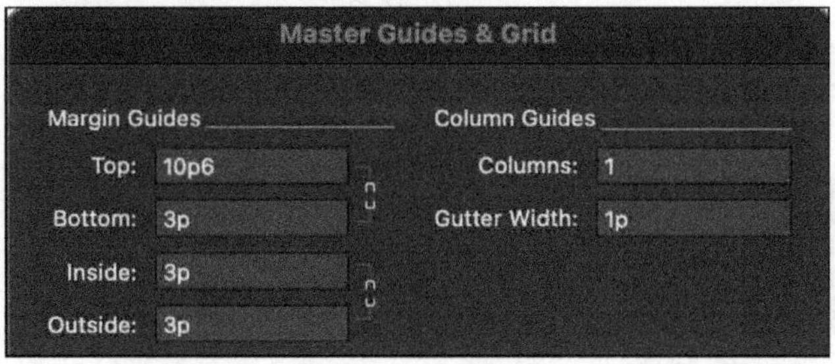

NOTES

NOTES

5. Using the **Text Content Tool**, draw a large text box that fills the page margins.

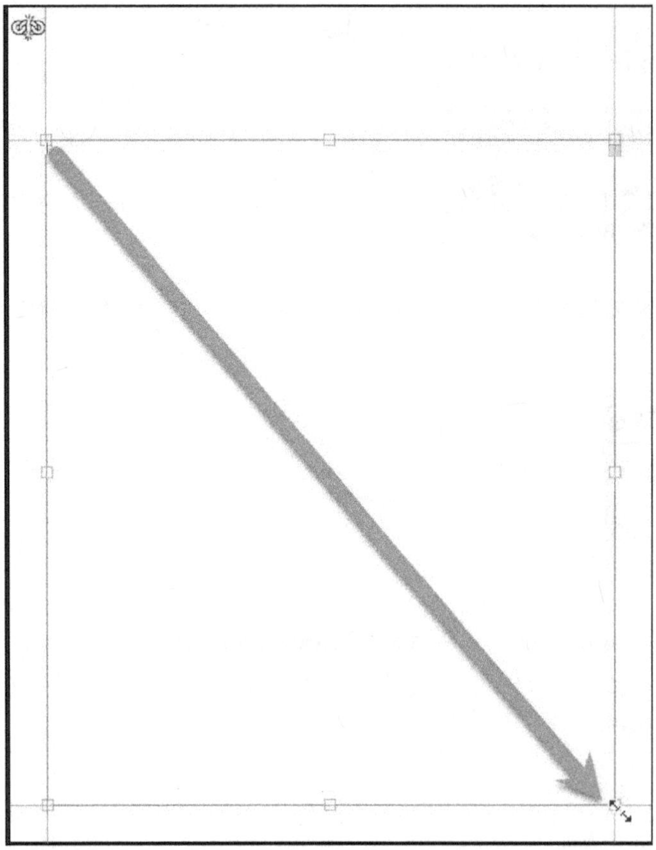

6. Use the **Measurements** window to change the number of columns to **2**.
7. Change the gutter width to **1p6**

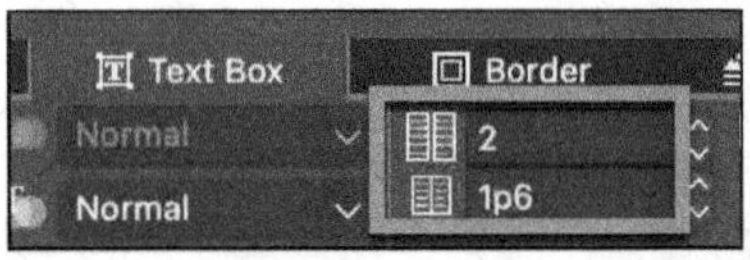

8. Notice that the broken link icon in the upper left of the new master.  The broken link icon means that this new master page does not contain an automatic text box. If you were to use this master page on any of your current document pages, the text on those pages would NOT flow in the text box you added to this page. To ensure text flows from page to page, you need to link your new text box to the automatic text boxes.
9. On the Tools window, select the **Text Linking Tool**. 
10. Click on the broken link symbol.
11. Click on the text box you added to the page.

The icon now appears as a link symbol. And just like that you've learned how to create an automatic text box on a master page.

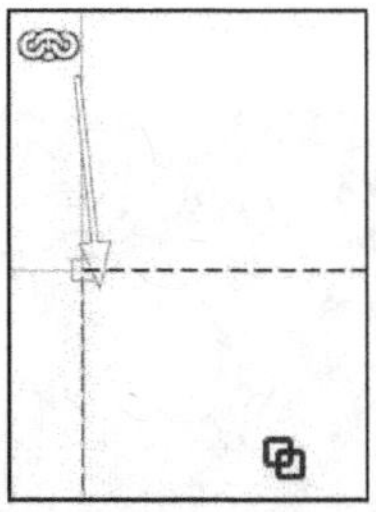

12. Add two new page guides to the C-Cover master page from the Horizontal ruler at the following positions: **3p** and **8p6**. (You learned how to add guides on page 151.)

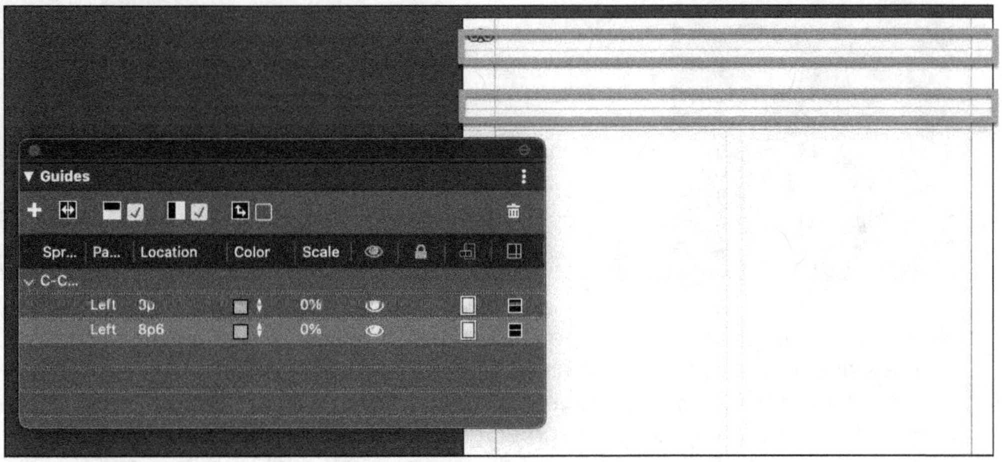

13. Open the **winerLibrary** (File > Open).
14. Drag the **Flag** object from the library and position it within the guides you just added to the page.
15. Drag the **Folio** object from the library and position it so that the text rests on the Page Guide at 8p6.

NOTES

NOTES

16. Apply the **C-Cover master** page to page 1. (You learned how to apply a master page to a layout page on page 161).

    Page 1 in your file should now look like the picture below.

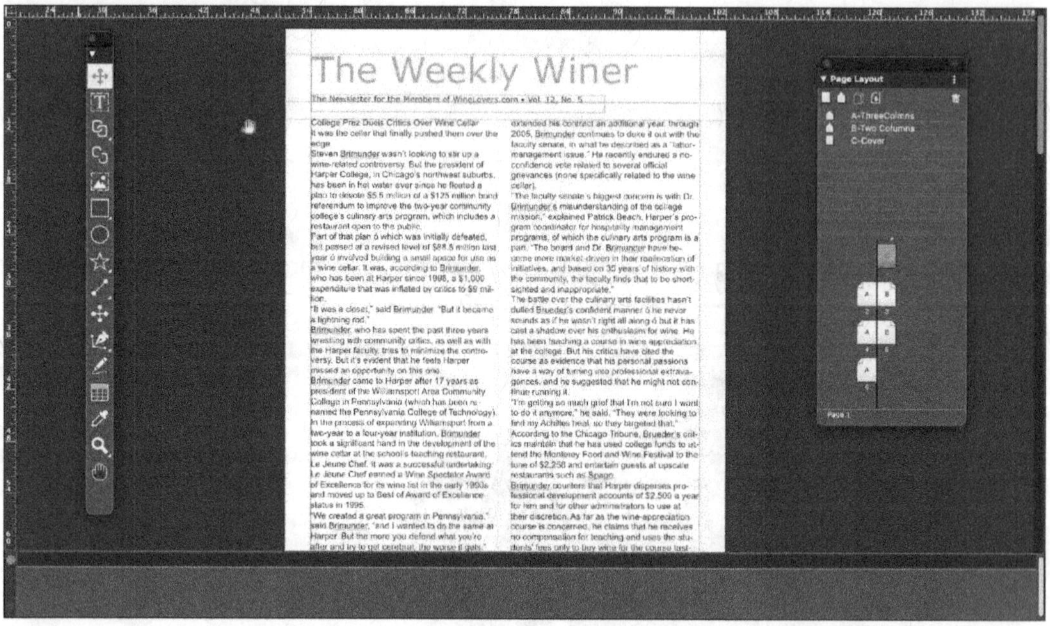

Note: When I applied master page **C** to page 1, I noticed that the green grapes image stayed on the page as an artifact from the other master pages. Select and delete the grapes image from page 1 if this happens to you. Reapply the master pages to the page. As you do, the green grapes image should appear on the page if you apply master pages A or B and disappear if you apply master page C.

17. Save and close the project.

ICONLOGIC
"Skills and Drills" Learning

Module 10: Advanced Style Sheets

In This Module You Will Learn About:

And You Will Learn To:

NOTES

Paragraph Style Sheets

You were first introduced to style sheets when you created a multi-column poster on page 109. During the activities in this module, you will delve deeper into style sheets by working with paragraph and character styles, the baseline grid, and drop caps.

Guided Activity 80: Create and Apply Paragraph Style Sheets

1. Open **styleMe** from the **QuarkXPress 2025 Book Assets** folder and save the project as **myStyles**.

2. Show the Style Sheets palette.

   ❒ choose **Window > Style Sheets**

   The Style Sheets palette opens.

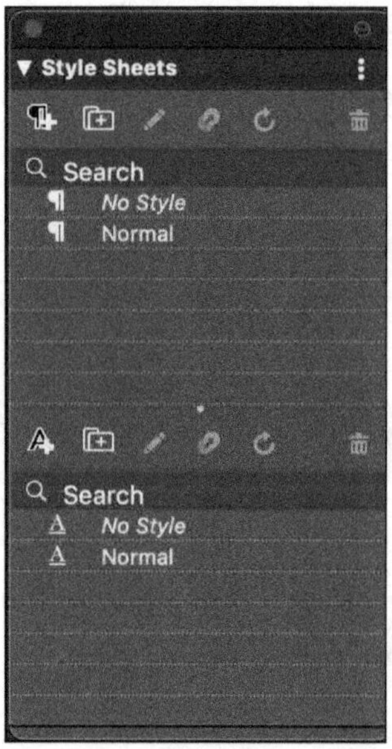

   Each new QuarkXPress layout begins with one paragraph style sheet and one character style. They are both called **Normal**, and they are both currently being used throughout the document.

3. Create a style sheet for the body text.

   ❒ click outside of the text flow to ensure that no text in the layout is selected

   ❒ choose **Edit > Style Sheets**

   The Style Sheets dialog box opens.

   ❒ click the **New** button and choose **Paragraph**

   The Edit Paragraph Style Sheet dialog box opens.

   ❒ change the Name to **BodyText**

4. Set the character attributes for the BodyText style sheet.

   ❒ in the **Character Style** area, click the **Edit** button

   The Edit Character Style Sheet dialog box opens.

   ❒ change the **Font** to either **Times New Roman** or **Times** (Macs typically have the Times New Roman and Times font—you can use either one)

   ❒ change the **Font Size** to **11**

   ❒ click **OK**

   You are now back in the Edit Paragraph Style Sheet dialog box. Notice the character attributes you just changed appear in the Description area.

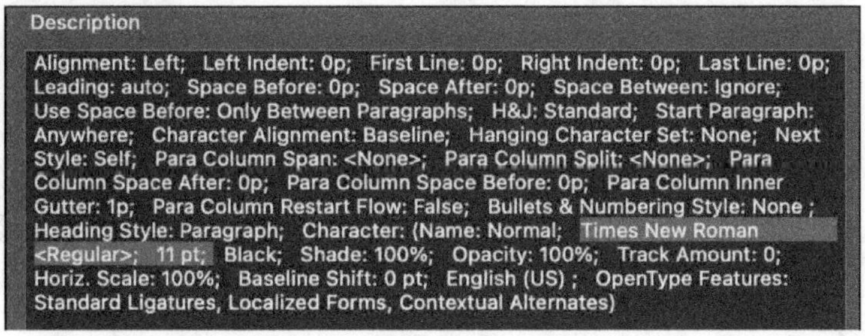

5. Set the paragraph attributes for the BodyText style.

   ❒ click the **Formats** tab

   ❒ change the **Leading** to **13**

   ❒ change the **Space After** to **1p1**

   ❒ change the **Alignment** to **Justified**

   ❒ click **OK**

   ❒ click **Save**

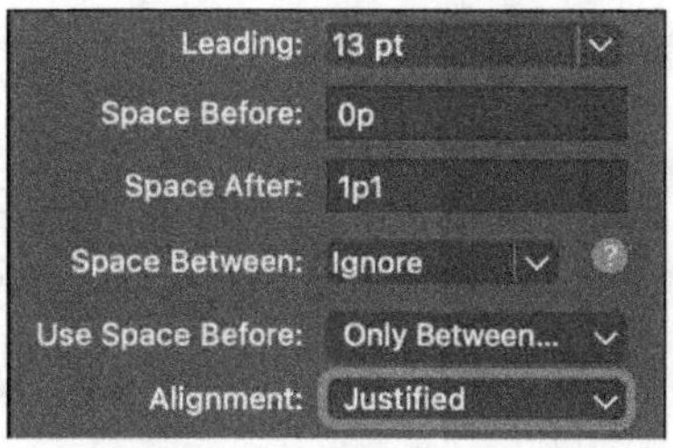

   Your new style appears in the Style Sheets palette, but is not yet being used.

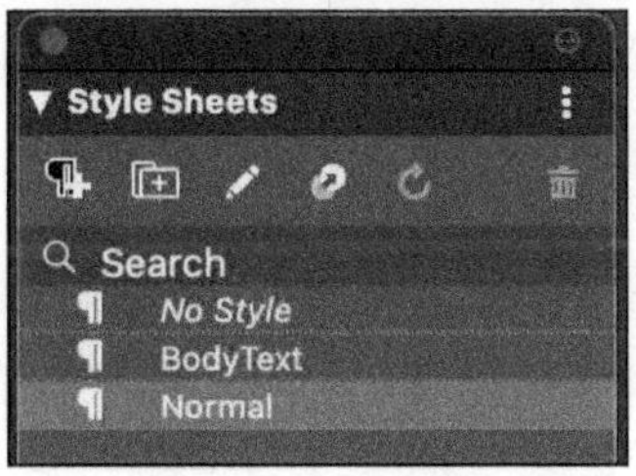

NOTES

6. Apply the BodyText style sheet to all of the text.

   - ❒ using the **Text Content Tool**, click anywhere in the text
   - ❒ press [**command**] [**a**] to select all of the text
   - ❒ on the Style Sheets palette, click the **BodyText** paragraph style sheet

   The selected text is instantly formatted with the attributes of the BodyText paragraph style sheet.

7. Create a headlines style sheet.

   - ❒ click outside of the text flow to ensure that no text in the layout is selected
   - ❒ at the top of the **Style Sheets** palette, click the **New** icon 

   The Edit Paragraph Style Sheet dialog box opens.

   - ❒ change the **Name** to **Headlines**
   - ❒ in the **Character Style** area, click the **Edit** button

   The Character Attributes dialog box opens.

   - ❒ change the **Font** to either **Arial Bold** or **Helvetica Bold** (Macs typically include both the Arial and Helvetica fonts—you can choose either one)
   - ❒ change the **Size** to **13**

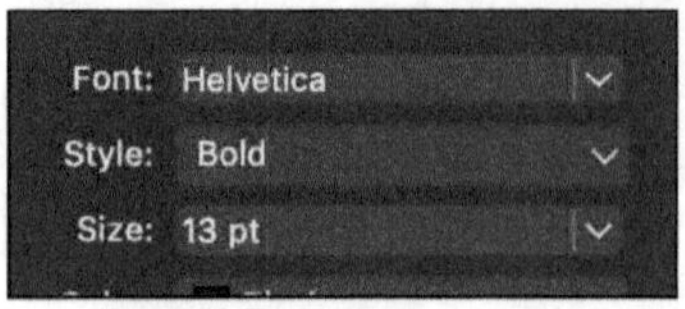

   - ❒ click **OK**

8. Set the paragraph attributes for the Headlines style sheet.

   - ❒ click the **Formats** tab

- ❒ change the **Leading** to **13 pt**
- ❒ change the **Space After** to **1p1**
- ❒ change the **Alignment** to **Left**

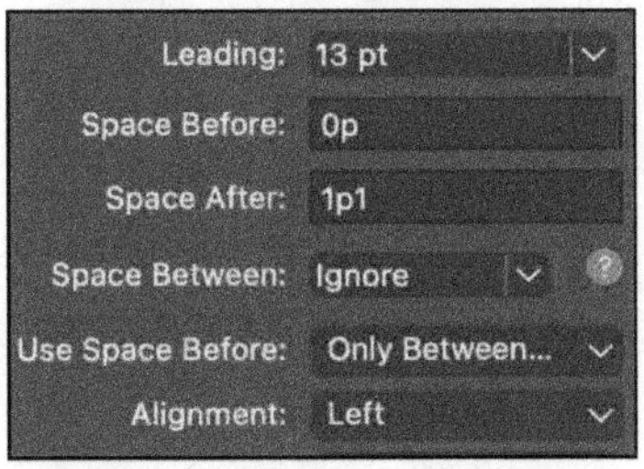

- ❒ click **OK**

Both of your paragraph style sheets are listed on the Style Sheets palette.

9. Apply the Headlines style to text.
   - ❒ click in the first paragraph ("College Prez Duels Critics Over Wine Cellar")
   - ❒ on the **Style Sheets** palette, click the **Headlines** style

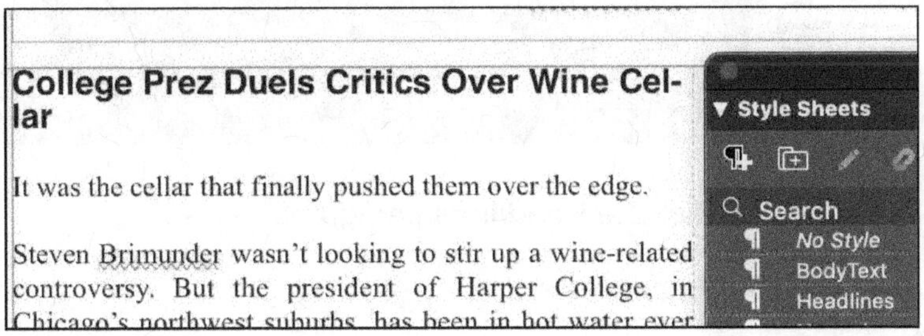

NOTES

Guided Activity 81: Use Find/Change to Locate a Phrase

1. The **MyStyles** project should still be open.

2. Find a phrase.

   ❒ choose **Edit > Find/Change**

   The **Find/Change** options appear.

   ❒ type **Latour and Cheval-Blanc** into the Find What area (check your spelling carefully)

   ❒ click **Find Next**

   Assuming you typed the phrase correctly, the paragraph "Latour and Cheval-Blanc Push Their 2000 Bordeaux Prices Even Higher" should be found on page 2 and the phrase highlighted.

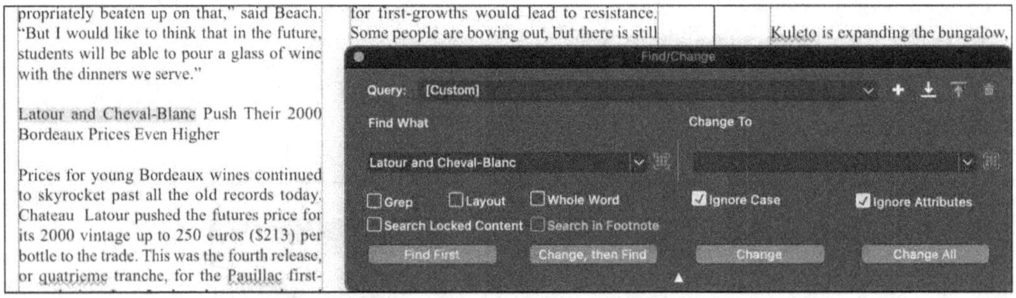

   ❒ on the Style Sheets palette, click the **Headlines** paragraph

   The paragraph is now using the Headlines style.

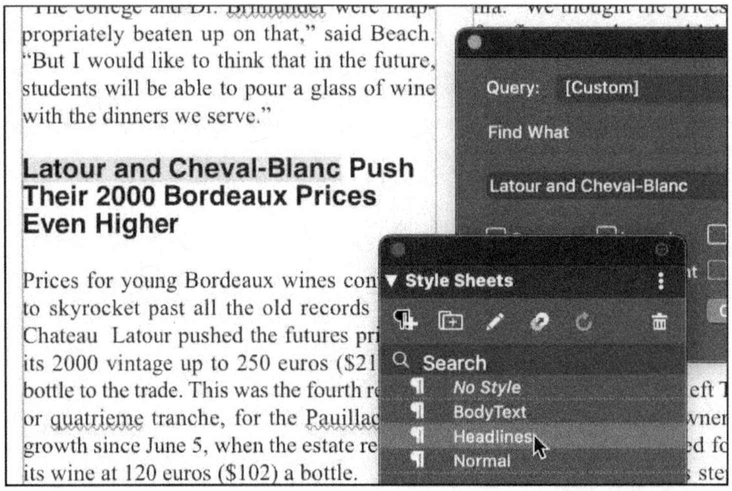

Confidence Check

1. Find the following text: **Three Top Napa** and apply the Headlines style to the text.
2. Find **Rolland Releases** and apply the Headlines style to the text.
3. Find **Wine Storage** and apply the Headlines style to the text.
4. With no text selected, create a **New Subheads Paragraph Style Sheet** that looks like this:

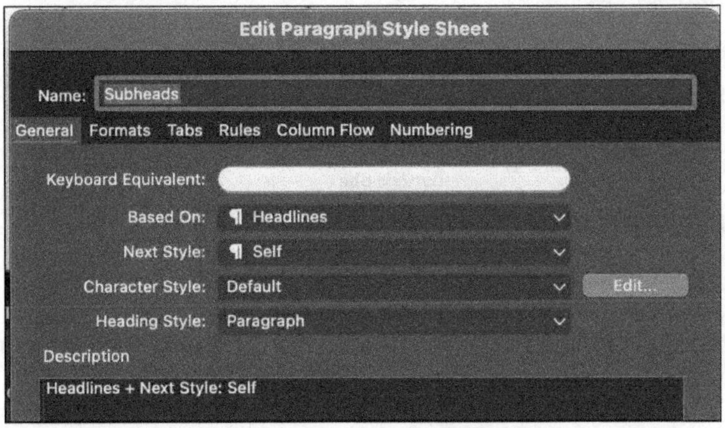

When you base a new style sheet **Based On** an existing style sheet, the new style sheet looks exactly like the original. You can modify the new style sheet as needed without affecting the original style. However, edits made to the original style sheet (in this case, Headlines) affect both style sheets.

5. Edit the Character Style for the Subhead style sheet to match these specifications (you can use either **Arial** or **Helvetica** for the Font and either **Bold Oblique** or **Bold Italic** for the style).

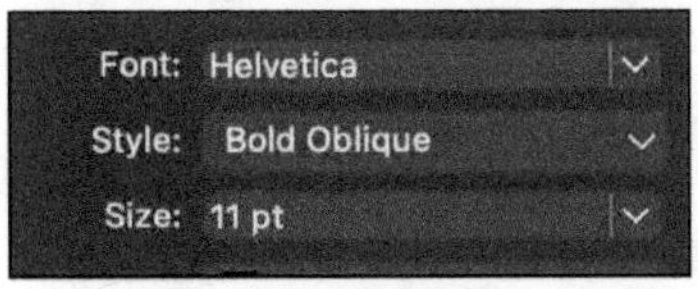

6. Find **Monthly Rental Rates** and apply the **Subhead** style to the text.

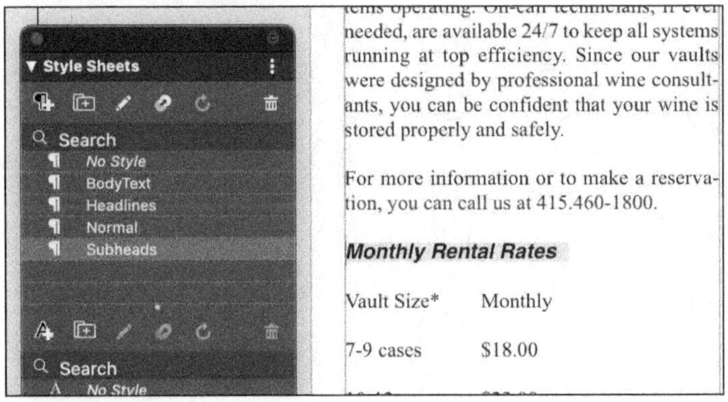

7. Save and close the project.

NOTES

NOTES

Guided Activity 82: Edit a Style Sheet

1. Open **changeMe** from the **QuarkXPress 2025 Book Assets** folder and save it as **myEditedStyles**.

2. Ensure that you're on page 1, viewing the page at Actual size, and that you can see the first headline: "College Prez Duels Critics Over Wine Cellar."

3. Edit the Character Attributes for the Headlines style.

   ❒ choose **Edit > Style Sheets**

   ❒ select **Headlines**

   ❒ click the **Edit** button

   The Edit Paragraph Style Sheet dialog box opens.

   ❒ to the right of **Character Style**, click the **Edit** button

   The Character Attributes for the Headlines style appear.

   ❒ change the **Font** to **Verdana**

   ❒ change the **Size** to **12**

   ❒ change the **Color** to **Pantone S 185-7**

   ❒ click **OK**

   ❒ click **OK**

   ❒ click **Save**

   All of the headlines throughout the layout have updated to the new font, font size, and color.

Controlling Bad Breaks

Scroll through the document and you will see some bad line breaks. For example, at the bottom of the second column on page 2, a line of text is stranded by itself. There's another bad break at the top of page 4. When one line from a paragraph appears at the bottom of a column without any other lines from the paragraph, it's known as a widow. One line appearing at the top of a column without any other lines from its paragraph is known as an orphan. You're about to learn how to set orphan and widow controls that will prevent these types of bad breaks.

Guided Activity 83: Set Orphan and Widow Controls

1. The myEditedStyles project should still be open.

2. Observe a bad break.

   ❒ scroll down to page 2 and observe the stranded line of text at the bottom of the page

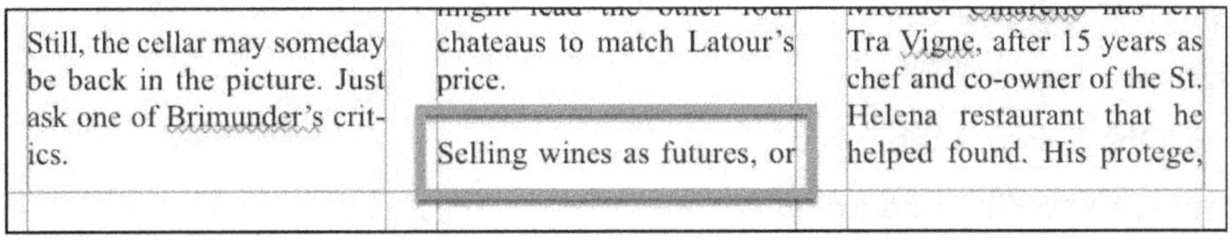

3. Eliminate orphans and widows.

   ❒ on the Style Sheets palette, right-click **BodyText** and choose **Edit Body Text**

   ❒ select the **Formats** tab

   ❒ on the right side of the dialog box, select **Keep Lines Together**

   ❒ select **Start 2 End 2** (click the radio button to the left of the word **Start**)

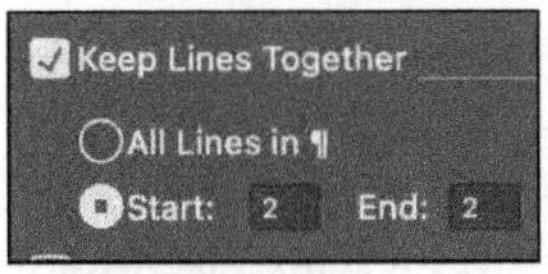

   ❒ click **OK**

   The BodyText bad breaks have been resolved document-wide.

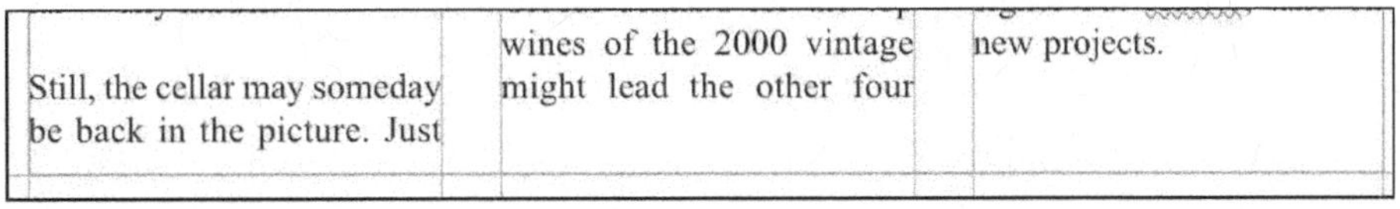

4. Save the project.

Keep Options

The Keep Options in QuarkXPress help prevent awkward breaks that can disrupt readability. For example, the Keep Lines Together option prevents headlines and subheads from appearing on a page or column different from the text they are associated with. The Keep with Next option allows you to link a paragraph with the one that follows, ensuring they appear together on the same page or column. Both options reduce the need for manual adjustments, column breaks, and page breaks.

Guided Activity 84: Set Keep Options

1. The myEditedStyles project should still be open.

2. Use the “Keep Lines Together” and “Keep With Next” commands.

   ❐ choose **Edit > Style Sheets**

   ❐ select **Headlines**

   ❐ click the **Edit** button

   ❐ click the **Formats** tab

   ❐ select **Keep Lines Together**

   ❐ select **All Lines in ¶**

   ❐ select **Keep with Next ¶**

   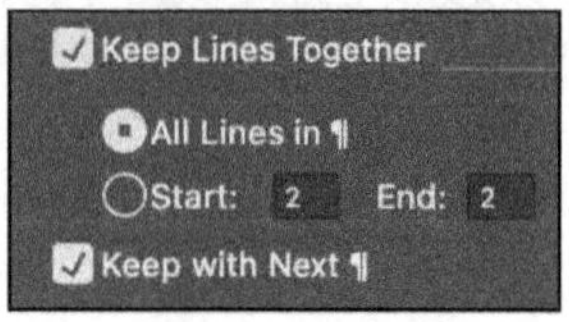

   ❐ click **OK**

   ❐ click **Save**

   If you scroll through your document you will see that there are no widows, orphans or stranded headlines.

3. Save the project.

Confidence Check

1. Edit the **BodyText** style making the following changes:

   First Line Indent: **1p1**

   Space After: **0**

   Alignment: **Left**

   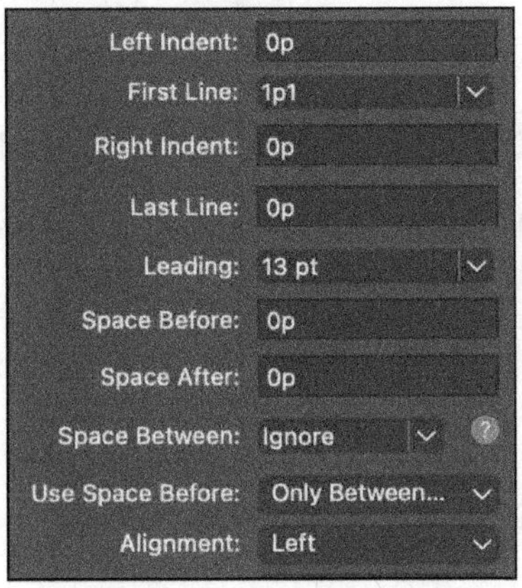

2. Scroll through the document and notice that the headlines have too much space below and not enough above. You will fix that next.
3. Edit the **Headlines** style sheet making the following changes:

   Space Before: **1p1**

   Space After: **0**

   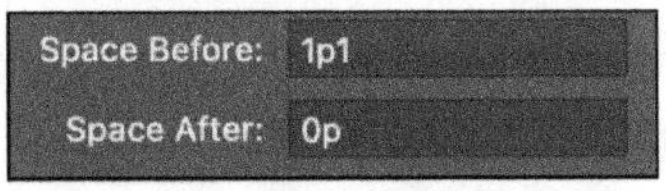

4. Save and close the project.

NOTES

NOTES

Inline Formatting

You can easily change the appearance of a paragraph assigned to a style sheet by using the Character tab in the Measurements window. When you manually format text that is already following a style sheet, those edits are referred to as inline or direct formatting. If a paragraph has both a style sheet applied and inline formatting, a plus sign will appear next to the style name in the Style Sheets palette. Earlier in this module, you learned how to edit a style sheet. Keep in mind that inline formatting remains unaffected when you make changes to the style sheet. You can choose to leave the inline formatting as is or create a new style based on the applied inline formatting.

Guided Activity 85: Apply Inline Formatting to a Paragraph

1. Open **addStyle** from the **QuarkXPress 2025 Book Assets** folder and save the project as **myDirectStyles**.

2. Apply inline styles to selected text.

   - ❐ select the **Text Content Tool**
   - ❐ on page 1, click in front of the fourth body paragraph "It was a closet..."
   - ❐ press **[return]** to insert a paragraph break
   - ❐ click in the white space you just created
   - ❐ type **It became a lightning rod...**

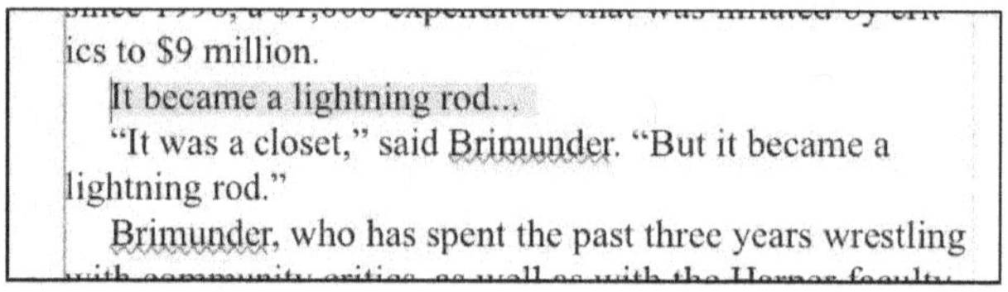
ics to $9 million.
It became a lightning rod...
"It was a closet," said Brimunder. "But it became a lightning rod."
Brimunder, who has spent the past three years wrestling

   - ❐ using the **Text Content Tool**, **triple-click** the text you just typed to highlight it
   - ❐ on the **Measurements** window, **Character** tab, change the **Font** to **Verdana**

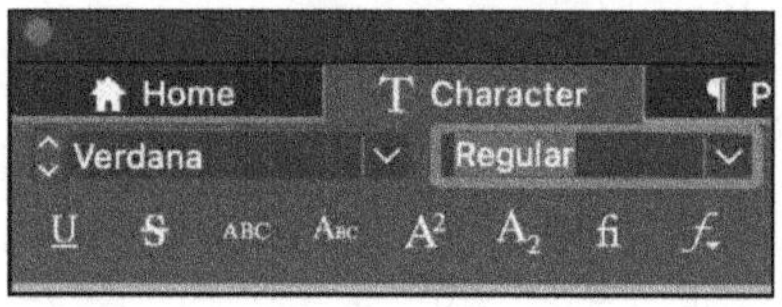

3. Change paragraph attributes.

   ❒ on the **Measurements** window, **Paragraph** tab, change the **First Line Indent** to **0**

   ❒ change the **Space Before** to **1p1**

   ❒ change the **Space After** to **1p1**

   ❒ change the **Alignment** to **Centered**

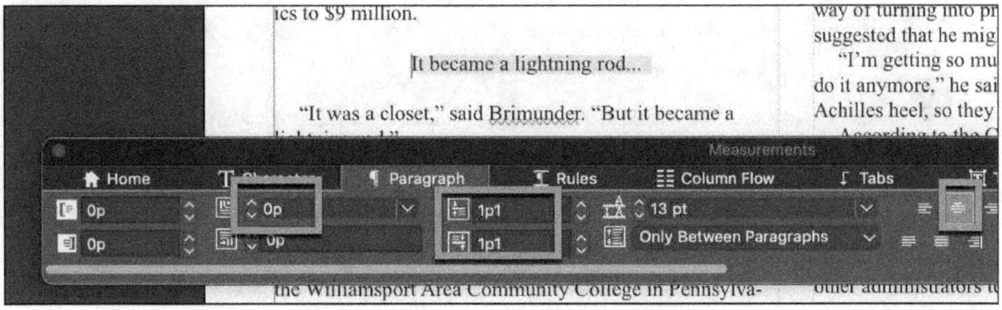

4. Add paragraph rules.

   ❒ ensure that the paragraph still selected,

   ❒ on the **Measurements** window, select the **Rules** tab

   ❒ select **Rule Above** and **Rule Below**

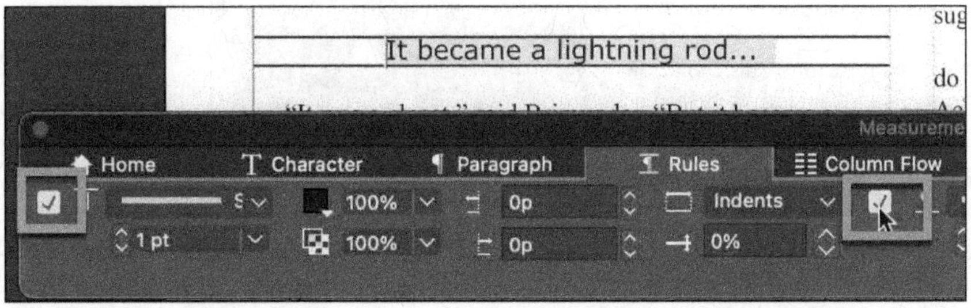

5. Edit the paragraph rules so that they are the width of the text instead of the paragraph.

   ❒ change the Length for both to **Text**

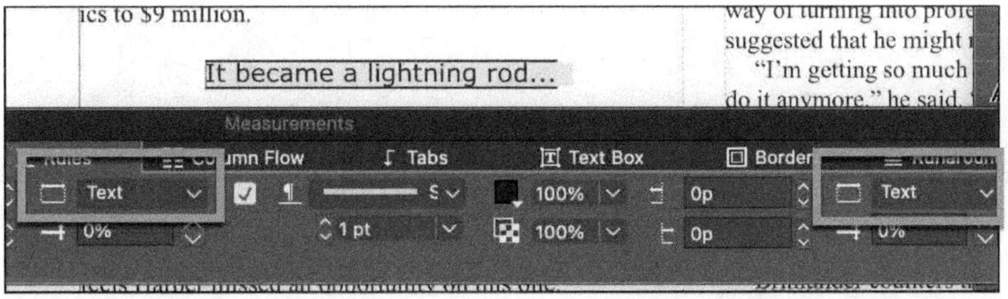

NOTES

6. Control the distance between the rules and the text and make the rules thicker.
   - ❐ change Offset for the Rule Above to **30%**
   - ❐ change Offset for the Rule Below to **20%**
   - ❐ change both Widths to **3 pt**

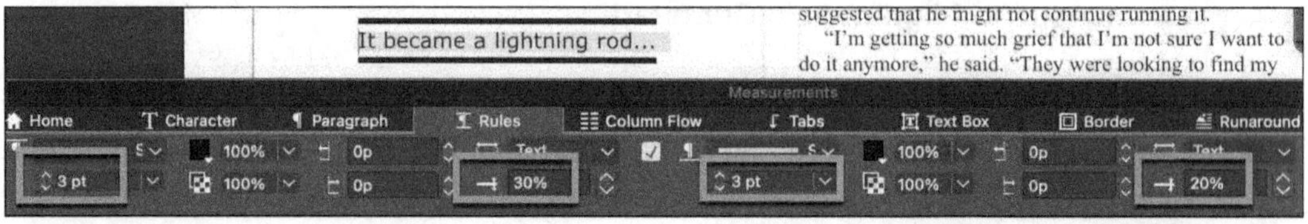

On the Style Sheets window, notice that the BodyText paragraph style has been overwritten with the direct formatting. How can you tell? Notice the **BodyText style** name in the Style Sheets palette now includes a plus sign (+) to the left of its name.

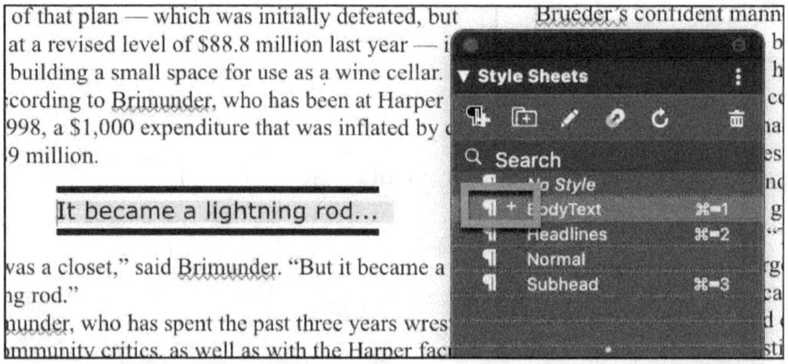

The plus sign is neither good nor bad, it is just informing you that direct formatting, not part of the style sheet, has been applied. If you wanted to remove the direct formatting, you would select the paragraph and then [alt]-click the **overwritten** style sheet in the Styles palette. Because you will be creating a new style sheet based on the inline formatting, leave the inline formatting as-is.

Guided Activity 86: Convert Inline Formatting into a Style Sheet

1. The myDirectStyles project should still be open.

2. Create a new style based on the paragraph you just formatted.

   ❒ ensure the paragraph you formatted is still selected (**It became a lighting rod...**)

   ❒ choose **Edit > Style Sheets**

   The Styles Sheets dialog box opens.

   ❒ click the **New** button and choose **Paragraph**

   ❒ type **PullQuotes** into the Name area

   Observe the information in the Description area. You'll find information about all of your direct formatting.

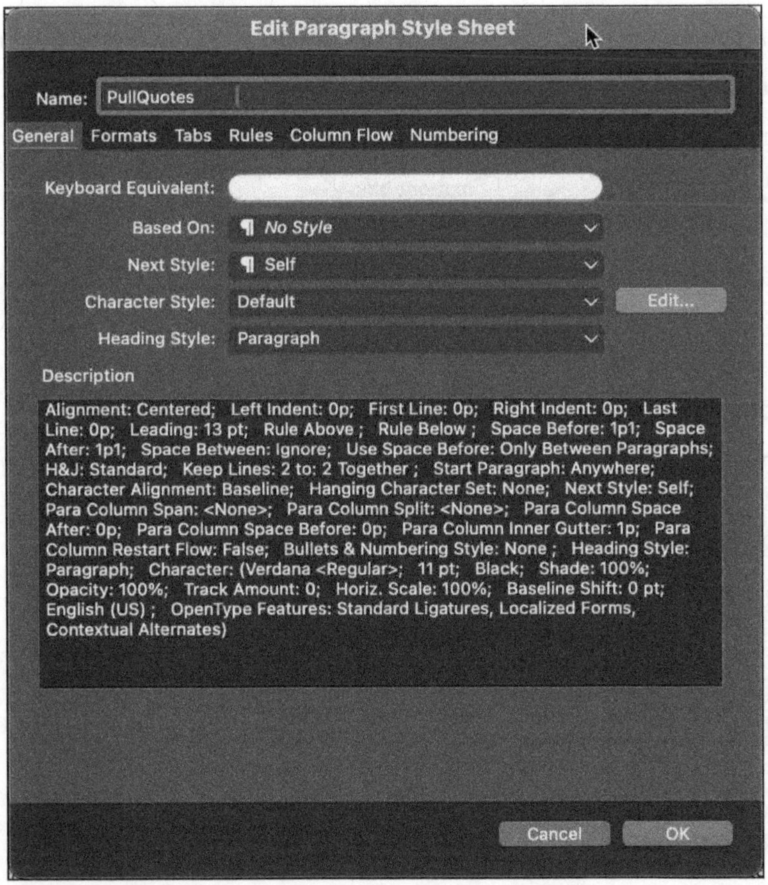

   ❒ click **OK**

   ❒ click **Save**

   Your new style sheet is now in the Style Sheets palette, but is not yet being used.

NOTES

NOTES

Confidence Check

1. Apply the PullQuotes style to the “It became a lightning rod…” paragraph.
2. Find the phrase **I’m getting so much grief**.
3. Click in front of the paragraph and type **“I’m not sure I want to do it anymore...”** and press [return].
4. Apply the **PullQuotes** style to the paragraph you just typed.

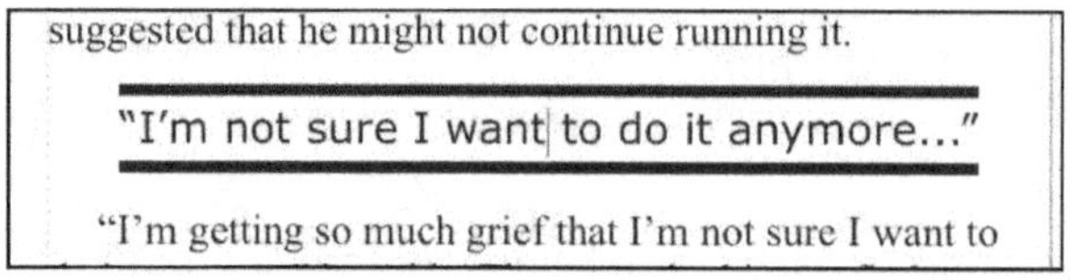

5. Find the phrase **Brimunder certainly has no fear**
6. Click in front of the paragraph and type **Brimunder has no fear...** and press [return].
7. Apply the **PullQuote** style to the paragraph you just typed.

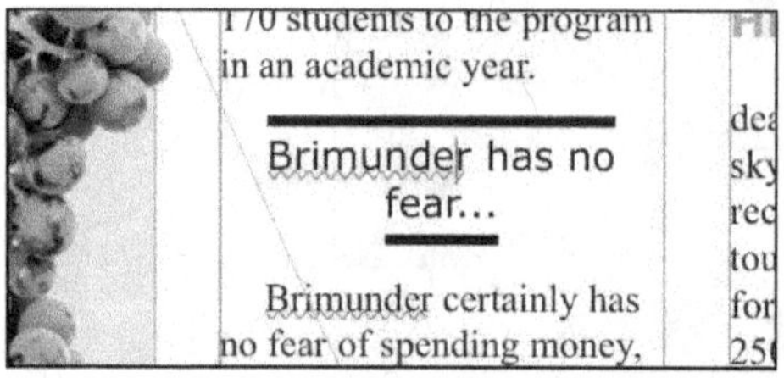

8. Edit the **PullQuotes** style sheet, changing its Font Size to **8**.

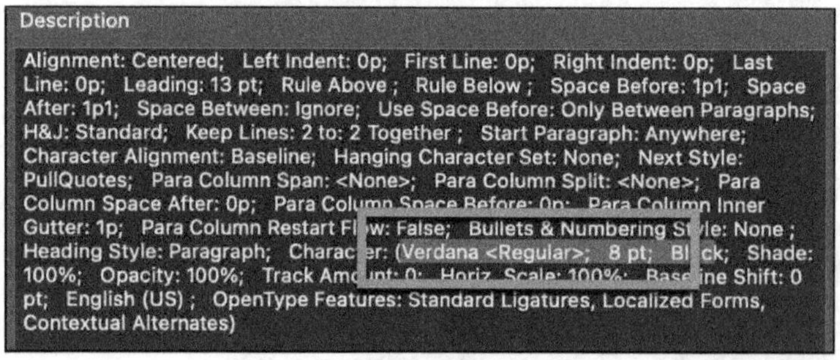

9. Save your work and close the project.

The Baseline Grid

When you work with text in QuarkXPress, the text sits on an invisible line known as a baseline. The baseline is a consistent reference point for aligning text across multiple columns in a layout, ensuring the text appears visually balanced and structured. QuarkXPress lets you set the size of the baseline in a grid and then lock text to that grid. In the "Weekly Winer" layout, you have consistently used 13 points as the leading (the space between the lines). The baselines do not line up across columns because different font sizes are used throughout the design. You will set the baseline grid to 13 points and then edit the style sheets to lock the text to the grid.

Guided Activity 87: Lock Text to a Page Grid

1. Open **gridme** and save the file as **myGrid**.

2. Ensure that you're on page 1 and viewing at Actual size.

3. Show the Baseline Grid.

   ❒ choose **View > Page Grids**

   Pink lines run straight across the page. Notice that the baselines of your text do not line up to the grid.

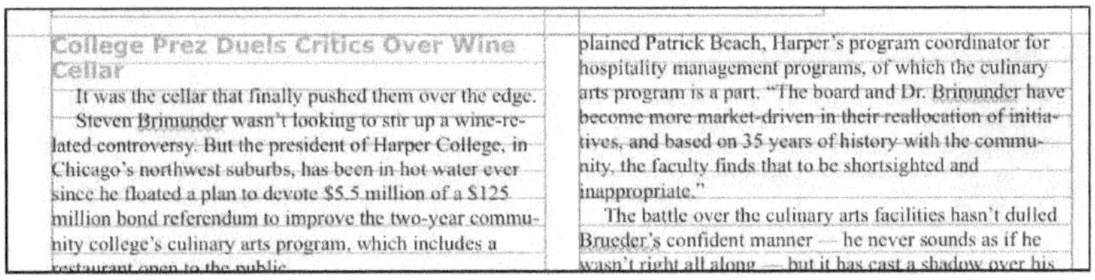

College Prez Duels Critics Over Wine Cellar

It was the cellar that finally pushed them over the edge.

Steven Brimunder wasn't looking to stir up a wine-related controversy. But the president of Harper College, in Chicago's northwest suburbs, has been in hot water ever since he floated a plan to devote $5.5 million of a $125 million bond referendum to improve the two-year community college's culinary arts program, which includes a restaurant open to the public.

plained Patrick Beach, Harper's program coordinator for hospitality management programs, of which the culinary arts program is a part. "The board and Dr. Brimunder have become more market-driven in their reallocation of initiatives, and based on 35 years of history with the community, the faculty finds that to be shortsighted and inappropriate."

The battle over the culinary arts facilities hasn't dulled Brueder's confident manner — he never sounds as if he wasn't right all along — but it has cast a shadow over his

4. Set up a Baseline Grid for the page on the Cover master page.

   ❒ choose **Page > Display > C-Cover**

   ❒ choose **Page > Master Guides & Grid**

   The Master Guides & Grid dialog box opens. Most of the text in your layout has a font size of 11 and leading of 13. On the Text Settings tab, you'll ensure that the Font Size is listed as 11 and the Line Spacing is 2 points—which would result in a leading value of 13. If you hope to line up the baselines, the grid increment must match the leading used throughout the document.

   ❒ change the Font Size to **11 pt**

   ❒ change the Line Spacing to **2 pt**

   Notice that the Leading value becomes 13.

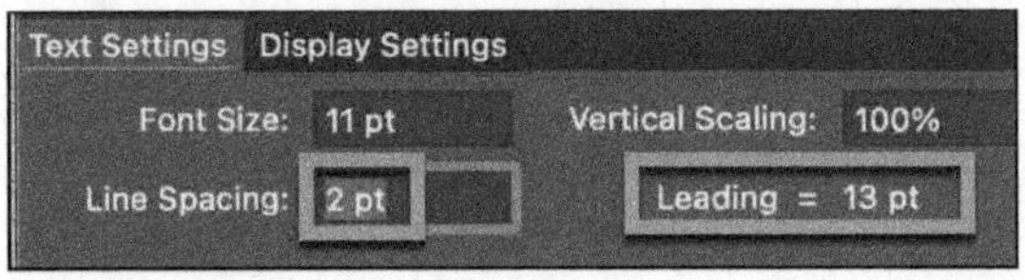

   ❒ click **OK**

NOTES

The baseline shifts and now there are 13 points of space between every pink line. The space is important because the leading throughout your document is also 13 points.

5. Return to the layout and observe the baseline alignment.

   ❒ choose **Page > Display > Layout** and, if necessary, go to page **1**

   The text is not yet locked to the edited baseline grid.

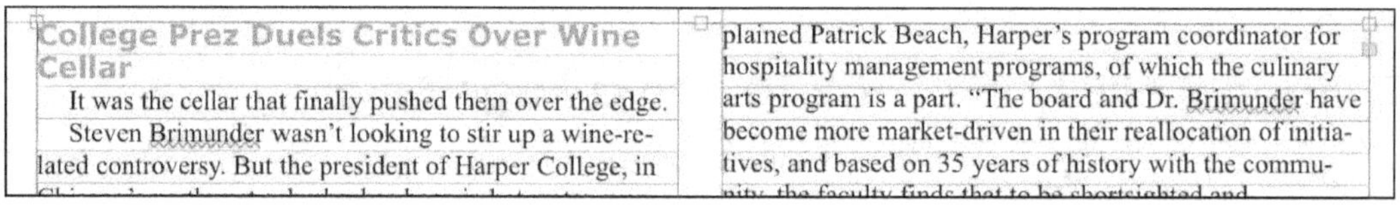

6. Edit the BodyText style to lock it to the baseline grid.

   ❒ choose **Edit > Style Sheets**

   ❒ double-click **BodyText** (to Edit the style)

   ❒ click the **Formats** tab

   ❒ select **Lock to Grid**

   ❒ ensure **Page Grid** is selected from the drop-down menu

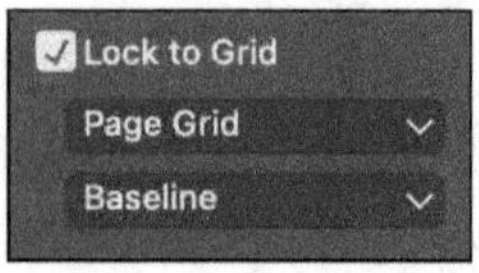

   ❒ click **OK**

   ❒ click **Save**

   All of the BodyText on page 1 locks to the baseline grid across both columns.

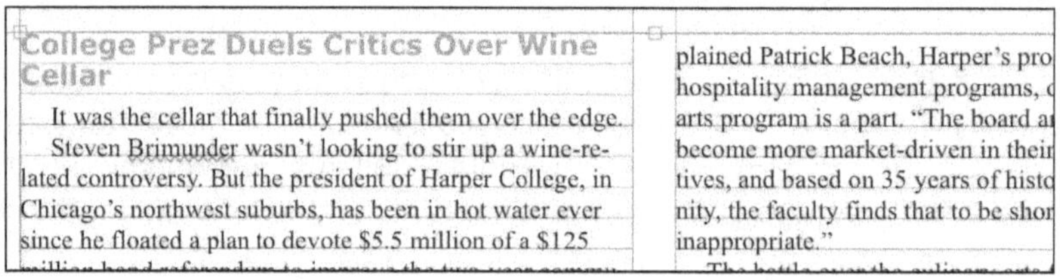

7. Save the project.

Confidence Check

1. Display the remaining master pages (Page > Display) and set the Master Guides & Grid to a Font Size of **11 pt** and Line Spacing of **2 pt**
2. Edit the **Headlines** style sheet so that it locks to the page grid.

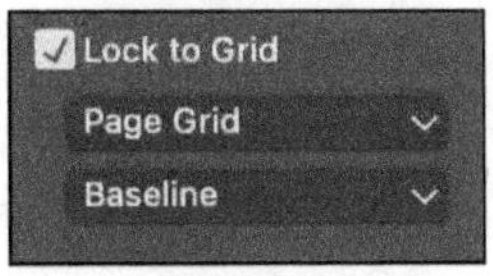

3. Edit the **PullQuotes** style so that it locks to the page grid.
4. Scroll through your document. Notice that the baselines for all of your text line up across the pages.

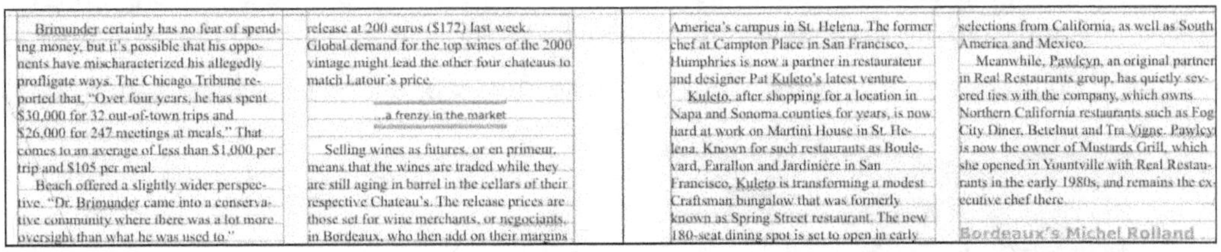

Brimunder certainly has no fear of spending money, but it's possible that his opponents have mischaracterized his allegedly profligate ways. The Chicago Tribune reported that, "Over four years, he has spent $30,000 for 32 out-of-town trips and $26,000 for 247 meetings at meals." That comes to an average of less than $1,000 per trip and $105 per meal.

Beach offered a slightly wider perspective. "Dr. Brimunder came into a conservative community where there was a lot more oversight than what he was used to."

release at 200 euros ($172) last week. Global demand for the top wines of the 2000 vintage might lead the other four chateaus to match Latour's price.

...a frenzy in the market

Selling wines as futures, or en primeur, means that the wines are traded while they are still aging in barrel in the cellars of their respective Chateau's. The release prices are those set for wine merchants, or negociants, in Bordeaux, who then add on their margins

America's campus in St. Helena. The former chef at Campton Place in San Francisco, Humphries is now a partner in restaurateur and designer Pat Kuleto's latest venture.

Kuleto, after shopping for a location in Napa and Sonoma counties for years, is now hard at work on Martini House in St. Helena. Known for such restaurants as Boulevard, Farallon and Jardinière in San Francisco, Kuleto is transforming a modest Craftsman bungalow that was formerly known as Spring Street restaurant. The new 180-seat dining spot is set to open in early

selections from California, as well as South America and Mexico.

Meanwhile, Pawlcyn, an original partner in Real Restaurants group, has quietly severed ties with the company, which owns Northern California restaurants such as Fog City Diner, Betelnut and Tra Vigne. Pawlcyn is now the owner of Mustards Grill, which she opened in Yountville with Real Restaurants in the early 1980s, and remains the executive chef there.

Bordeaux's Michel Rolland

5. Hide the page grids (View menu).
6. Save and close the project.

NOTES

NOTES

Drop Caps

A drop cap is a typographic design element where the first letter of a paragraph extends down two or more lines into the text. Drop caps break up the monotony of a text-heavy layout and serve as visual markers, providing readers with a clear and comfortable starting point for reading.

> **Note:** When creating Drop Caps, you can have a Character Count of up to **127** and a Line Count of up to **16**.

Guided Activity 88: Insert Drop Caps

1. Open **dropMe** and save it as **myDropCaps**.

2. Insert a drop cap.

   - ❐ go to the top of page **1**
   - ❐ using the **Text Content Tool**, click in the first paragraph "Steven Brimunder wasn't looking to stir up a wine-related controversy."
   - ❐ on the **Measurements** window, **Paragraph** tab, change the **First Line Indent** to **0**

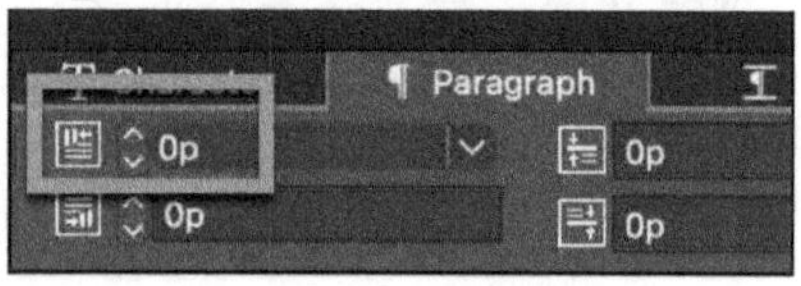

   - ❐ on the **Measurements** window, **Paragraph** tab, select **Drop Caps**
   - ❐ ensure the **Character Count** is **1**
   - ❐ change the **Line Count** to **2**

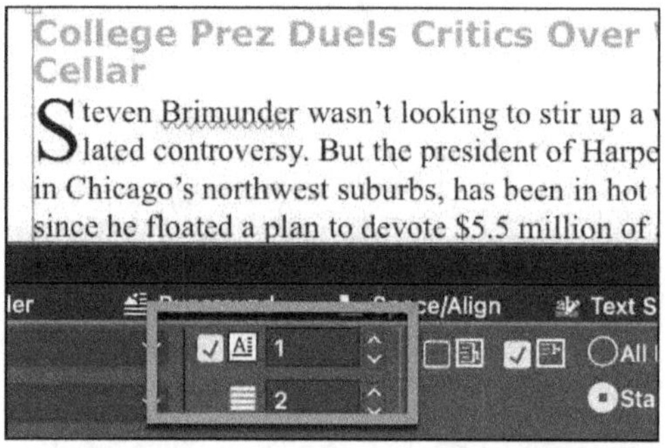

   There is now a two-line drop cap in the first paragraph.

3. Add some white space above the drop-cap paragraph.

   - ❐ with the drop-cap paragraph still selected, on the **Measurements** window, **Paragraph** tab, change the **Space above** to **0**

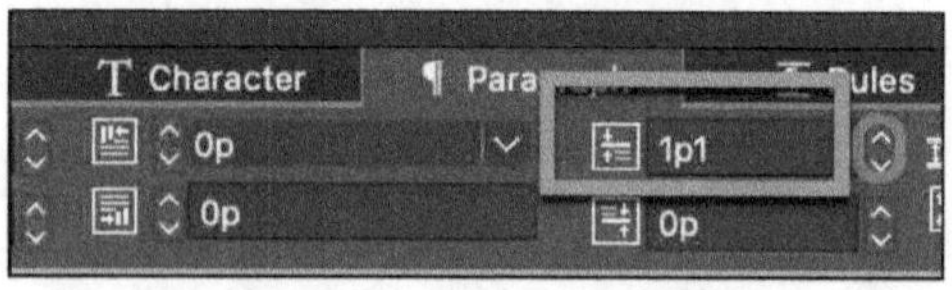

Confidence Check

1. Select the paragraph you just formatted and create a New Paragraph Style sheet called **DropCaps** that uses [command] [keypad 6] as its Keyboard Equivalent.

   (You learned how to create paragraph style sheets based on selected text on page 181.)

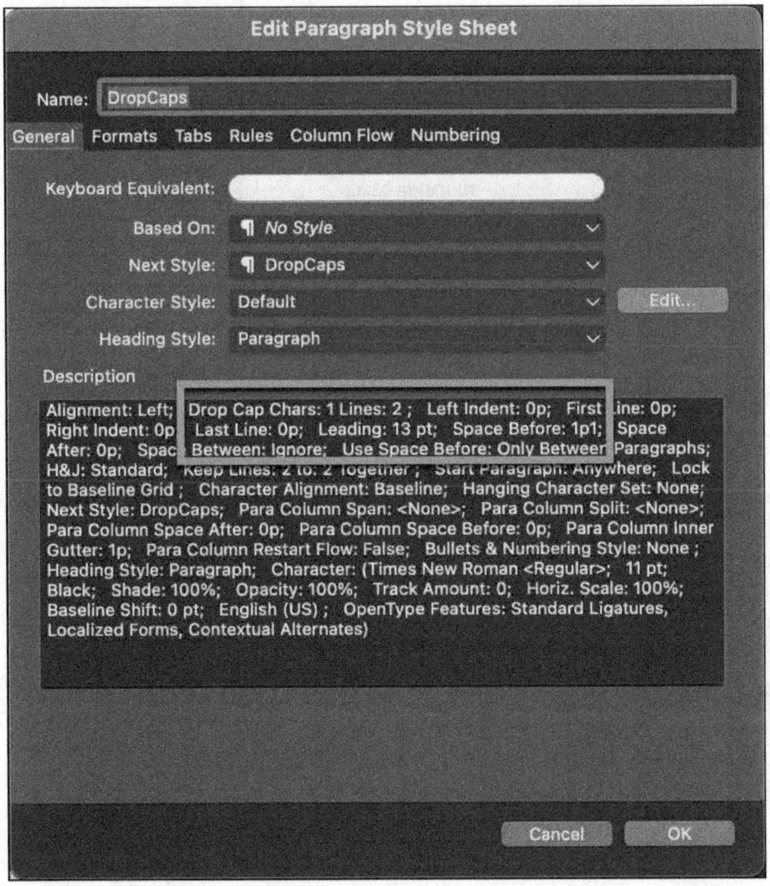

2. Apply the new style sheet to one or two paragraphs per page throughout your layout as you see fit.

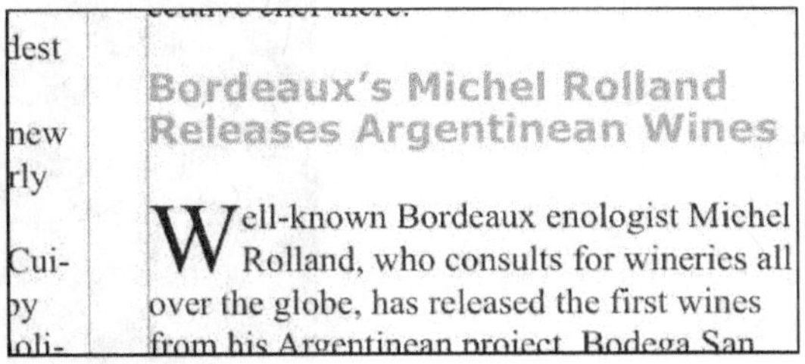

Bordeaux's Michel Rolland Releases Argentinean Wines

Well-known Bordeaux enologist Michel Rolland, who consults for wineries all over the globe, has released the first wines from his Argentinean project, Bodega San

3. Save the project.

NOTES

Character Style Sheets

You have spent significant time during the lessons in this book creating paragraph-style sheets. As you have seen, a paragraph style sheet applies formatting to an entire paragraph, including alignment, indentation, line spacing, and paragraph spacing. You have seen that paragraph style sheets contain character-level formatting like font, size, and font color. Now, let's focus on character style sheets. While paragraph style sheets define a paragraph's overall look and structure, character style sheets allow for precise formatting of smaller text elements within the paragraph, such as controlling the color of just the drop cap character.

Guided Activity 89: Create a Character Style Sheet

1. Ensure that the **myDropCaps** project is still open.

2. Create a character style sheet.

    ❒ choose **Edit > Style Sheets**

    ❒ click **New > Character**

    ❒ name the new style sheet **DropCapLetterStyle**

    ❒ change the **Style** to **Bold**

    ❒ change the **Color** to **Pantone S 185-7**

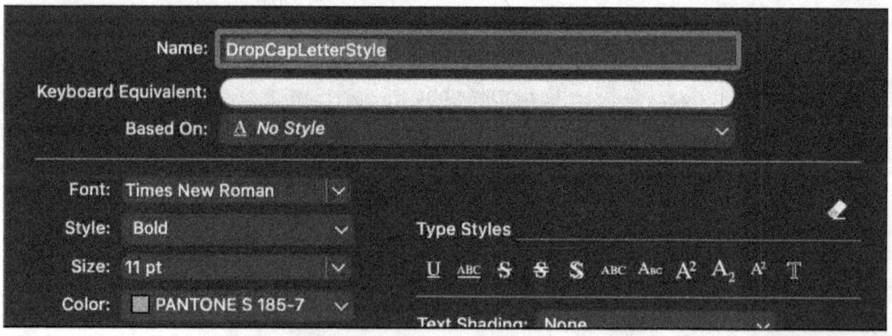

    ❒ click **OK**

    ❒ click **Save**

    The new style sheet appears in the bottom section of the Style Sheets palette.

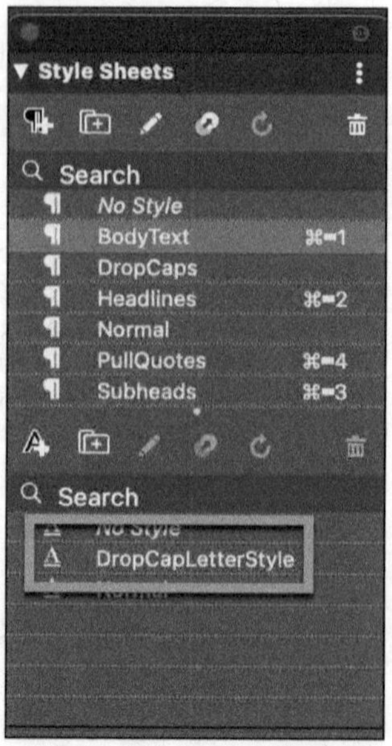

Confidence Check

1. Go to page **1** and select the large "S" in the first paragraph.
2. With the letter selected, select **DropCapLetterStyle** from the Style Sheets palette.

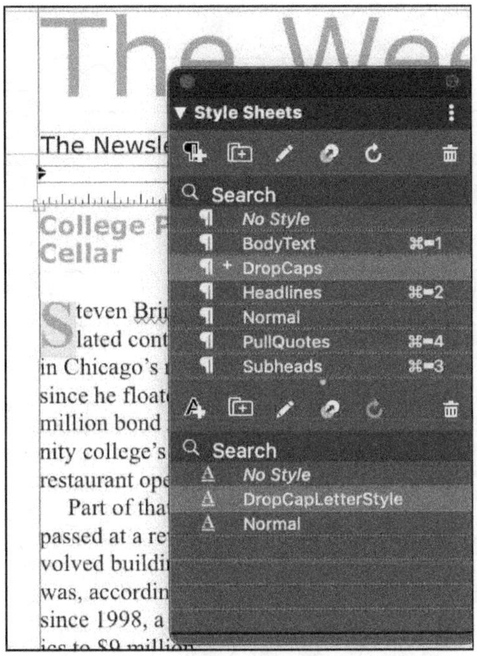

Because you've just applied a character style sheet to the text, only the selected letter changes.

3. Apply the DropCapLetterStyle to all of the drop caps in your layout.
4. Save and close the project.

NOTES

Notes

ICONLOGIC

"Skills and Drills" Learning

Module 11: Item Styles

In This Module You Will Learn About:

And You Will Learn To:

NOTES

Applying, Creating, and Editing Item Styles

You can create item styles that save myriad attributes such as frame width, style, color, picture scale, background color, runaround, and text inset. Similar to text styles, which you learned about on page 167, item styles appear on a palette and can be applied to layout items with a mouse click or a keyboard shortcut. A usage feature allows you to quickly determine where the style is being used and how often. As with text styles, you can quickly update any item style and make global changes to the items in seconds.

Guided Activity 90: Apply an Item Style

1. Open **itemStyleMe** from the **QuarkXPress 2025 Book Assets** and save the project as **myItemStyles**.

2. Scroll through the document and notice that there are captions positioned in the outside margins of most of the pages.

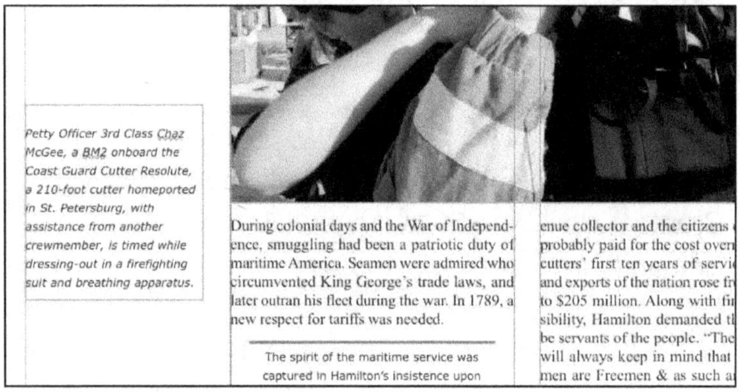

The appearance of the text within the text boxes is being controlled by a paragraph style. The appearance of the text boxes themselves is being controlled in large part by an item style.

3. Draw a text box in the margin of page 2.

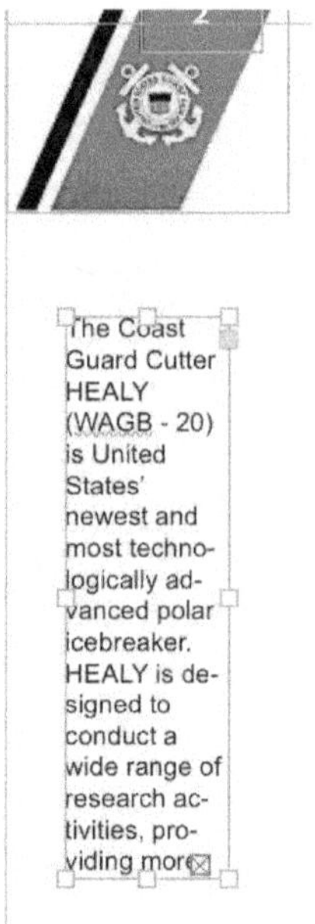

   - ❒ go to page 2 of the layout
   - ❒ using the **Text Content Tool**, draw a text box at the left of the page in the margin beneath the Coast Guard racing stripe that is approximately one-half inch wide and 2 inches tall
   - ❒ click inside the new text box and choose **File > Import**
   - ❒ from **QuarkXPress 2025 Book Assets** > **textFiles**, open **healyCaption.txt**

   There is more text than will fit in the box. You will fix that soon enough.

4. Apply a paragraph style sheet to text.

   ❒ using the **Text Content Tool**, highlight all of the healyCaption text you just imported

   ❒ on the Style Sheets window, click **Caption_Left**

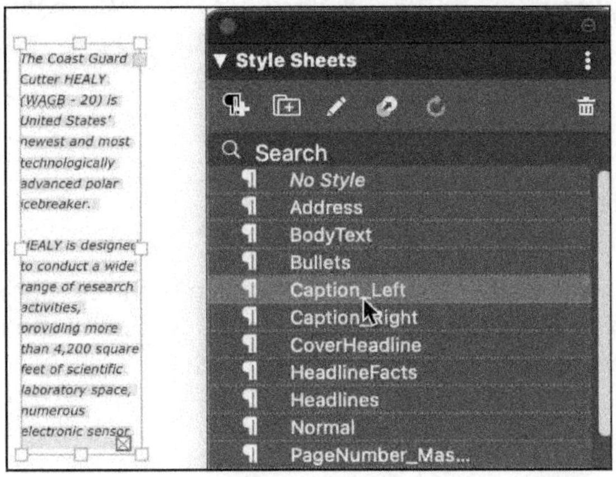

   While the text takes on the appearance of the Caption_Left style, the text box is unchanged.

5. Apply an existing item style to the caption text box.

   ❒ choose **Window > Item Styles**

   By default, new QuarkXPress projects do not contain item styles. I created the **CaptionBoxes** style for you.

   ❒ with the **healyCaption** text box selected, click **CaptionBoxes**

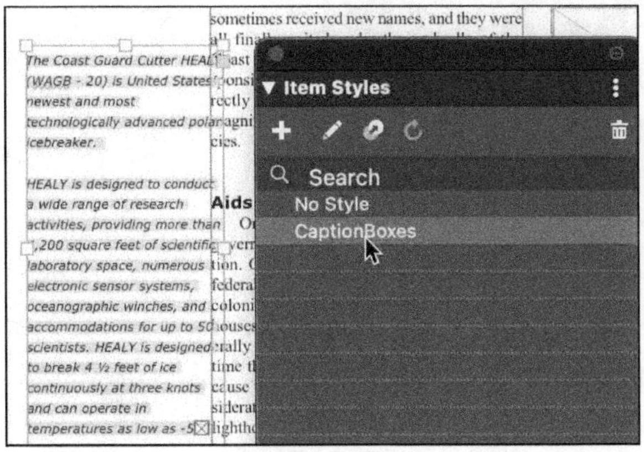

   The text box resizes.

NOTES

NOTES

6. Reposition and resize the text box.

   - ❒ using the **Item Tool**, drag the healyCaption text box **left** until its left edge lines up with the green guide
   - ❒ stretch the bottom, center resizing handle down until all of the caption text appears

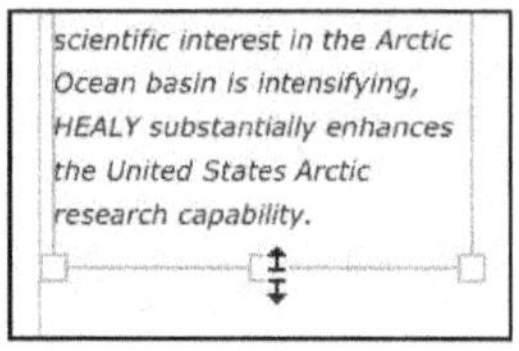

Notice that the text in the text box is vertically aligned to the bottom of the text box. No matter how deep you make the box, the text will always align to the bottom of the box, not the top. This formatting option is part of the CaptionBoxes item style.

7. Check item style usage.

   - ❒ on the **Item Styles** window, right-click the **CaptionBoxes** item style and select **Usage** from the menu

The **Items Styles Usage** dialog box opens. This handy dialog box lets you know where the item style is used throughout the layout. Keep an eye on the **Status** column. As you can see in the image below, everything is fine. You will soon see what happens if you change something about the text box that is not part of the item style's properties.

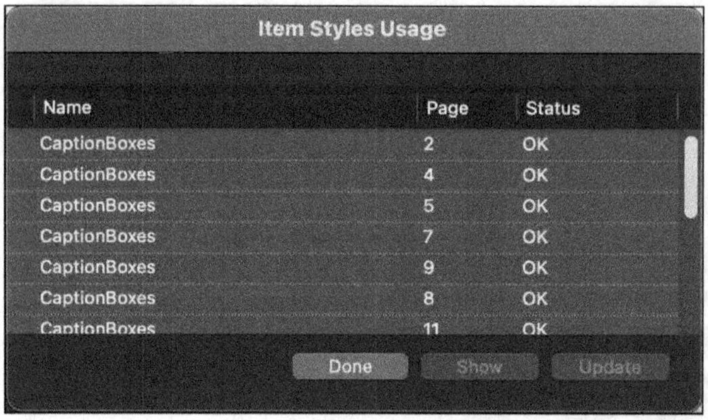

   - ❒ click **Done**

Guided Activity 91: Override and Reapply an Item Style

1. Override an item style.

   ❒ go to page 4 of the layout and, using the **Item Tool**, resize the width of the caption's text box so that the box is more narrow

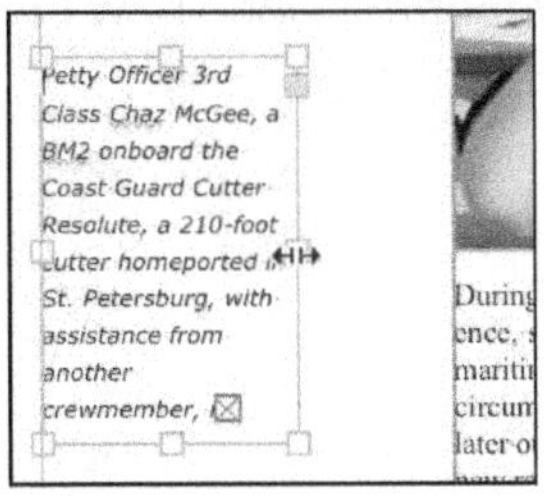

2. Check item style usage.

   ❒ on the **Item Styles** window, right-click the **CaptionBoxes** style and select **Usage**

   The Items Styles Usage dialog box opens again. This time, notice the word **Modified** in the Status column. As you have seen, you can change the properties of an item, such as its size, without any problems. However, if the item is using an item style, you will always see a Modified alert in the Usage dialog box.

3. Remove item style overrides.

   ❒ click the word **Modified**

   ❒ click **Update**

   Notice that the Status column once again reads OK.

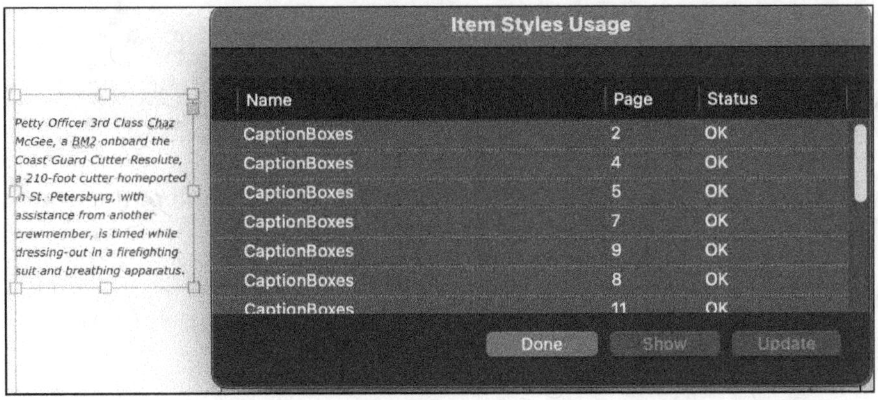

   ❒ click **Done**

   The resized text box returns to the size specified by the item style.

NOTES

NOTES

Guided Activity 92: Create a New Item Style

1. The **myItemStyles** project should still be open.

2. Create a new item style.

❒ ensure no items are selected in the layout (this is very important since new Item styles pick up attributes of selected items)

❒ on the **Item Styles** window, click the **New** icon +

The Edit Item Style dialog box opens.

❒ on the **General** tab, type **BoxRunaround** into the **Name** field

❒ select the **Runaround** tab

❒ enable **Apply** (put a check in the box)

❒ enable **Type**

❒ if necessary, change the **Type** to **Item**

❒ select **all four** options beneath Type (Top, Left, Bottom and Right)

❒ change the **Top** to **13**

❒ change the **Left** to **0**

❒ change the **Bottom** to **13**

❒ change the **Right** to **0**

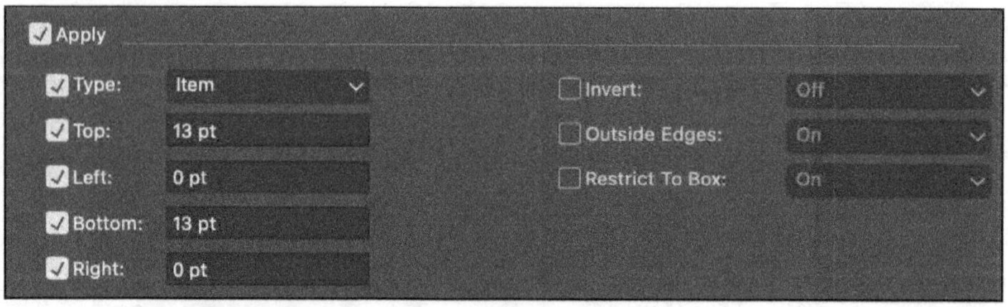

Review all of the other tabs in the dialog box and ensure that **none of the other options are selected**.

❒ click **OK**

The new item style appears on the **Item Styles** window.

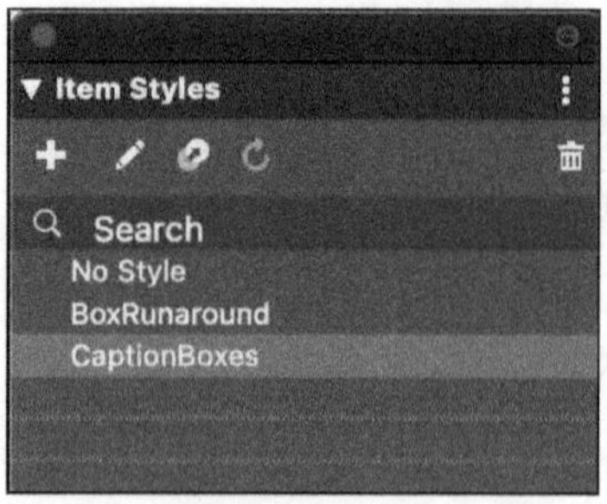

3. Apply the item style to a picture box.

- ❒ go to **page 5**
- ❒ at the **bottom** of **page 5**, select the **picture**
- ❒ on the **Item Styles** window, click the **BoxRunaround** style

Notice that white space is added above the picture box.

Confidence Check

1. With the exception of the large picture of the cutter on page 6 or the boxes containing the racing stripes on the master pages, apply the **BoxRunaround** item style to all of the picture boxes throughout the layout.
2. Go to page 2 and import the **healy.jpg** picture from the Images folder into the large picture box.

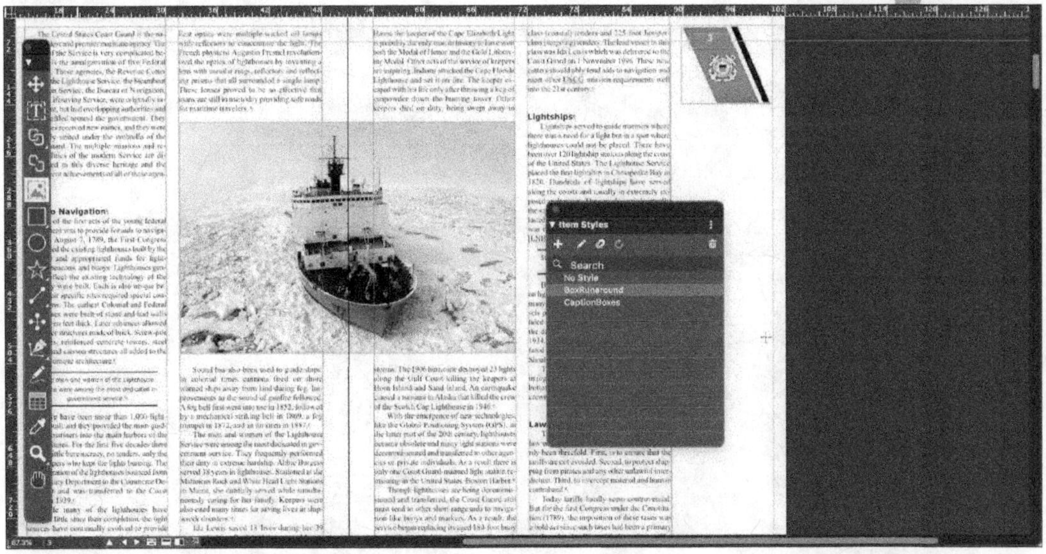

3. Resize and crop the image as you like.
4. Save the project.

NOTES

Guided Activity 93: Edit an Item Style

1. The **MyItemStyles** project should still be open.

2. Edit an item style.

   - ❒ choose **Edit > Item Styles**
   - ❒ select **BoxRunaround**
   - ❒ click **Edit**
   - ❒ select the **Border** tab
   - ❒ select **Apply** (put a check in the box)
   - ❒ select **Style**
   - ❒ confirm that the **Style** is **Solid**
   - ❒ select **Color**
   - ❒ change the Color the **Coast Guard Red**
   - ❒ select **Width**
   - ❒ change the **Width** to **2 pt**

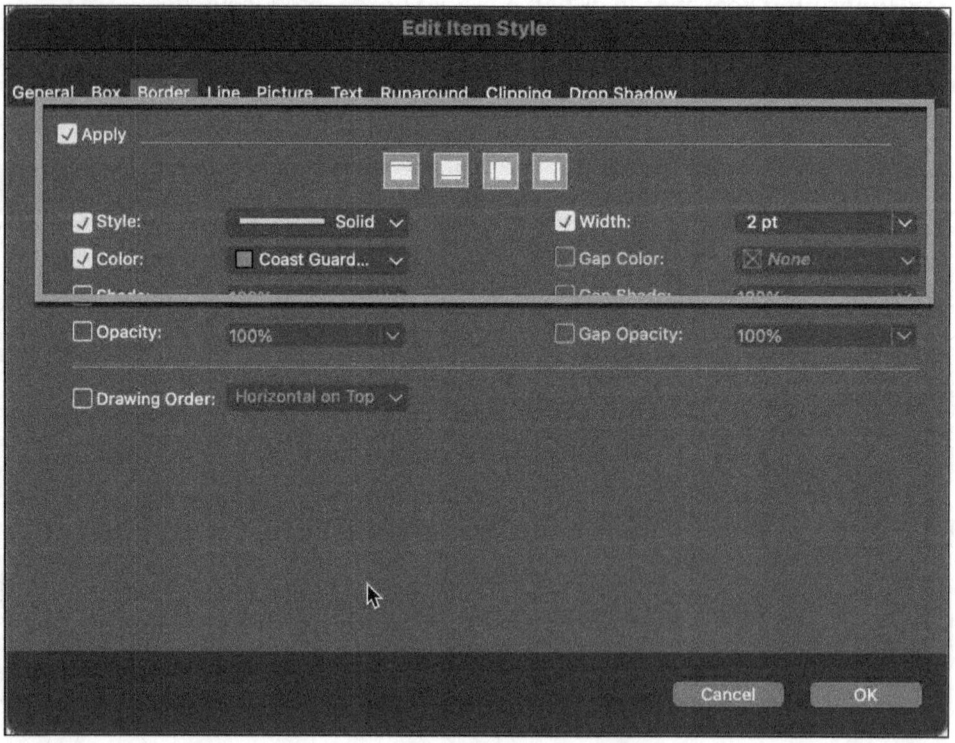

   - ❒ click **OK**
   - ❒ click **Save**

   Scroll through the document and notice that every item using the BoxRunaround style now includes a red, 2 pt border.

3. Save and close the project.

ICONLOGIC
"Skills and Drills" Learning

Module 12: Tracking, Kerning and Hyphenation

In This Module You Will Learn About:

And You Will Learn To:

NOTES

Tracking and Kerning

Tracking and kerning both control character spacing, but they serve different purposes. Tracking allows you to adjust spacing for selected text or for an entire layout. Kerning is meant to adjust or fine-tune the spacing between individual pairs of characters to ensure they fit together as needed.

Guided Activity 94: Track Text

1. Open **trackKernMe** and save the file as **myTrackKern**.

2. Use tracking to change the letter spacing for selected text.

    ❒ using the **Text Content Tool**, select all of the text

    ❒ on the **Measurements** window, select the **Character** tab

    ❒ locate the **Track Amount** area 

    ❒ type **-50** as the Track Amount area and press [**enter**]

    Yikes! All of the letters are smashed together. Perhaps -50 was a *just a bit* too much tracking!

Confidence Check

1. Change the tracking to **-25**.
2. Change the tracking to **-18**.

   How does the character spacing look? Larger display text is typically tracked until it is *tight but not touching*.

3. Spend a moment tracking the text so that the spacing looks good to you—tight but not touching.

   Note: You can track text using keyboard shortcuts. Use the following shortcuts to track the text:

   Decrease 1/20 em space: [**command**] [**shift**] [{]

   Increase 1/20 em space: [**command**] [**shift**] [}]

   Decrease 1/200 em space: [**command**] [**alt**] [**shift**] [{]

   Increase 1/200 em space: [**command**] [**alt**] [**shift**] [}]

4. Change the tracking to **-9**.

5. Save the project.

NOTES

NOTES

Guided Activity 95: Kern Letter Pairs

1. The **myTrackKern** project should still be open.

2. Use kerning to adjust the space between two letters.

   ❒ click between the "G" and the "o" in Goodness

   ❒ On the **Measurements** window, notice that the Track amount area has automatically become the Kern amount area

   ❒ in the Kern amount area, type **-50** and press [enter]

   You probably could have guessed that **-50** was going to be just a bit too tight.

Confidence Check

1. Change the kerning between the two letters until the spacing is tight but not touching.
2. Spend the next few moments changing the kerning between any characters that need attention. Remember, you are striving for *tight but not touching*.
3. *Now try this:* Assuming you have changed the tracking and kerning for all of the text, and spent some time getting the spacing just right, what do you think would happen if you changed the font?

   Change the font to Times or Times New Roman.

   How does the letter spacing look now? It should have changed, and now you've got more tracking and kerning work to do. There is a moral to this exercise. Track and kern the text after making font and font size choices, never before.

4. Save and close the project.

Project-Wide Tracking

Once you've learned how to track and kern, you've got tremendous power over how your text flows in your document. If you find yourself short by a couple of lines of text, you can highlight several paragraphs, track them to +1 or +2, and gain your needed lines. The same is true if your text is running a little long. Tracking to -2 or -3 can save several lines over a long document.

Guided Activity 96: Add Tracking to a Style Sheet

1. Open **trackAndHyphenateMe** and save the file as **myTrackedAndHyphenatedLayout**.

2. Add tracking to a style sheet.

   ❐ on the Style Sheets window, edit the **BodyText** style sheet.

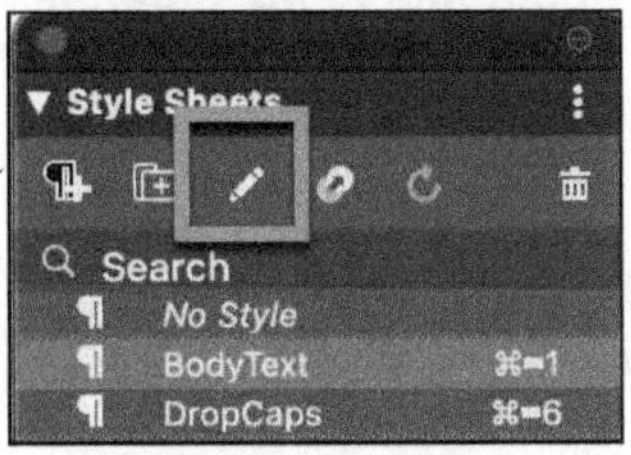

   ❐ to the right of **Character Style**, click **Edit**

   ❐ change the **Track Amount** to **-2**

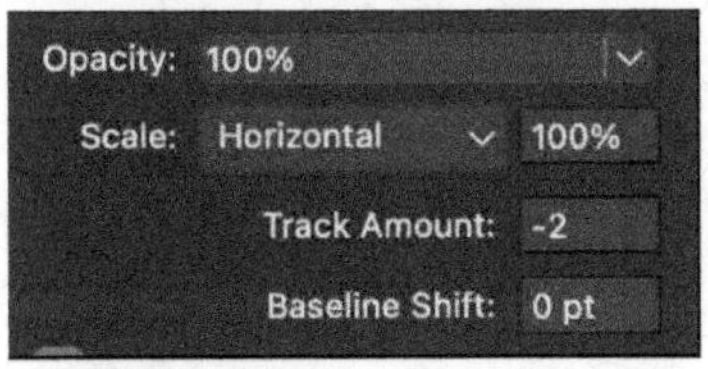

   ❐ click **OK**

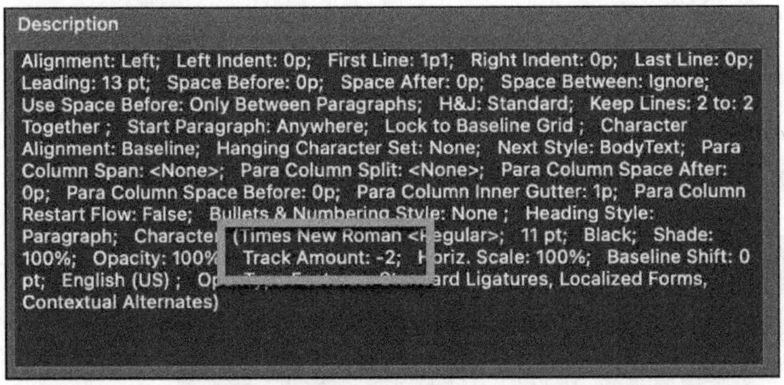

   ❐ click **OK**

   The layout's main body text is now a bit tighter. Because the lines have been tightened up, the document is also a few lines shorter than before.

3. When finished, save the project and keep it open for the next activity.

NOTES

Hyphenation

You can control how QuarkXPress hyphenates words in a couple of ways. You can edit the hyphenation settings that tell QuarkXPress whether or not to break capitalized words, how many characters are allowed to appear after a hyphen, and how many hyphens are allowed in a row. You can also set up hyphenation exceptions that contain words you don't want QuarkXPress to ever hyphenate in any project.

Guided Activity 97: Edit Hyphenation Settings

1. The **myTrackedAndHyphenatedLayout** should still be open.

2. On page 1, column two, find the paragraph "According to the Chicago Tribune..."

   The paragraph is left aligned and there are white gaps at the end of the sentences.

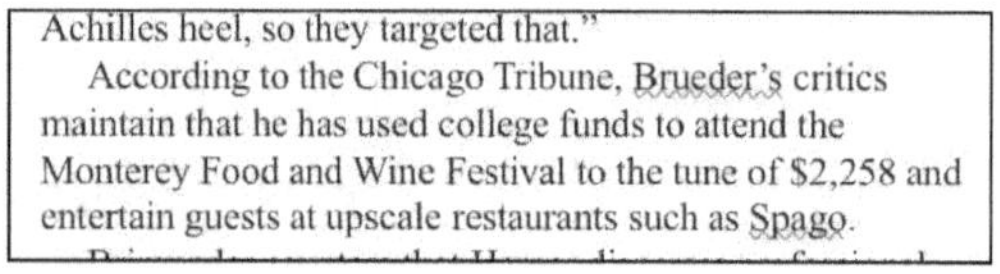
Achilles heel, so they targeted that."
According to the Chicago Tribune, Brueder's critics maintain that he has used college funds to attend the Monterey Food and Wine Festival to the tune of $2,258 and entertain guests at upscale restaurants such as Spago.

   Notice that the word "Monterey" in the third sentence is not hyphenated. No capitalized words are hyphenated anywhere in the document. If the word "Monterey" were hyphenated, the sentence above would not have quite as large of a white gap. Let's use hyphenation controls to remove some of the end-of-sentence gaps.

3. Edit the hyphenation settings to allow capitalized words to hyphenate.

   ❒ choose **Edit > H&Js**

   The **Edit Hyphenation & Justification** options open.

   ❒ click the **New** button

   The Edit Hyphenation & Justification dialog box opens.

   ❒ type **breakCaps** into the Name area

   ❒ select **Break Capitalized Words** (turn the option on)

   ❒ confirm that **Hyphens in a Row** is set to **2**

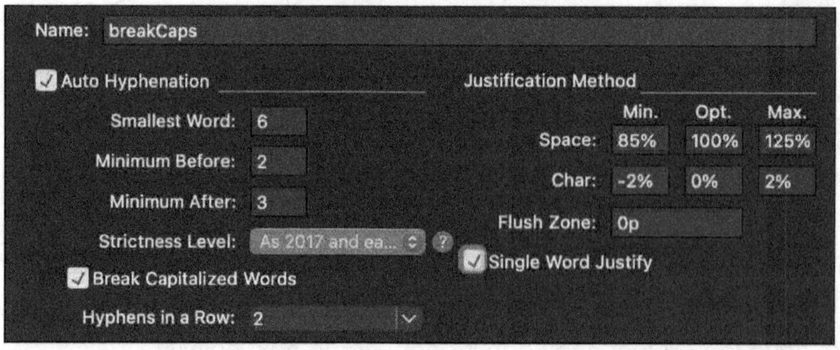

   ❒ click **OK**

❒ click **Save**

While you've created the breakCaps H&J, it is not currently being used. You'll take care of that next.

4. Add the new H&J to a style sheet.

❒ choose **Edit > Style Sheets**

❒ double-click the **BodyText** style

❒ click **Formats** tab

❒ from the **H&J** drop-down menu, choose **breakCaps** 

❒ click **OK**

❒ click **Save**

Examine your document. While not every capitalized word has been hyphenated, some have (including the word "Monterey" in the paragraph we were discussing a moment ago).

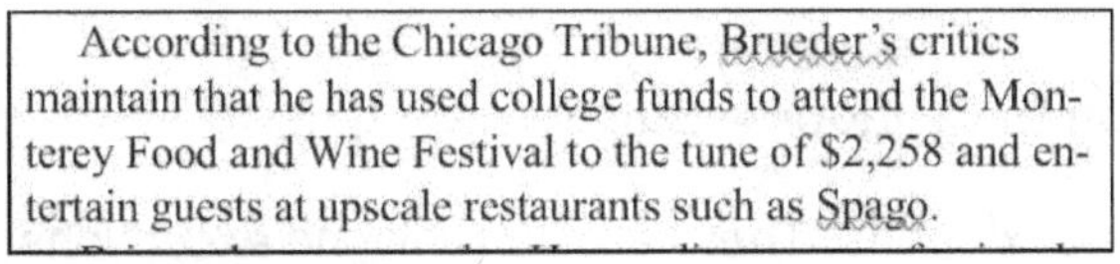
According to the Chicago Tribune, Brueder's critics maintain that he has used college funds to attend the Monterey Food and Wine Festival to the tune of $2,258 and entertain guests at upscale restaurants such as Spago.

Confidence Check

1. Edit the H&J's again.

   Notice that QuarkXPress comes with an H&J called **No Hyphenation**. If you use this H&J, you'll prevent some specific content from hyphenating (such as headlines and pull quotes).

2. Edit both the **Headlines** and **PullQuotes** style sheets so that they use the **No Hyphenation** H&J.

3. Save the project.

NOTES

Hyphenation Exceptions

There may be certain words that you don't want QuarkXPress to hyphenate. You can easily create a hyphenation exception list in QuarkXPress that contains any words you don't want hyphenated.

You may also come across a single instance of a word you don't want to hyphenate, but you don't want to add to the exceptions list. QuarkXPress allows you to designate discretionary hyphens that easily insert or stop hyphenation.

The difference between creating a discretionary hyphen and the hyphenation exceptions list is that with discretionary hyphens you can choose to stop (or change) the hyphenation of one occurrence of a single word. The hyphenation exceptions list affects every occurrence of a word in the project.

Guided Activity 98: Set Hyphen Exceptions

1. The **myTrackedAndHyphenatedLayout** should still be open.

2. Create a hyphenation exception.

   ❐ choose **Utilities > Hyphenation Exceptions > Edit**

   The Hyphenation Exception dialog box opens. There are currently no exceptions.

   ❐ type **monterey** and then click **Add**

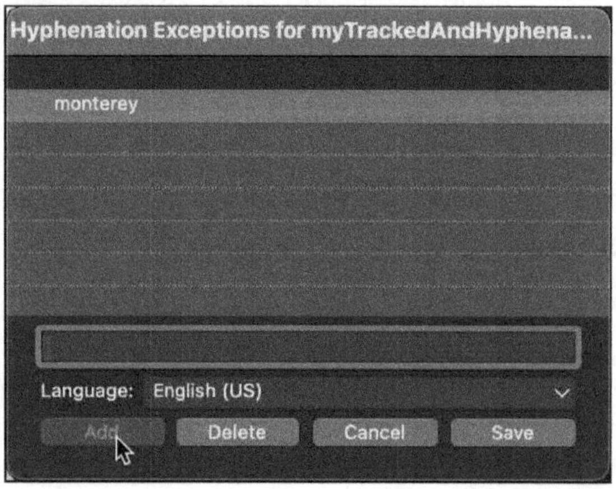

   ❐ click **Save**

   The word "Monterey" is no longer hyphenated anywhere in this project (or any other QuarkXPress file on your computer).

3. Add a discretionary hyphen character.

   ❐ scroll around the layout until you find a word that is hyphenated (there are several)

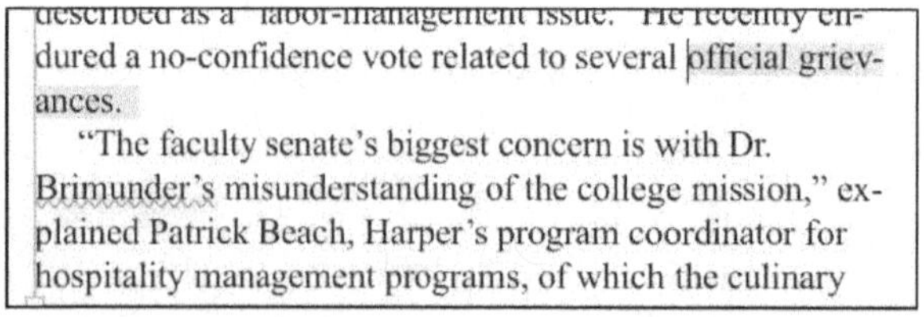
dured a no-confidence vote related to several official griev-
ances.
"The faculty senate's biggest concern is with Dr.
Brimunder's misunderstanding of the college mission," ex-
plained Patrick Beach, Harper's program coordinator for
hospitality management programs, of which the culinary

❒ click in front of the hyphenated word

❒ choose **Utilities > Insert Character > Special > Discretionary Hyphen**

The word is no longer hyphenated. You've just placed an invisible code in front of the word that does allow that one occurrence of the word to hyphenate.

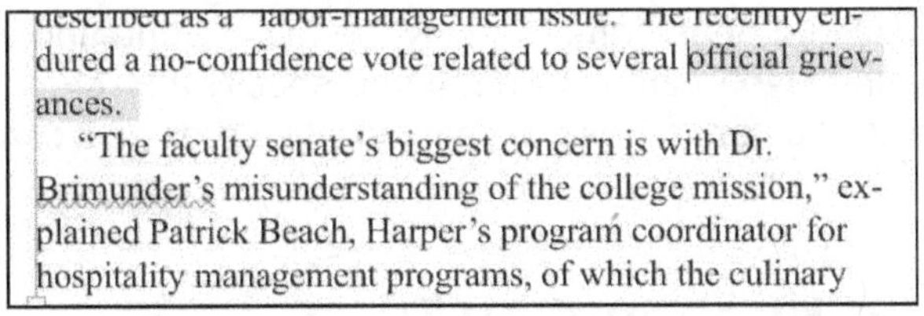
described as a "labor-management issue." He recently en-
dured a no-confidence vote related to several official griev-
ances.
"The faculty senate's biggest concern is with Dr. Brimunder's misunderstanding of the college mission," ex-
plained Patrick Beach, Harper's program coordinator for
hospitality management programs, of which the culinary

4. Remove the discretionary hyphenation character.

❒ ensure you're still in front of the same word

❒ **Mac users**, press [**delete**]; **PC users**, press [**backspace**]

When you pressed [delete/backspace], you removed the discretionary hyphen character. The word should once again be hyphenated.

Confidence Check

1. Delete the word **Monterey** from the Hyphenation Exceptions list. (Utilities > Hyphenation Exceptions > Edit.)
2. Find a multi-syllable word that is currently hyphenating.

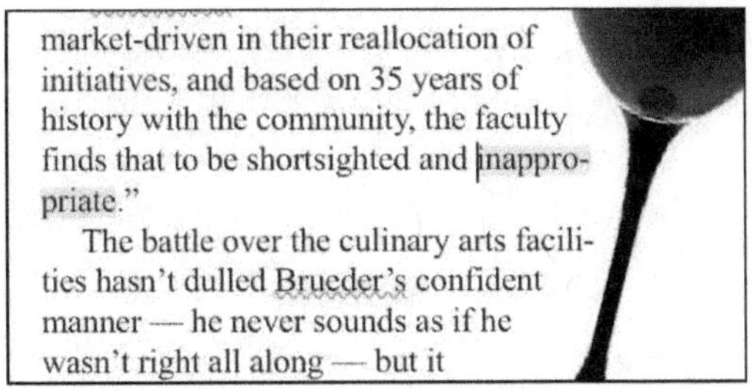

3. Highlight the word.
4. Choose **Utilities > Suggested Hyphenation**.

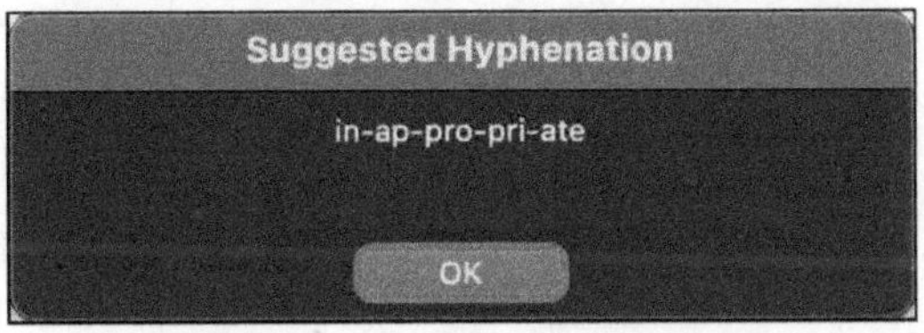

5. If you'd like, add a discretionary hyphen as suggested.

NOTES

NOTES

Hyphenation Zones

You can set a Hyphenation Zone for any text that does not use justified alignment. The Hyphenation Zone, measured from the right indentation to the end of a line, tells QuarkXPress where hyphenation can occur.

Suppose you specify a Hyphenation Zone greater than 0. In that case, QuarkXPress will hyphenate a word only when the previous word ends before the Hyphenation Zone and an acceptable hyphenation point falls within the Hyphenation Zone. If you specify a Hyphenation Zone of 0, there is no Hyphenation Zone, and QuarkXPress will hyphenate words as it can (based on other settings in the H&J).

Guided Activity 99: Create a Hyphenation Zone

1. Create a Hyphenation Zone in the BreakCaps H&J.

   ❒ choose **Edit > H&Js**

   ❒ double-click the **breakCaps H&J** you created earlier to open it for editing

   ❒ change the Hyphenation Zone to **1p**

   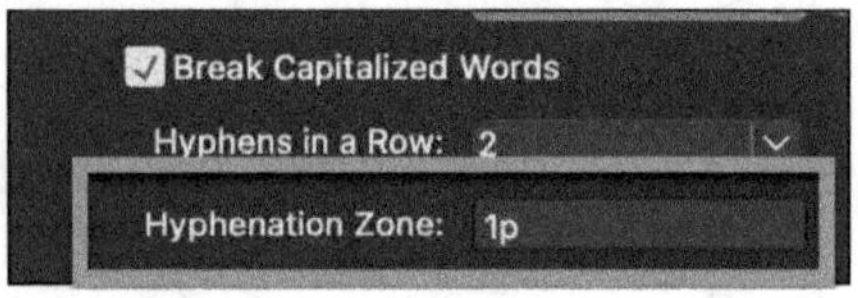

   ❒ click **OK**

   ❒ click **Save**

   Since the value you specified was greater than 0, fewer words than before are hyphenating. Generally speaking, the larger the Hyphenation Zone, the fewer hyphens you will get.

2. Save and close the project.

ICONLOGIC

"Skills and Drills" Learning

Module 13: Tables, Lists, and Templates

In This Module You Will Learn About:

And You Will Learn To:

Inserting Tables

There are a few ways to add tables to a QuarkXPress layout. You can use the Table Tool on the Tools window to draw a table of any size you need. When you use the Table Tool, you'll get a dialog box asking you how many columns and rows you need. After the table appears, you can add your data and format the table as appropriate. You can easily add rows and columns to existing tables on the fly. Another way to create a table, assuming you already have text in the QuarkXPress layout, is to convert selected text into a table.

Table Terms You Should Know

Cell, the rectangle shapes where you'll enter your data	**Row,** a collection of cells across your table	**Column,** a collection of cells down your table
Here is how you can move around a QuarkXPress table.		
[command] [tab]: move from cell to cell	**[command] [shift] [tab]:** move backward from cell to cell	**[direction arrow keys]:** move from cell to cell in any direction
click just above any cell (after getting a black, down arrow): selects the entire column	**click just to the left of any cell (after getting a black, down arrow):** selects the entire row	

Guided Activity 100: Draw a Table

1. Create a New project that matches the specifications shown in the picture below.

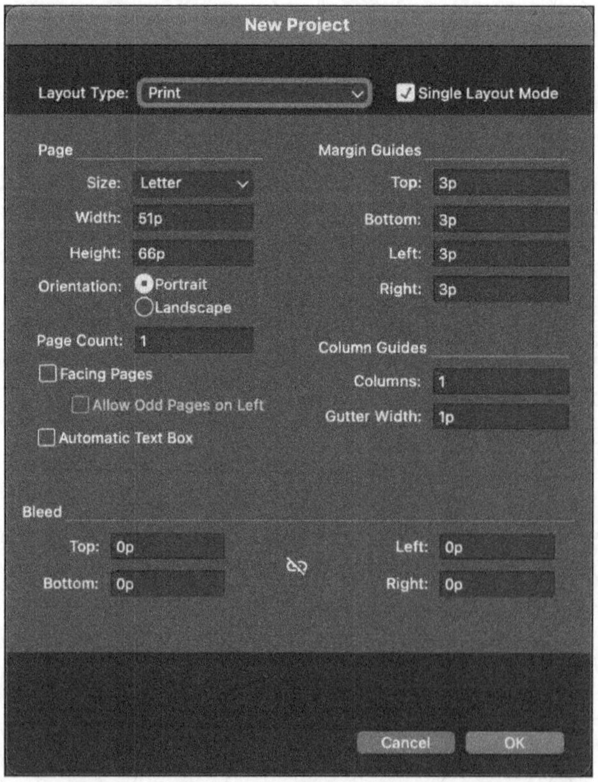

2. Save the project to the **QuarkXPress 2025 Book Assets** folder as **myFirstTable**.

3. Draw a table.

   - ❒ from the Tools window, select the **Table Tool** 
   - ❒ using the Tables tool, draw a table on the page that is approximately **three** inches (18p) **wide** and **three** inches (18p) **tall**

   When you finish drawing the table, the Table Properties dialog box opens.

   - ❒ change the number of **Body Rows** to **2**
   - ❒ change the number of **Columns** to **3**

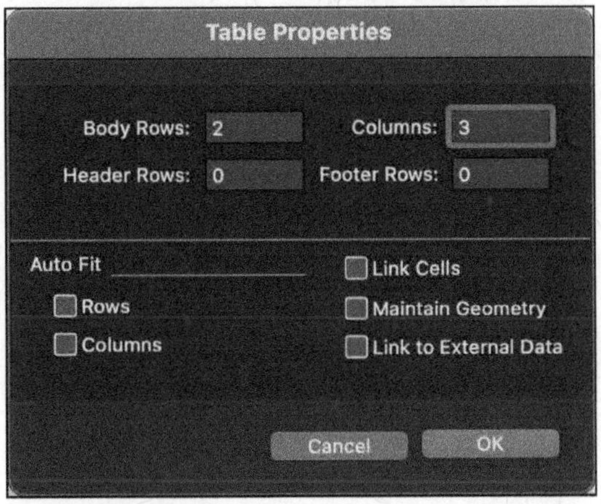

   - ❒ click **OK**

   A three column, two row table is inserted into your layout. By default, the table includes a thin border.

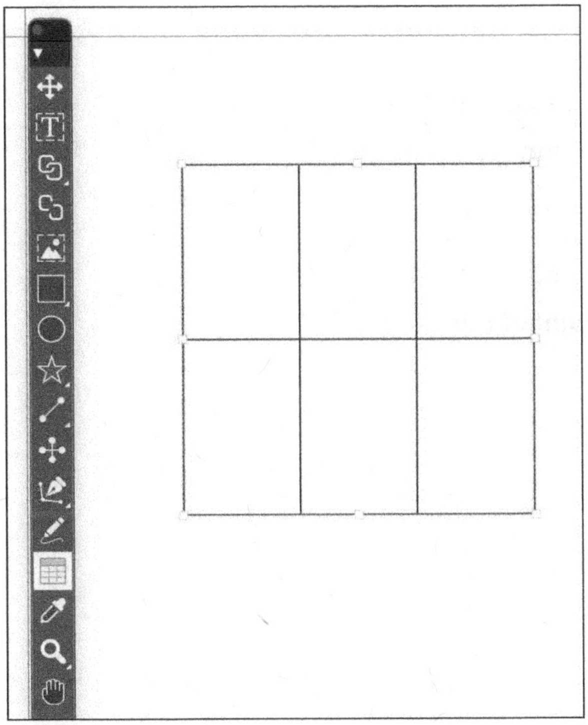

NOTES

NOTES

Guided Activity 101: Add Columns and Rows to a Table

1. The MyFirstTable project you were working on during the last activity should still be open.

2. Add text content to a cell.

   ❒ select the **Text Content Tool** and click in the first cell

   ❒ type **Projected Wine Sales (by region)**

   ❒ click in the first cell in the second row and type **North**

   ❒ click in the next cell in the second row and type **South**

   ❒ click in the last cell in the second row and type **East**

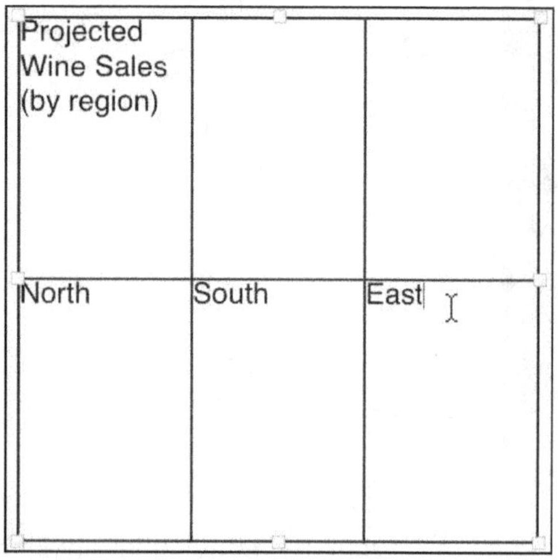

   You are going to need another column for West. You will take care of that next.

3. Insert a column.

   ❒ click in the cell containing the word **East**

   ❒ choose **Table > Insert > Column**

   The Insert Table Columns dialog box opens.

   ❒ ensure the **Number of Columns** is set to **1**

   ❒ if necessary, select **Insert Right of Selection**

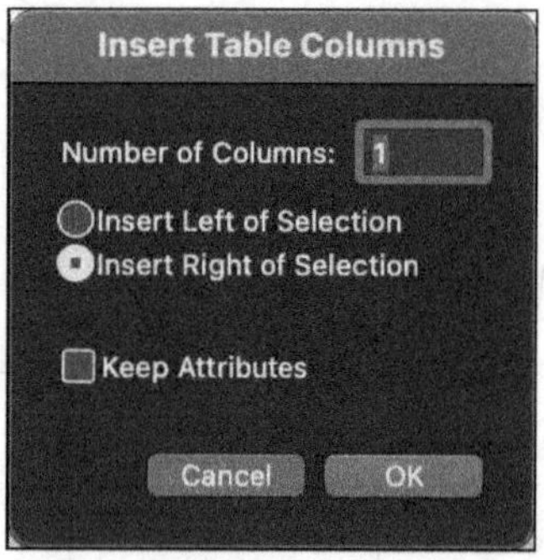

   ❒ click **OK**

- ❒ click in the last cell
- ❒ type **West**

Projected Wine Sales (by region)			
North	South	East	West

4. Insert a row.
   - ❒ click in the cell containing the word **West**
   - ❒ choose **Table > Insert > Row**
   - ❒ ensure Number of Rows is set to **1**
   - ❒ if necessary, select **Insert Below Selection**

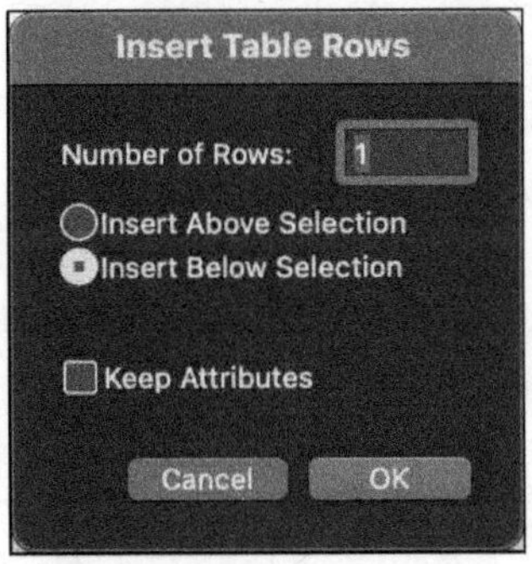

   - ❒ click **OK**

5. Save the project.

NOTES

Confidence Check

1. Insert a new column to the left of the cell containing the text **Projected Wine Sales (by region)**.
2. Use the picture shown below as your guide to add the text and rows necessary to fill out the rest of the table.

	Projected Wine Sales (by region)			
	North	South	East	West
Roserock Pinot Noir	5000	20000	15000	8000
California Cabernet Sauvignons	6500	12000	11000	9500

3. Save the project.

Guided Activity 102: Combine Cells

1. The MyFirstTable project you were working on during the last activity should still be open.

2. Move cell contents from one cell to another.

   ❒ using the **Text Content Tool**, select the text **Projected Wine Sales** text

   ❒ choose **Edit > Cut**

   ❒ using the **Text Content Tool**, click in the first cell

   ❒ choose **Edit > Paste**

   The contents of the second cell should now be in the first cell of the table.

3. Combine the cells in the first row into a single cell.

   ❒ click anywhere in the first row of the table

   ❒ choose **Table > Select > Row**

   The entire row should now be selected.

   ❒ choose **Table > Combine Cells**

   The entire first row is now one large cell.

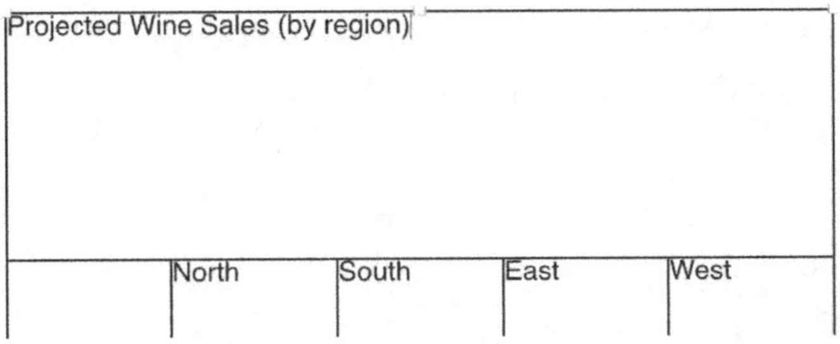

4. Use the Quick Access bar to change the character attributes for the contents in the first row.

   ❒ using the **Text Content Tool**, select the words **Projected Wine Sales (by region)**

   ❒ choose **Windows > Quick Access Bar**

   ❒ using the **Quick Access Bar**, change the **Font** to **Verdana Bold**

   ❒ change the **Size** to **18**

Note: The Quick Access bar changes dynamically depending upon what is selected in the layout. For instance, Picture tools appear when working with images. You can customize the Quick Access bar by clicking the three dots at the right and choosing **Preferences**.

NOTES

NOTES

Guided Activity 103: Format a Table

1. The MyFirstTable project you were working on during the last activity should still be open.

2. Change the vertical alignment and text inset for the entire table.

   - ❒ using the **Text Content Tool**, click anywhere in the table
   - ❒ choose **Table > Select > All Cells**
   - ❒ on the **Measurements** window, select the **Text Box** tab
   - ❒ change the **Vertical Alignment** to **Centered**
   - ❒ change the **Text Inset All Edges** to **12**

   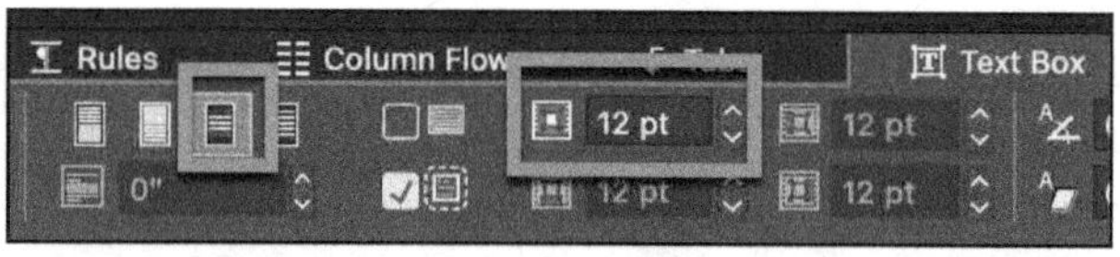

   - ❒ click **OK**

   All of the table's content has been centered vertically in their respective cells; and 12 points of white space has been added between the edge of the cells and cell contents.

3. Resize the size of the table using the Measurements window.

   - ❒ using the **Item** tool, **select the table**
   - ❒ on the **Measurements** window, select the **Home** tab
   - ❒ change the **W** to **20p**
   - ❒ change the **H** to **16p**

   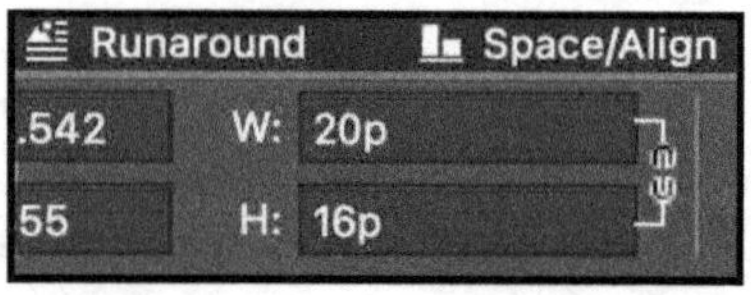

   The table is much smaller. Notice that much of the text no longer fits within the table cells and there are text overflow alerts (the red boxes).

   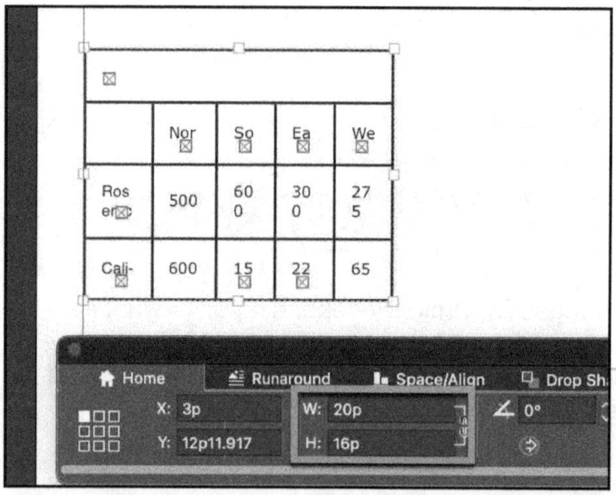

4. Resize a row manually.
   - ❒ select the **Text Content Tool**
   - ❒ position your mouse pointer on the line separating row one from row two (you'll see a vertical, two-headed arrow)
   - ❒ drag the line **down**, making the row tall enough to see the row's content

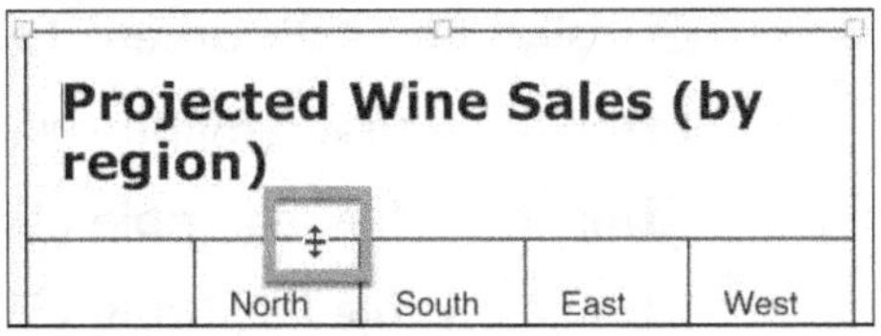

5. Resize a column manually.
   - ❒ position your mouse pointer on the line separating column one from column two
   - ❒ drag the line **right** to make the column wide enough to see the cell contents

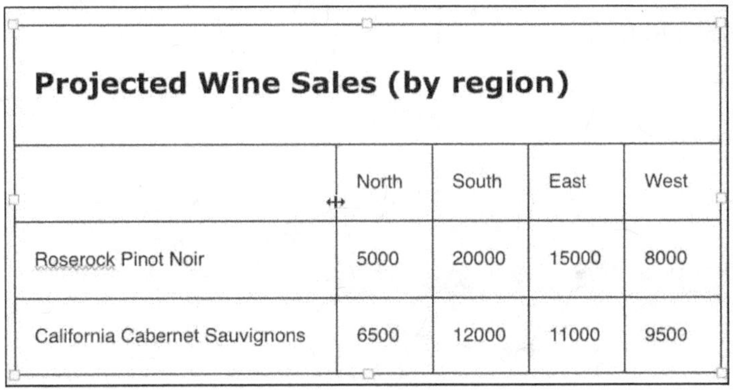

Projected Wine Sales (by region)				
	North	South	East	West
Roserock Pinot Noir	5000	20000	15000	8000
California Cabernet Sauvignons	6500	12000	11000	9500

6. Change the color of a row.
   - ❒ resize the remaining columns and rows to ensure the table content appears
   - ❒ using the **Text Content Tool**, click within the first row
   - ❒ on the **Measurements** window, **Cells** tab, change the **Box Color** to any color

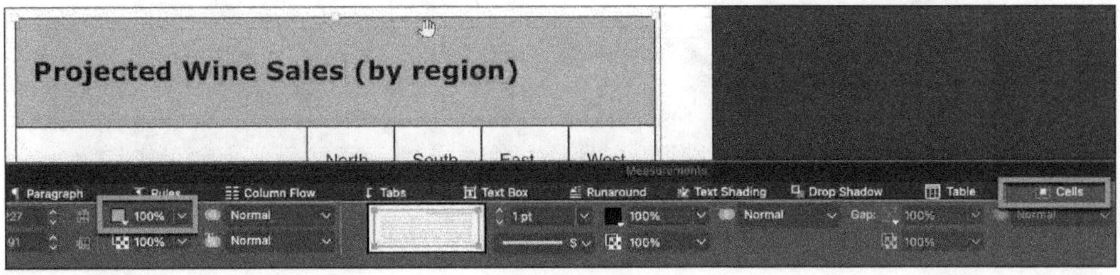

Confidence Check

1. Spend a few moments changing the colors of selected rows and cells as you see fit.
2. Select the text in all of the rows except the first row and then format the text as **Verdana**, **11 pt**.
3. When finished, save the project.
4. Keep the project open for the next activity.

NOTES

NOTES

Guided Activity 104: Modify Table Gridlines

1. The myFirstTable project should still be open.

2. Change table gridline properties.

   ❒ using the **Text Content Tool**, click in any table cell

   ❒ on the **Measurements** window, select the **Table** tab

   ❒ on the **Table** tab, **triple-click** the grid icon to **disable** the borders option

   ❒ on the **Table** tab, **triple-click** the grid icon again to **enable** the borders option

   If the borders area is light blue, the feature is enabled and you can modify the table's borders

   ❒ change the **Grid Width** to **2**

   ❒ ensure the **Style** is **Solid**

   ❒ select **any Grid Line Color**

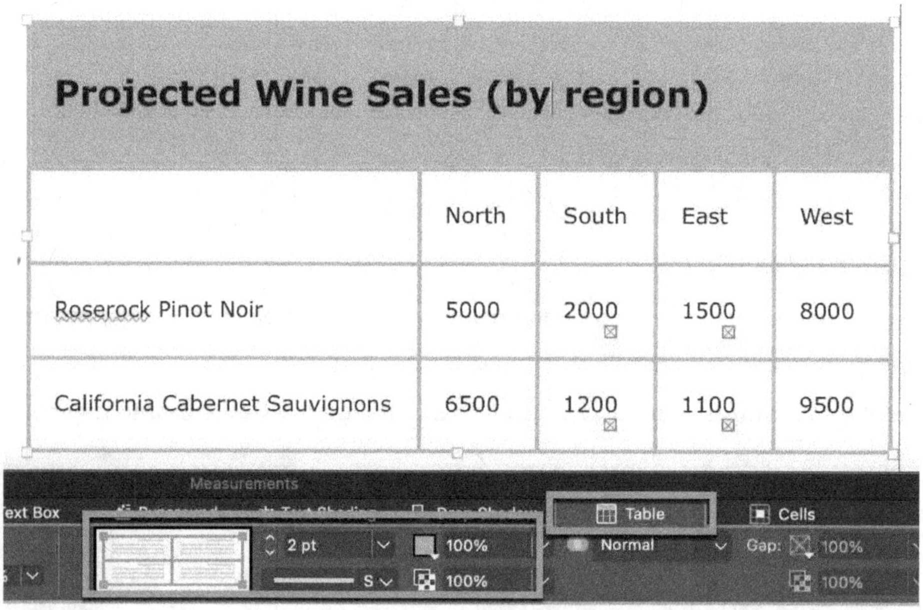

3. Resize the table as needed to account for any overflow text.

4. Save the project.

Guided Activity 105: Change a Cell's Content from Text to Picture

1. Change a text cell into a picture cell.

   ❒ using the **Text Content Tool**, click in the cell containing **Roserock Pinot Noir**

   ❒ choose **Item > Content > Picture**

   You will be alerted that moving forward will delete the text content.

   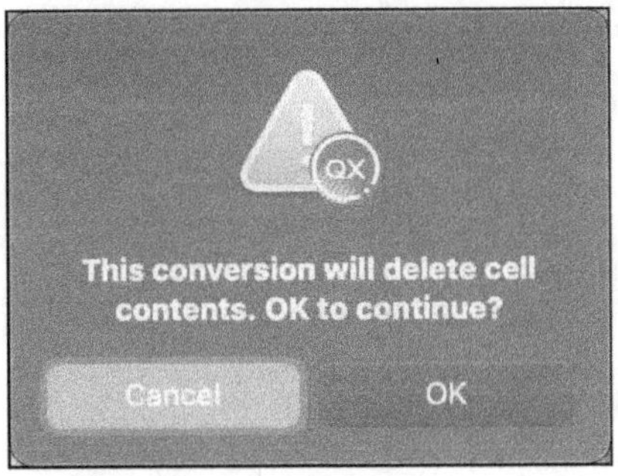

   ❒ click **OK**

   The text content is gone, and the cell now has an X—a visual indicator that the cell is now a picture cell.

Projected Wine Sales (by region)				
	North	South	East	West
	5000	20000	15000	8000
California Cabernet Sauvignons	6500	12000	11000	9500

2. Import a picture into the cell.

   ❒ click in the picture cell you just created

   ❒ choose **File > Import**

   ❒ from the **QuarkXPress 2025 Book Assets > images**, open **roseRock**

   The wine bottle image is imported. The image is huge and it needs to be resized and repositioned within the cell. You will take care of both tasks next.

NOTES

NOTES

Confidence Check

1. Resize both the wine bottle and the table to accommodate the content.

Projected Wine Sales (by region)				
	North	South	East	West
	5000	20000	15000	8000
California	6500	12000	11000	9500

2. Change the cell containing "California Cabernet Sauvignons" to picture content.
3. Import the **calCab** picture into the picture cell.
4. Resize both the wine bottle and the table to accommodate the content.

Projected Wine Sales (by region)				
	North	South	East	West
	5000	20000	15000	8000
	6500	12000	11000	9500

5. Save and close the project.

Converting Text to a Table

You now know how to create a table on the fly. If there is already text in the QuarkXPress layout, the text can be converted into a table. The secret to converting text into a table is how the text is separated. Data can be separated with spaces, tabs, commas, or paragraph returns. The most common separator is a tab. Each separator becomes a new table column when you convert the text to a table.

Guided Activity 106: Convert Text into a Table

1. Open **tableListMe** and save the file as **myTableList**.

2. Go to page **4**.

   There is a list in the first column that you will convert into a table.

3. Show invisible characters.

   ❒ choose **View > Invisibles**

   Notice that the text is separated with a tab character—the arrow between the cases and the dollar value. Each tab character is a separator and will become a table column.

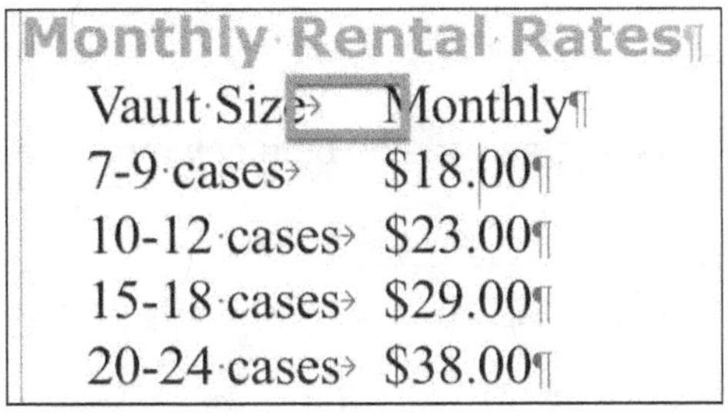

4. Convert text into a table.

   ❒ using the **Text Content Tool,** highlight all text from the "Monthly Rental Rates" headline through "$132.00."

   Note: Don't select the paragraph mark after the "$132.00" or you will end up with an extra row in the upcoming table.

   ❒ choose **Table > Convert Text to Table**

   The Convert Text to Table dialog box opens.

   ❒ select **Paragraphs** from the **Separate Rows With** drop-down menu

   ❒ select **Tabs** from the **Separate Columns With** drop-down menu

   ❒ ensure **Rows** is set to **15**

   ❒ ensure **Columns** is set to **2**

NOTES

❒ ensure **Cell Fill Order** is set to **Left to Right, Top Down**

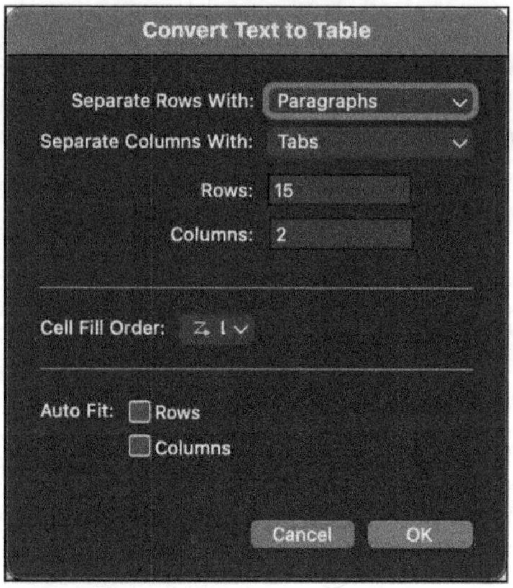

❒ click **OK**

The selected text has been copied into a large table. Notice that the original text does not get removed from the layout. You will remove the original text and resize the table next.

5. Resize the table.

   ❒ using the **Item Tool**, resize the table so that it is as wide as both columns and position it similar to the image below

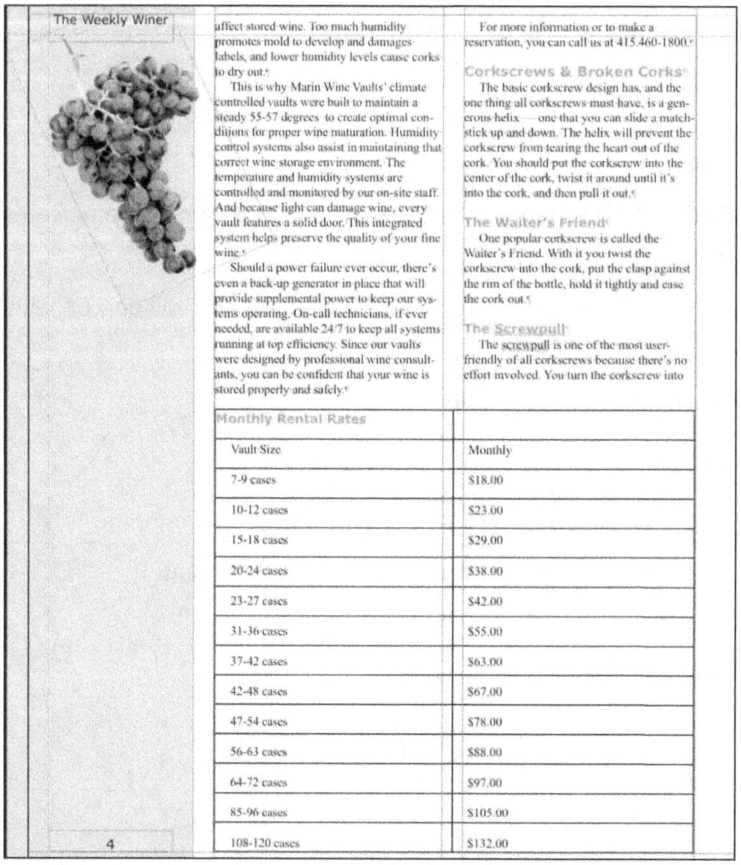

Confidence Check

1. Delete the original table text.
2. Select and combine the first two table cells. (You learned how to do this on page 215.)
3. Center the "Monthly Rental Rates" heading horizontally within the row.
4. Change the text inset for the entire table to **3 points**. (You learned how on page 216.)
5. Vertically align the cell contents to **Center Alignment**.
6. Resize the table as appropriate to account for any text overflow.
7. Create a new paragraph style sheet named **TableText** using the attributes as shown below.

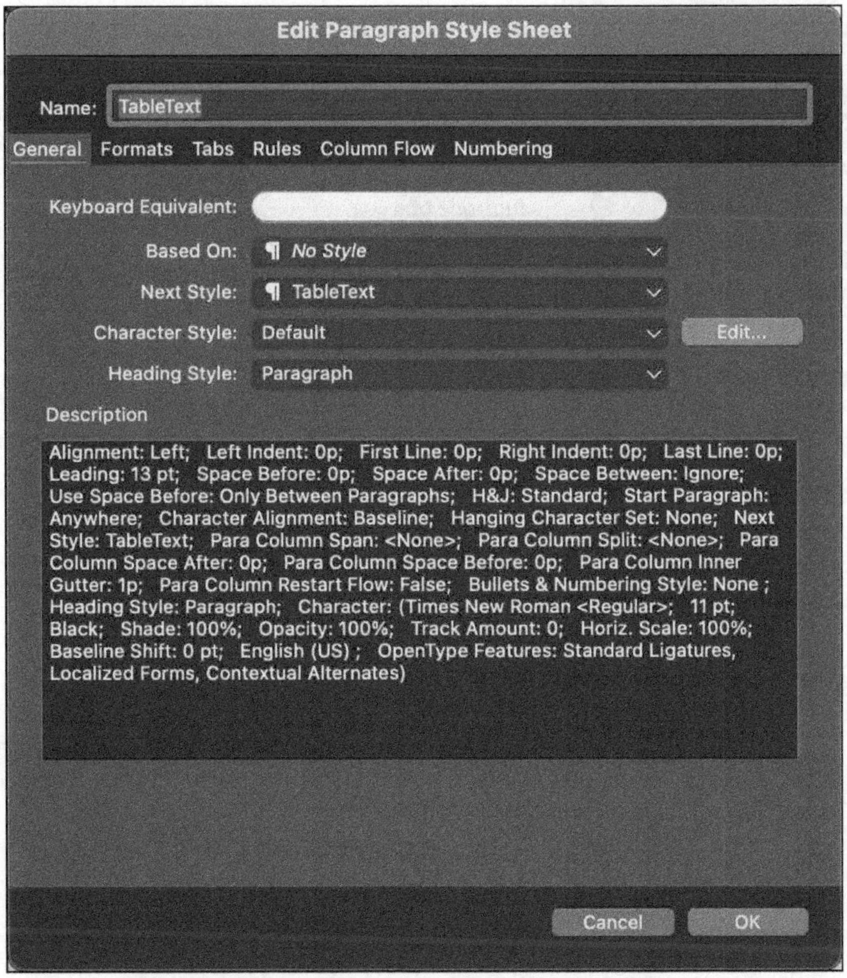

8. Apply the **TableText** style to all of the table contents except the first row.
9. Save the project and keep it open for the next activity.

NOTES

NOTES

Table Styles

Table styles speed up the table formatting process by allowing you to define and instantly apply consistent design for cell borders, fills, and other formats. Unlike paragraph styles, which are focused solely on text formatting—such as font, size, alignment, and spacing—table styles manage the structure and design of entire tables, integrating cell and text styling.

Guided Activity 107: Apply Preset Table Styles

1. Ensure that the **myTableList** project is still open.

2. Apply a preset table style to a table.

   ❒ click anywhere on the table that you worked with during the last activity

   ❒ choose **Window > Table Styles**

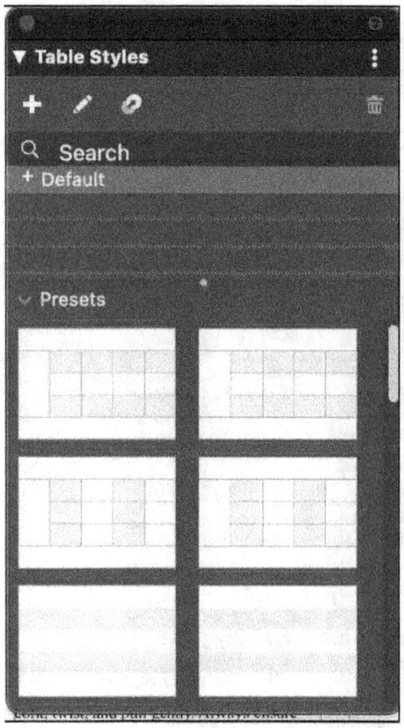

   ❒ from the **Presets** area, click any of the existing table styles

   The table takes on the attributes of the preset. While the appearance of a table can vary widely from preset to preset, the appearance of the table's content is based on the TableText style you created during the last activity.

Guided Activity 108: Create a Table Style

1. Ensure that the **myTableList** project is still open.

2. Create a table style.
   - ❐ on the **Table Styles** window, click the **New** icon 
   - ❐ name the new style **winerTables**
   - ❐ from the list at the left, click **Table**
   - ❐ select the **Border and Fill** tab
   - ❐ from the border **Color** drop-down menu, choose **Pantone S 185-7**

   - ❐ select the **Text** tab
   - ❐ from the **Paragraph Style** drop-down menu, select **TableText**
   - ❐ from the Insets area, deselect **Multiple Insets**
   - ❐ in the **All Edges** area, type **3**

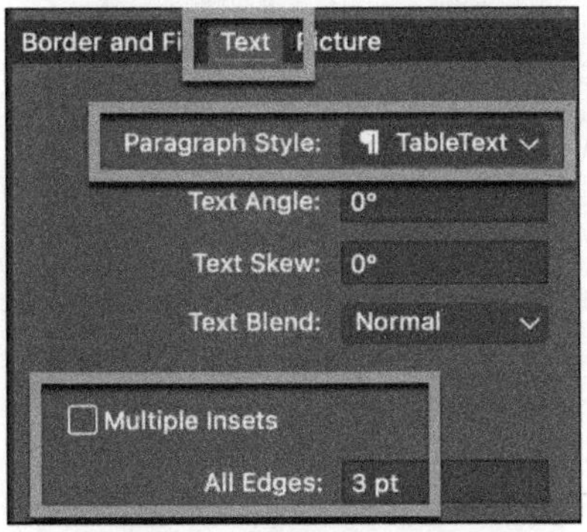

   - ❐ click **OK**

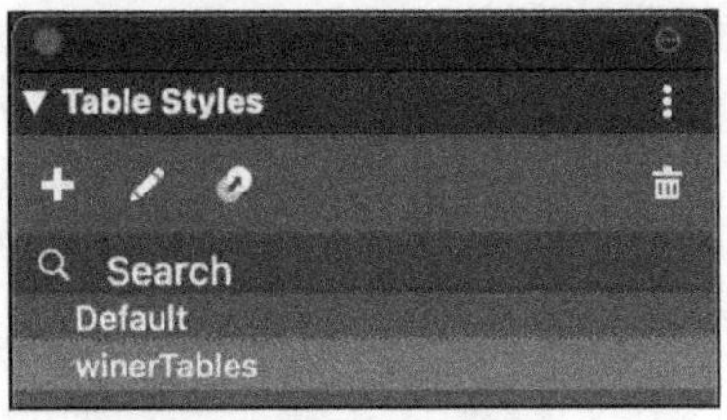

NOTES

NOTES

Confidence Check

1. Edit the **winerTables** style.
2. From the list at the left, select **Row**.
3. From beneath **Formatting Rules**, click the **plus sign**
4. Choose **All Even**.
5. On the **Border and Fill** tab change the **Fill** color to **Pantone S 185-7**.
6. Change the **Fill Opacity** to **50%**.

7. Apply the **winerTable** style to the table you've been working with.

   The table takes on the attributes of the table style. Most notably, the table borders are using the Pantone 185-7 color along with the fill for the even rows.

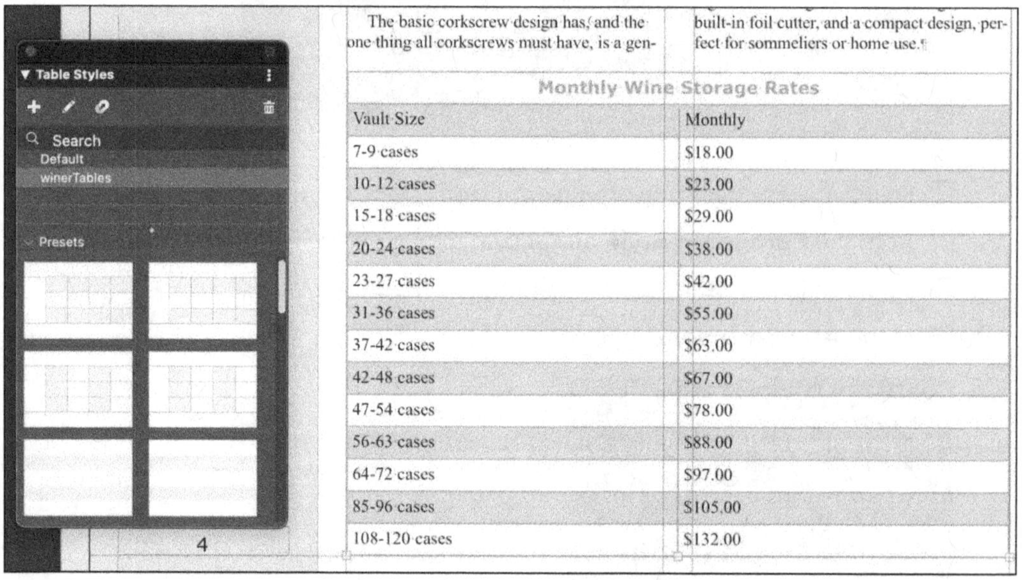

Vault Size	Monthly
7-9 cases	$18.00
10-12 cases	$23.00
15-18 cases	$29.00
20-24 cases	$38.00
23-27 cases	$42.00
31-36 cases	$55.00
37-42 cases	$63.00
42-48 cases	$67.00
47-54 cases	$78.00
56-63 cases	$88.00
64-72 cases	$97.00
85-96 cases	$105.00
108-120 cases	$132.00

8. Add a two column, six row table to the layout.
9. Apply the winerTable style to the new table.

   The new table takes on the same attributes as the existing table.

10. Edit the winerTable style, changing the color of the even rows to any color that you like. After saving the style, notice that both tables update instantly.
11. Edit the winerTable style again, returning the color of the even rows back to Pantone S 185-7.
12. Delete the extra table and then save the project.

Numbered and Bulleted Lists

Numbered and bulleted lists add structure and clarity to content, making creating and managing organized information easier. Changes to the list, such as adding or removing items, automatically update the numbering, saving time and reducing errors.

Guided Activity 109: Create a Numbered List

1. Ensure that the **myTableList** project is still open.

2. Apply a numbered list to selected text.

   ❒ using the **Text Content Tool**, select the list of corkscrews in the "Top Five Corkscrews" section (depending upon the height of the table, the list is either above the table or at the top of page **5**)

   ❒ on the **Measurements** window, **Paragraph** tab, **Bullets & Numbering Style** drop-down menu, choose **Default Numbering Style**

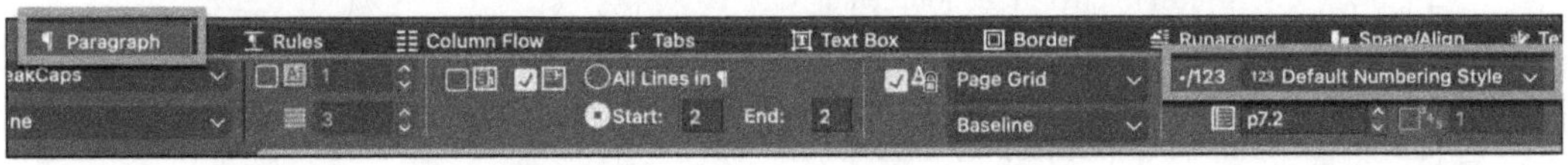

   The selected text is instantly numbered.

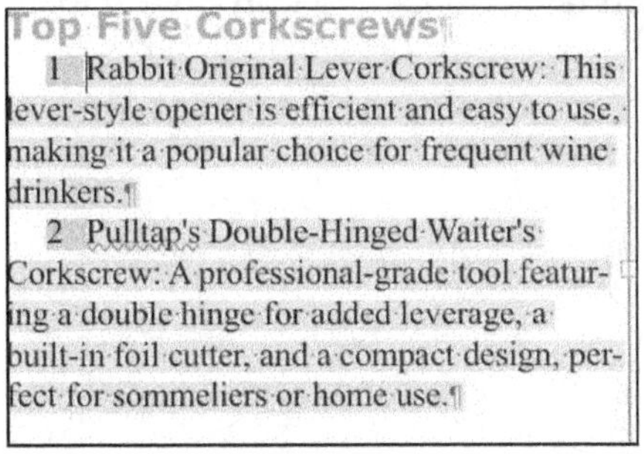

3. Add a period after each number in the list.

   ❒ choose **Edit > Bullet, Numbering and Outline Styles**

   ❒ select **Default Numbering Style**

   ❒ click **Edit**

   The Edit Numbering Style options open.

   ❒ in the **Suffix** area, type a **period**

   ❒ click **OK**

   ❒ click **Save**

   There is now a period after each number in the list.

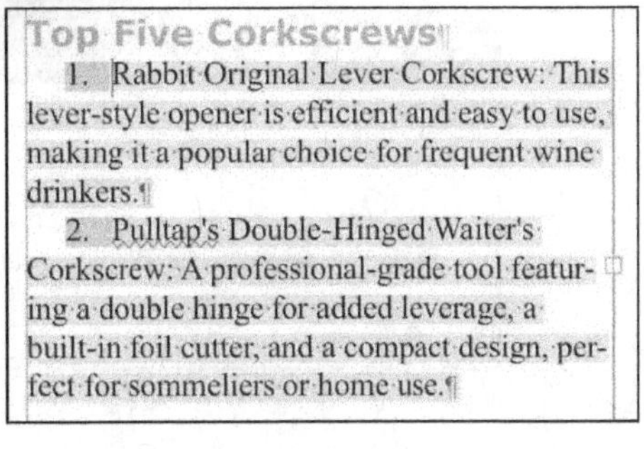

NOTES

4. Create a hanging indent.

   ❒ choose **Edit > Bullet, Numbering and Outline Styles**

   ❒ select **Default Numbering Style**

   ❒ click **Edit**

   ❒ change the **Outset** to **-1p1** 

   ❒ click **OK** and then click **Save**

   The first line indent for the body is currently 1p1. Because you set the numbering outset to -1p1, the numbers appear to the left of the body text.

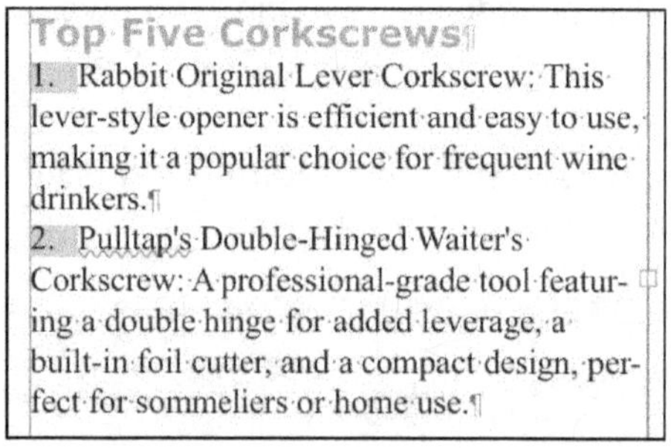

   ❒ select the first paragraph in the list ("Rabbit Original Lever...")

   ❒ on the **Measurements** window, **Paragraph** tab, change the **Left Indent** to **1p1**

   ❒ change the **First Line Indent** to **0**

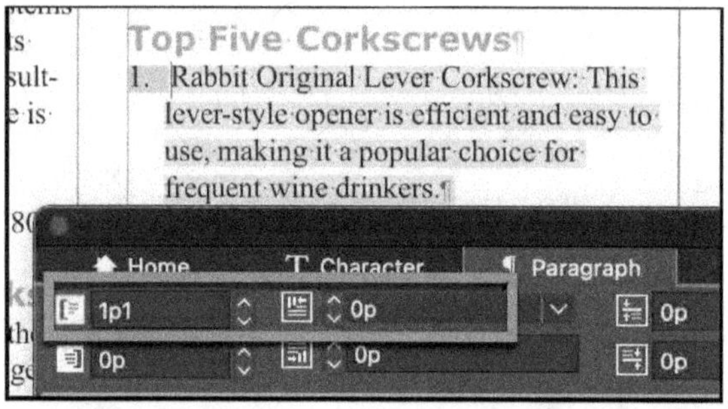

   The hanging indent is nearly perfect for the selected paragraph. You just need to move the text in the first line a bit more left.

   ❒ on the **Measurements** window, **Paragraph** tab, change the **Minimum Bullet/Number Distance From Text** to **0**

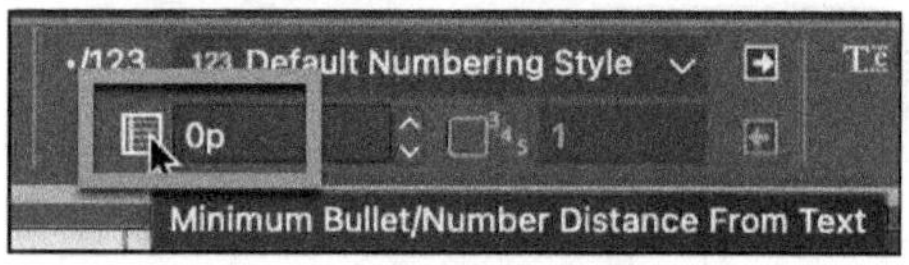

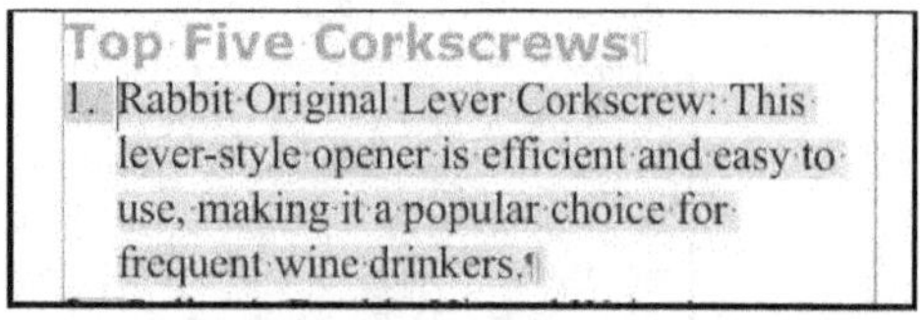

Confidence Check

1. With the paragraph still selected, create a new paragraph style sheet named **NumberedList**. (Use the Description shown below as your guide.)

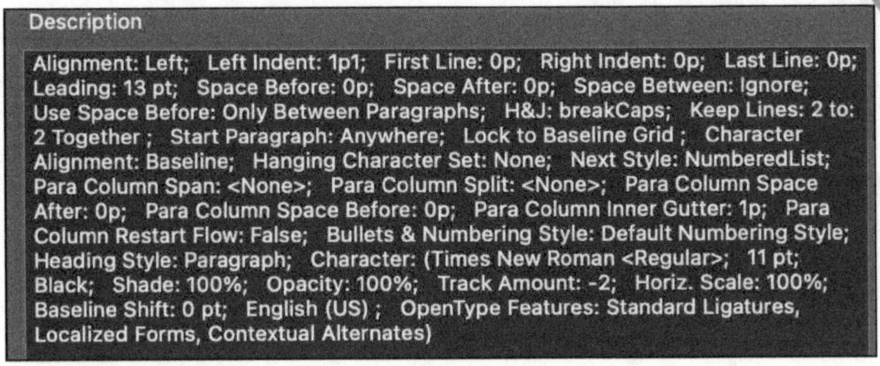

Description

Alignment: Left; Left Indent: 1p1; First Line: 0p; Right Indent: 0p; Last Line: 0p; Leading: 13 pt; Space Before: 0p; Space After: 0p; Space Between: Ignore; Use Space Before: Only Between Paragraphs; H&J: breakCaps; Keep Lines: 2 to: 2 Together ; Start Paragraph: Anywhere; Lock to Baseline Grid ; Character Alignment: Baseline; Hanging Character Set: None; Next Style: NumberedList; Para Column Span: <None>; Para Column Split: <None>; Para Column Space After: 0p; Para Column Space Before: 0p; Para Column Inner Gutter: 1p; Para Column Restart Flow: False; Bullets & Numbering Style: Default Numbering Style; Heading Style: Paragraph; Character: (Times New Roman <Regular>; 11 pt; Black; Shade: 100%; Opacity: 100%; Track Amount: -2; Horiz. Scale: 100%; Baseline Shift: 0 pt; English (US) ; OpenType Features: Standard Ligatures, Localized Forms, Contextual Alternates)

2. Apply the **NumberedList** style to all of the list items.

   After applying the style sheet to the text, you'll likely see a **plus sign** next to the NumberedList style sheet name. The plus sign indicates paragraph formatting that is not part of the style sheet.

3. Right-click the style sheet and choose **Apply Style Sheet & Remove Local Paragraph Formatting**.

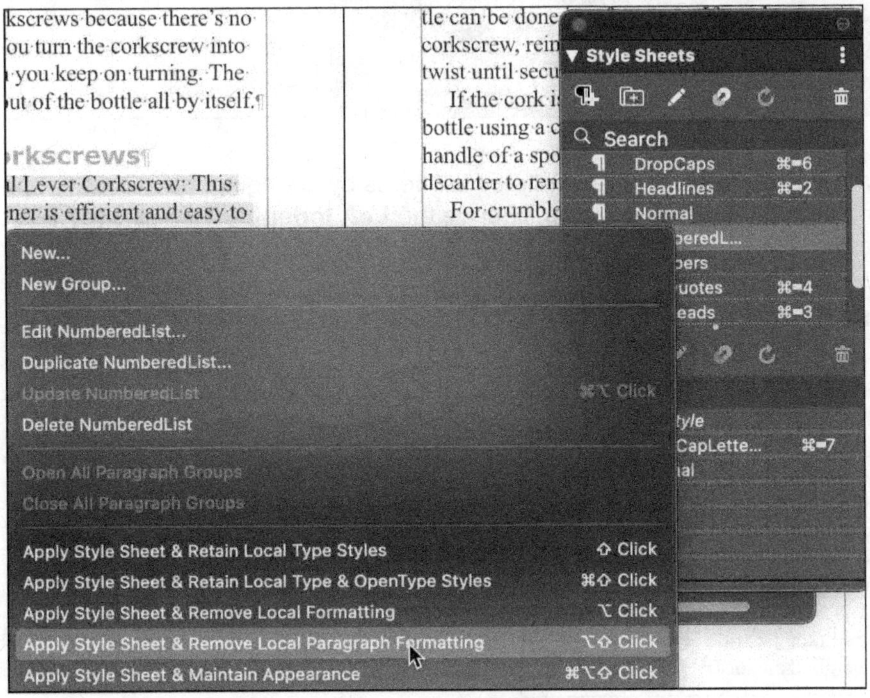

NOTES

NOTES

4. At the end of the story, select the items in the **Pro Tips** section and apply the **Default Bullet Style**.

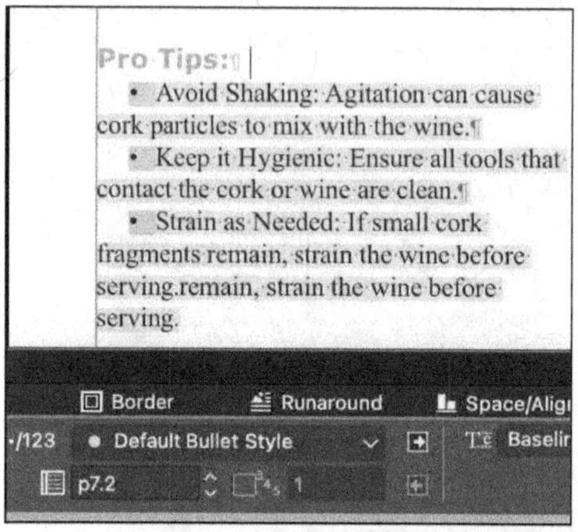

5. Change the bullet **Outset** for the **Default Bullet Style** to **-1p1**. (Hint: Edit > Bullets, Numbering, and Outline Styles)

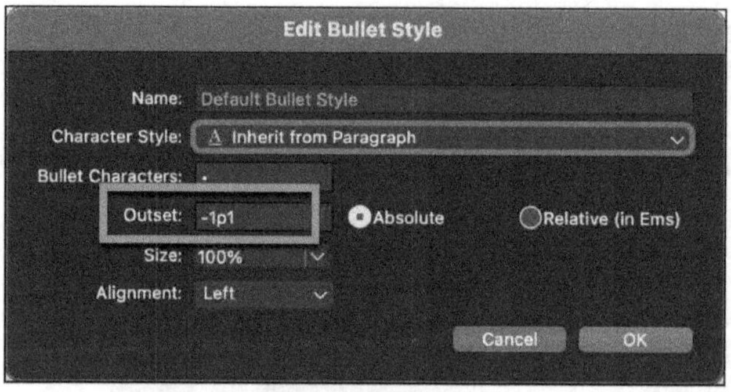

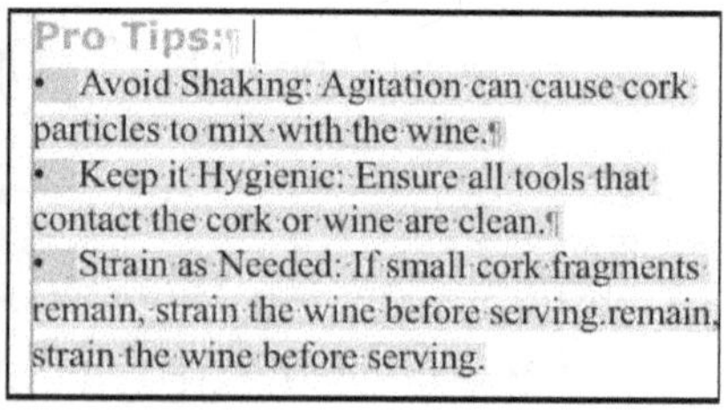

6. Create a **hanging indent** for the bulleted list items by changing the minimum space between the bullet and the text to **0**, change the **Left Indent** to **1p1**, and the **First Line Indent** to **0.**

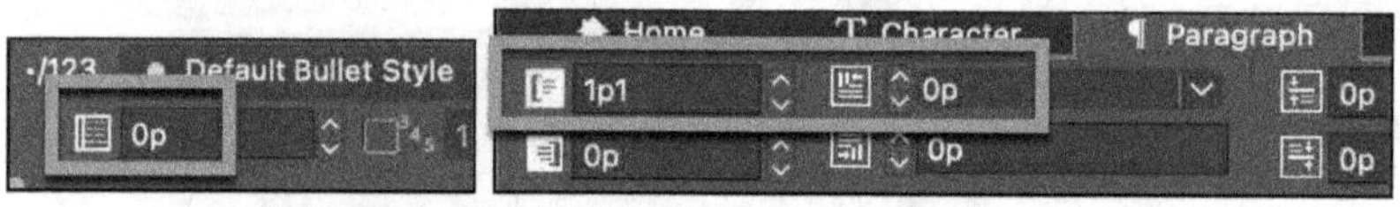

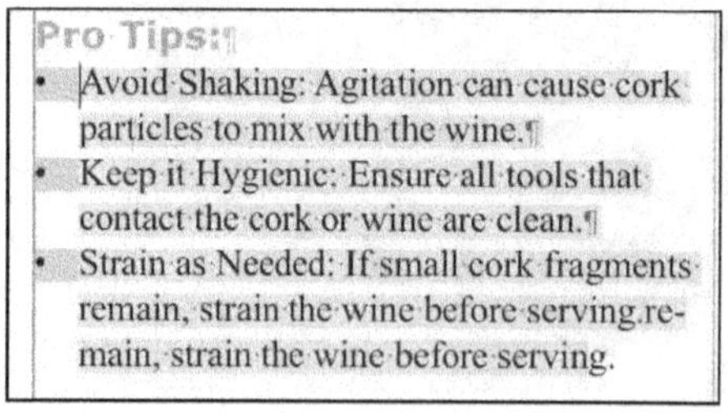

7. With the bulleted items selected and now formatted with a hanging indent, create a new paragraph style named **Bullets**.

8. Apply the **Bullets** style to the bulleted list, removing any local paragraph formatting (if necessary).

9. Save and close the project.

Font Usage

If you plan to share your QuarkXPress projects with other users or intend to send your completed output to a commercial printer for high-end printing, you must ensure your fonts and graphics are in good order and printable. QuarkXPress provides a Usage utility that tracks the status of both fonts and images.

Guided Activity 110: Use Font Usage to Replace a Font

1. Open **letterHead** from the **QuarkXPress 2025 Book Assets** folder.

2. Save the project as **myLetterhead**.

   Notice a red X in the text box at the top of the layout, indicating that some text is missing. The text has “accidentally” been formatted using Courier (New) when it should use Times New Roman. You will use the Usage command to replace Courier with Times New Roman. You could have easily seen the problem, selected the text, and changed the font. However, the Usage command will save you much time working on a large document.

3. Use the Font Usage utility to replace a font.

   ❒ choose **Utilities > Usage**

   The Usage dialog box opens.

   ❒ select **Fonts** from the list at the left

   Notice that three fonts are being used in the document. Times New Roman, Arial and Courier (New). You are going to replace Courier with Times New Roman.

   ❒ select **Courier (New)**

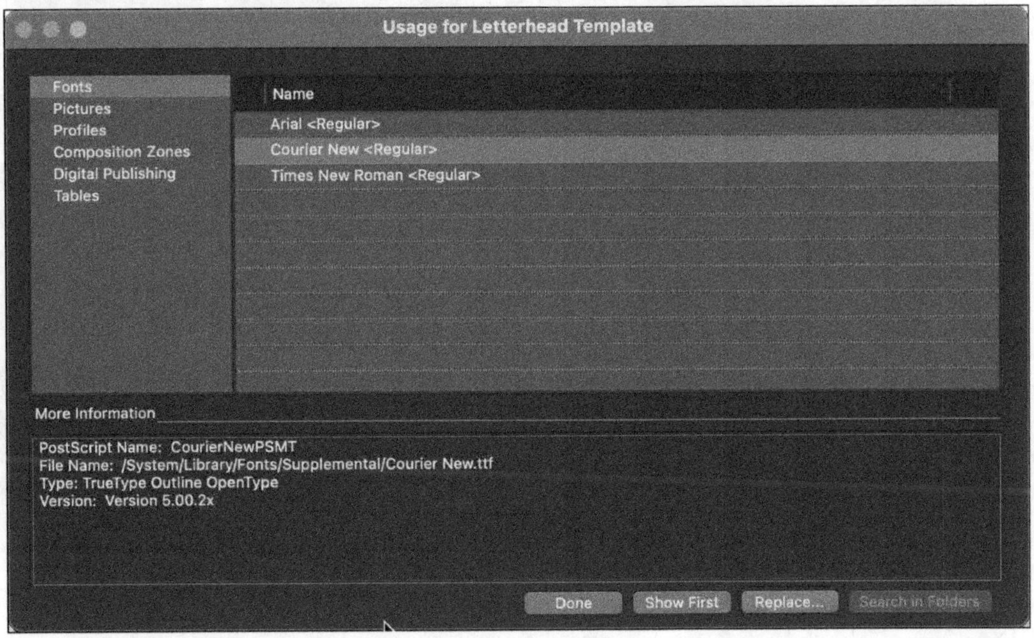

   ❒ click the **Replace** button

   The Replace Font dialog box opens.

NOTES

❐ select **Times New Roman** as the **Replacement Font**

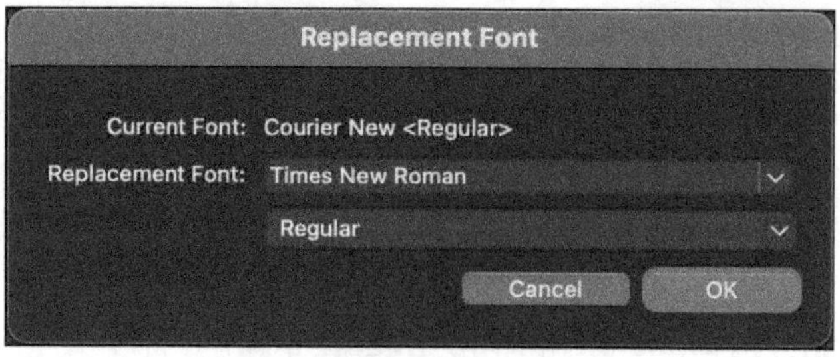

❐ click **OK**

You'll be asked to confirm the action.

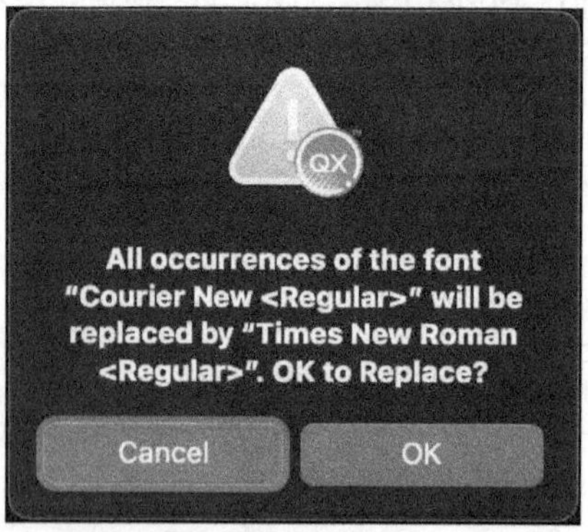

❐ click **OK**

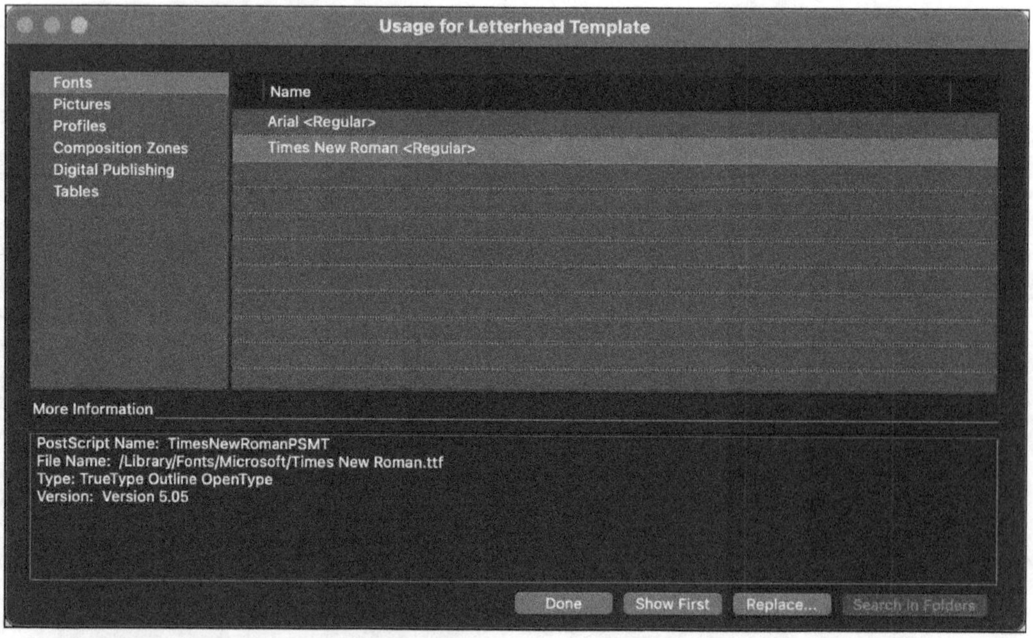

❐ click **Close** (Mac users, click **Done**)

❐ if necessary, deselect all text by clicking away from the selection

All occurrences of the Courier font have been replaced. And now that the font has been replaced, you can see the missing text in the text box.

Picture Usage

After importing an image or multimedia into QuarkXPress, tracking whether the original asset has been renamed, updated, or moved is essential. If these changes occur, QuarkXPress may lose its link to the asset, and the picture might not print accurately.

To make working with images easier, keeping the original files in a central location, such as an images folder on a server, is helpful. Importing all images from this central location into your QuarkXPress documents will make updating links much more straightforward than if the original files are scattered across multiple locations. Additionally, when using the Picture Usage feature to replace an original file with a new one, ensure that both the original and replacement files are the exact same size (both in width and height). If the replacement file differs in size, the images in your document may become distorted.

Guided Activity 111: Use Picture Usage to Update a Picture

1. The myLetterhead project should still be open.

2. Show picture usage.

   ❒ choose **Utilities > Usage**

   ❒ select **Pictures** from the list at the left

   There is only one image in the project: **oldlogo**. While the status of the image is currently OK, there is a newer version of the logo available.

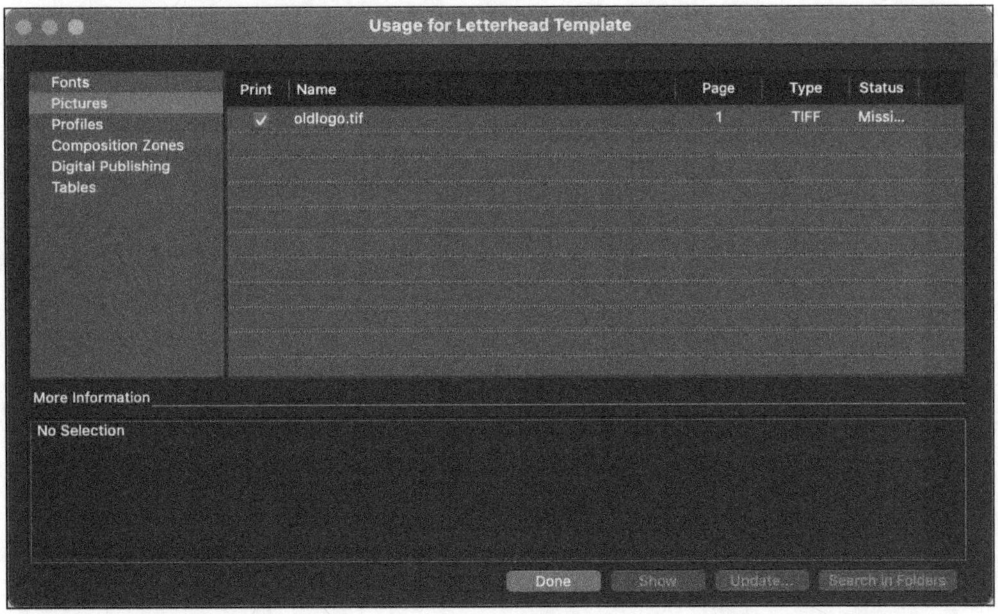

3. Update an image.

   ❒ click one time on the words **oldlogo.jpg**

   ❒ click **Update**

   ❒ from **QuarkXPress 2025 Book Assets** > images, open **newLogo**

   Because you're actually changing the old logo with a completely different file, the Status now says **Modified**.

NOTES

❒ click the **Update** button and then click **Close/Done**

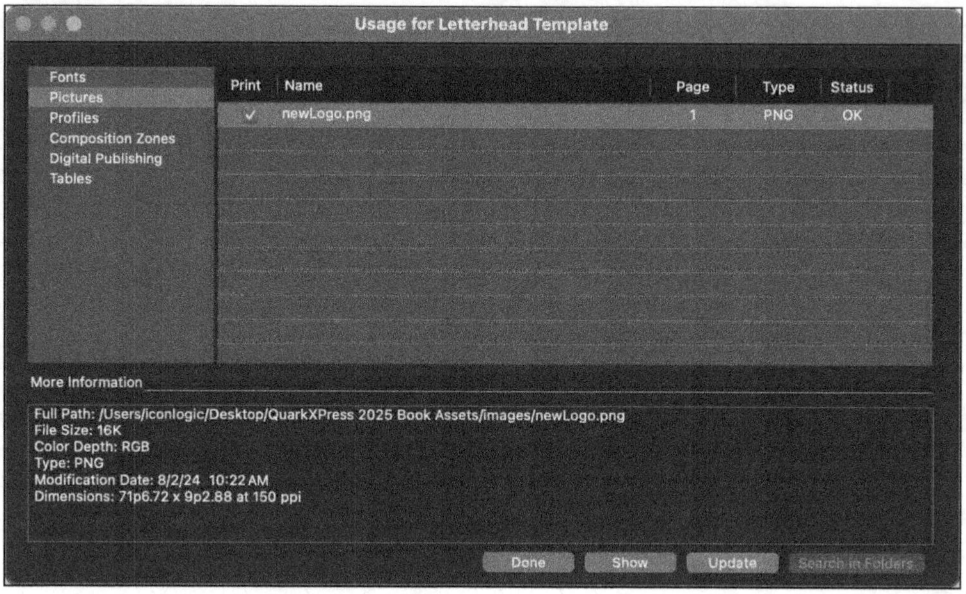

The logo has been updated.

❒ click the **Close** (Done) button

4. Save the project.

Confidence Check

1. Resize and position the new logo similar to the image below.

2. Save the project.

Templates

A template is a pre-designed project that serves as the foundation for creating consistent layouts. Templates can include placeholders for text, images, styles, master pages, and even project settings such as page size, margins, and colors.

Starting a new project based on a template is useful when working on recurring projects like newsletters, brochures, or magazines, where consistency is critical. Templates reduce the need to recreate projects from scratch and ensure your designs remain consistent.

Guided Activity 112: Create and Use a Template

1. Save a document as a template.

   ❒ ensure **myLetterhead** is still open

   ❒ choose **File > Save As**

   ❒ name the file **myTemplate**

   ❒ from the **Save as type/Type** area, select **Project Template**

   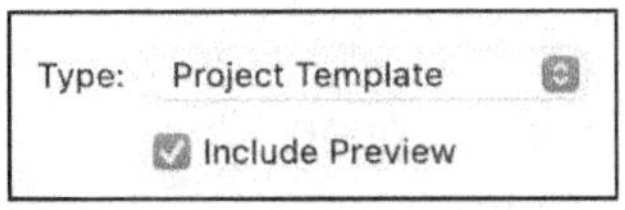

   ❒ save the template to the **QuarkXPress 2025 Book Assets** folder

2. Close the template.

3. Create a new project based on a template.

   ❒ choose **File > Open**

   ❒ from **QuarkXPress 2025 Book Assets,** open **MyTemplate**

   Notice that the project is **untitled**—it's a copy of the template. If you wanted to, you could now replace the text on the page with real text.

4. Close the project without saving.

NOTES

NOTES

Congratulations, you've completed this book. At a high level, you have learned about the following QuarkXPress concepts:

You can learn more about my books, instructor-led training classes (onsite or virtual), and QuarkXPress support options by visiting my website, **www.iconlogic.com**, emailing me at **ksiegel@iconlogic.com**, or by calling **888.812.4827**.

ICONLOGIC

"Skills and Drills" Learning

Lab 2: Images

Add Images to an Existing Project

Skill Level: **Basic-Intermediate**

1. Open the **finishedWeeklyWiner** project.
2. Scroll through the layout and notice the images that have been added throughout.
3. Open the **lab2** project and save it as **myLab2**.
4. Using the finished project as your guide, import the images, resize them, and set the runaround properties as appropriate.

The Weekly Winer

The Newsletter for the Members of WineLovers.com • Vol. 12, No. 5

College Prez Duels Critics Over Wine Cellar

Steven Brimunder wasn't looking to stir up a wine-related controversy. But the president of Harper College, in Chicago's northwest suburbs, has been in hot water ever since he floated a plan to devote $5.5 million of a $125 million bond referendum to improve the two-year community college's culinary arts program, which includes a restaurant open to the public.

Part of that plan — which was initially defeated, but passed at a revised level of $88.8 million last year — involved building a small space for use as a wine cellar. It was, according to Brimunder, who has been at Harper since 1998, a $1,000 expenditure that was inflated by critics to $9 million.

It became a lightning rod...

"It was a closet," said Brimunder. "But it became a lightning rod."

Brimunder, who has spent the past three years wrestling with community critics, as well as with the Harper faculty, tries to minimize the controversy. But it's evident that he feels Harper missed an opportunity on this one.

Brimunder came to Harper after 17 years as president of the Williamsport Area Community College in Pennsylvania (which has been renamed the Pennsylvania College of Technology). In the process of expanding Williamsport from a two-year to a four-year institution, Brimunder took a significant hand in the development of the wine cellar at the school's teaching restaurant, Le Jeune Chef. It was a successful undertaking: Le Jeune Chef earned a Wine Spectator Award of Excellence for its wine list in the early 1990s and moved up to Best of Award of Excellence status in 1995.

"We created a great program in Pennsylvania," said Brimunder, "and I wanted to do the same at Harper. But the more you defend what you're after and try to get cerebral, the worse it gets."

Although the Harper Board of Trustees recently extended his contract an additional year, through 2005, Brimunder continues to duke it out with the faculty senate, in what he described as a "labor-management issue." He recently endured a no-confidence vote related to several official grievances.

"The faculty senate's biggest concern is with Dr. Brimunder's misunderstanding of the college mission," explained Patrick Beach, Harper's program coordinator for

NOTES

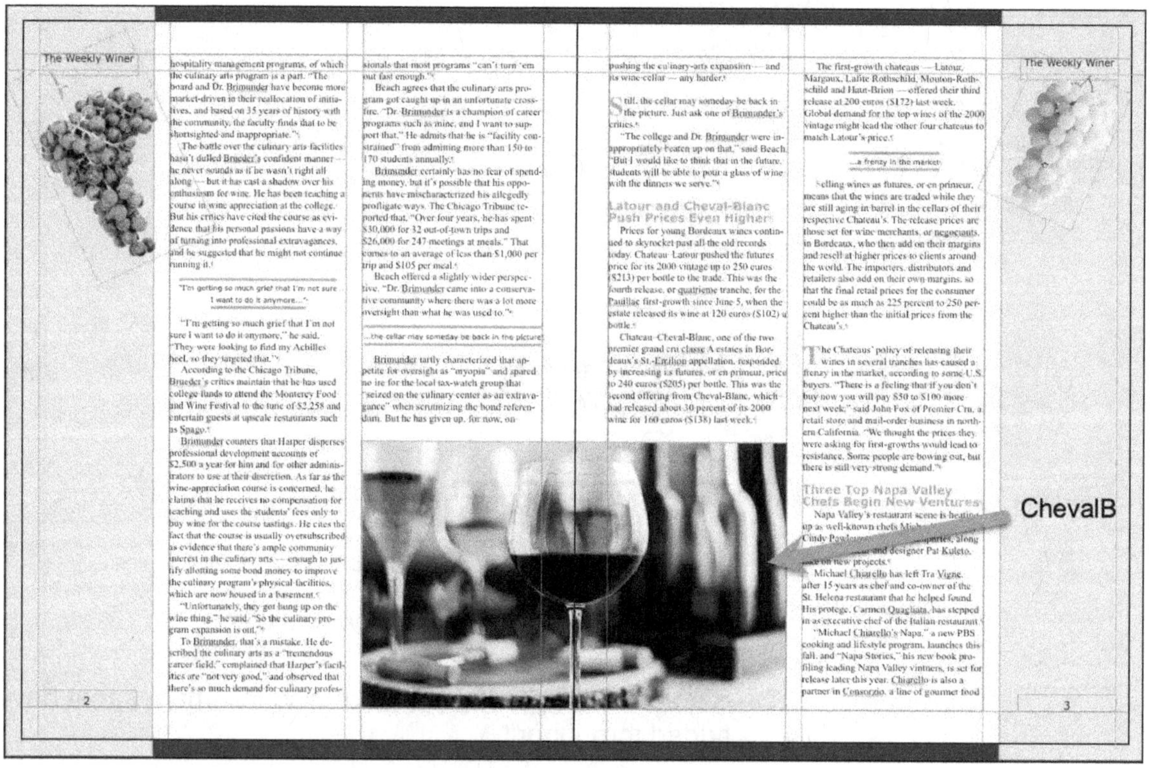

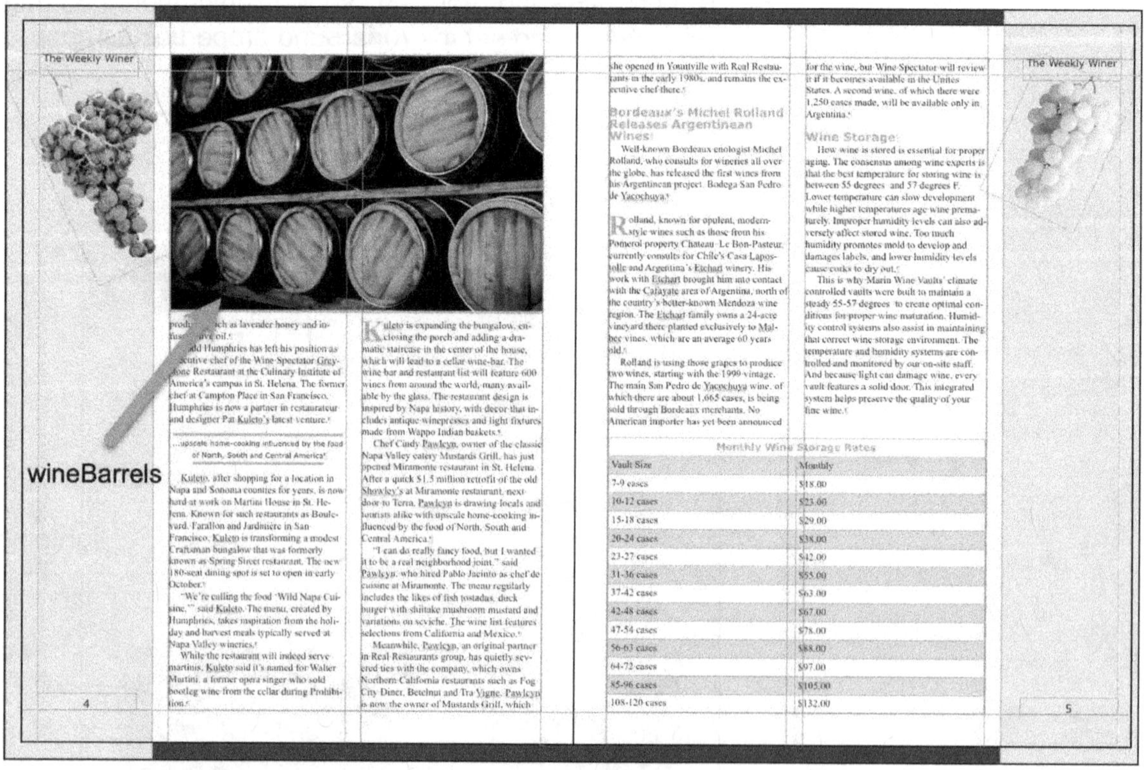

The Weekly Winer
Tips of the Week
Opening the Bottle
Cutting the capsule
Pouring Wine: The Dos and Don'ts
Corkscrews
The Waiter's Friend
The Screwpull
Broken Cork in the Bottle?
Pro Tips:
wineglas
cork2
cork3
6

NOTES

Notes

Index

NOTES

NOTES

NOTES

Notes

www.ingramcontent.com/pod-product-compliance
Lightning Source LLC
LaVergne TN
LVHW060447061126
851857LV00016B/1756
* 9 7 8 1 9 6 0 6 0 4 3 2 3 *